If the project of European unification is not to lose its power, its momentum and its vivacity, it must necessarily contain perspectives for further development. Political, economic and currency union, a strong European market simply cannot do *without the social element*.

Otto Schulz (1996: p 3)

Also by Adrian Adams, Peter Erath and Steven Shardlow as part of the same series of books:

Adams, A., Erath, P. and Shardlow, S.M. (Eds.) (2000). *Key Themes in European Social Work*. Lyme Regis: Russell House.

Shardlow, S.M. and Cooper, S. (2000). *A Bibliography of European Studies in Social Work*. Lyme Regis: Russell House.

Fundamentals of Social Work in Selected European Countries

Historical and Political Context, Present Theory, Practice, Perspectives

Edited by Adrian Adams, Peter Erath and Steven Shardlow

Russell House Publishing

First published in 2000 by:
Russell House Publishing Ltd.
4 St. George's House
Uplyme Road
Lyme Regis
Dorset DT7 3LS

Tel: 01297-443948
Fax: 01297-442722
e-mail: help@russellhouse.co.uk

Adrian Adams, Peter Erath, Steven Shardlow, Oldřich Chytil, Radka Popelková, Juha Hämäläinen, Pauli Niemelä, Emmanuel Jovelin, Evelyne Tully, Wolfgang Klug, Horst Sing, Rino Fasol, Geert van der Laan and Montserrat Feu have asserted their rights under the Copyright, Designs and Patents Act 1988 to be identified as the authors of this book.

British Library cataloguing-in-publication data:
A catalogue record for this book is available from the British Library.

ISBN: 1-898924-68-6

Typeset by The Hallamshire Press Limited, Sheffield

Printed by Cromwell Press, Trowbridge

Russell House Publishing

Is a group of social work, probation, education and youth and community work practitioners and academics working in collaboration with a professional publishing team. Our aim is to work closely with the field to produce innovative and valuable materials to help managers, trainers, practitioners and students. We are keen to receive feedback on publications and new ideas for future projects.

Contents

Figures

Tables

Acknowledgements

A large number of people are involved in the production of any book, and this is no exception. Many of the names go unrecorded but we would like to thank all who have been involved, in particular those who have translated chapters, and the staff at Russell House who have been enthusiastic and helpful as this book and the project of which it forms a part have developed. We would like to extend our thanks to the following who have influenced the development of the ideas in this book: Willi Fischges, Jordi Sabater i Garcia, and Francesco Villa. Individually, the authors have been influenced by many others, too numerous to mention, and to all of them we offer our thanks.

We also wish to thank the European Union without whose financial support this book would not have been possible. The EU provided the opportunity for us to come together as a group, and enabled us, through mobility programmes, to build good working relationships.

As ever, the editors and the authors of the book gratefully acknowledge the help of others but accept responsibility for the book's contents—including any mistakes!

The Authors

Adrian Adams is Senior Lecturer in Social Work at Canterbury Christ Church University College. Previously he has worked as a social worker and as a Social Work Education Advisor for the Central Council for Education and Training in Social Work (CCETSW). Current research and teaching interests are in the role and contribution of social work in community care. He is editor of the *Kent Journal of Practice Research*, an annual publication, sponsored by the Kent Consortium for Education and Training in Social Work Education.

Oldřich Chytil is Director of Social Work Studies at the Medico-Social Faculty, Ostrava University, Czech Republic. He is interested in the theory and methods of social work and social work training. He is President of the Association of Social Work Schools in the Czech Republic.

Peter Erath is Professor of Social Work Theory at the Catholic University of Eichstaett, Department of Social Work. He has previously worked as a teacher in the field of special education. He is a member of the German Society for Social Work and has been head of several research projects with large welfare organisations in Bavaria. He was co-ordinator of the European Module Project, 'Social Security Systems and Social Work Theories'. Current research and teaching interests are in the area of social work theories, social work with young people and comparative social work.

Rino Fasol is a researcher at the Dipartimento di Sociologia e Ricerca Sociale and Professor of Organization of Social Services at the Corso di diploma in Servizio sociale of the Universita' degli Studi di Trento (Italy). His current research interests are in the field of the organization of the social and health care systems at national and local level.

Montserrat Feu is Professor of Social Work and co-ordinator of international relations at the School of Social Work, Ramon Llull University, (Barcelona). She has worked as a social worker in the Catalonian Local Administration. She is also responsible for several training projects at the Catalan Official College of Social Workers. She is interested in the intercultural and interdisciplinary dimensions of social work.

Juha Hämäläinen is Professor of Social Work (special area Social Pedagogy), Head of Department of Social Sciences at the University of Kuopio, Finland. He is interested in theoretical questions concerning social work, especially the development of ideas therein.

Emmanuel Jovelin is Doctor of Sociology and diplomate of political sciences. He is a researcher and Professor in Sociology at the Social Institute of Lille-Vauban (Catholic University of Lille). He has published *Devenir travailleur social aujourd'hui, vocation ou repli?* (Ed. L'harmattan, 1999).

Wolfgang Klug is Professor of Social Work (Methods) at the Catholic University of Eichstaett (Department of Social Work). He has previously worked as a head of a centre of social aid. His special areas of research are adult education, management of social organizations and quality management. He is a member of the German Society of Social Work (Community of research) and the German Association of Social Work (Community of practitioners). In 1999 he was elected as the Dean of his department.

Geert van der Laan is Professor of Social Work at the University of Utrecht, (Department of General Social Sciences), Netherlands. He is conducting research on 'Street Children' in Romania. He is Chairman of the One Europe Foundation and Member of the editorial board of the *European Journal of Social Work*.

Pauli Niemelä is Professor of Social Policy, with particular reference to social work, and Dean of the Faculty of Social Sciences at the University of Kuopio. He is a permanent expert used by the Social and Health Ministry (the National Research and Development Centre for Welfare and Health). His particular interests include human security/insecurity and coping methods, health and social policy, social ethics, social work in public health and the inter-generational questions.

Radka Popelková is Senior Lecturer at the Medico-Social Faculty, Ostrava University, Czech Republic. Her main interests are social policy, especially housing and employment policy.

Steven Shardlow is Director of Social Work Studies at the University of Sheffield, United Kingdom. Previously he has worked as a social work practitioner and manager in both field and residential work. He is ex-chairperson of the Association of Teachers in Social Work Education, (UK), and Editor of the *Journal of Social Work*, (a new journal to be published by Sage in 2001). In addition, he is a member of the Executive Committee of the European Association of Schools of Social Work, representing the UK. He has been involved in international social work, particularly in Europe through development work, consultancy and research. Current research and teaching interests are in the areas of social work values and ethics, comparative social work practice and social work education, especially practice learning. He has published widely in these fields and his work has been translated into several languages.

Horst Sing is Professor of Political Science at the Catholic University of Eichstaett, Department of Social Work. He is responsible for the 'Studienschwerpunkt interkulturelle/internationale Sozialarbeit' of the faculty and is Director of the 'Institut fuer vergleichende Sozialarbeitswissenschaft und interkulturelle/internationale Sozialarbeit' (ISIS), Eichstaett. Current research and teaching interests are in the area of International and Intercultural Social Work, especially in the Third World under different aspects of globalization.

Evelyne Tully is Professor of social work at Social Institute of Lille-Vauban (Catholic University of Lille).

Preface

Adrian Adams, Peter Erath and Steven Shardlow

This book is the result of three years of co-operation by a multi-national group, sponsored by the Socrates Programme of the European Union. The initial aim of the group was to develop and then implement into the curricula of their respective educational institutions a common module on Theories and Models of Social Security Systems and Social Work Practice in Europe. Inevitably, in such a time consuming and demanding project, not all European countries could be taken into account; nevertheless, the group does include representatives from the range of different models of social security systems across Europe. One result of the work of the group has been to produce three books. The first is this book, which explores the historical and political contexts of social work in several European countries. The second book builds upon this analysis and provides critical analyses of key themes in social work across Europe. Third, a bibliography of materials published in English about social work in Europe. These publications are intended to complement each other in the development of understanding about social work across Europe, and to promote the development of better practice through the exchange and sharing of ideas.

During this programme of work, there has been an active exchange of lecturers and students from the participating universities within a framework of a student and staff mobility programme, with the texts, that comprise the contents of this book, emerging from a process of continuous development, discussion and refinement by the group. These texts have been devised to form the basis of lectures and seminars for social work students with an interest in the European dimension of social work and who undertake visits abroad as part of their studies. However, the texts are not solely aimed at students. Practitioners, managers and policy makers within the various countries within Europe cannot afford to ignore the ways in which social work practice is developing elsewhere in Europe. Hence, this book is intended to inform current debates about policy and practice and to help in the creation and exchange of ideas about new and innovative practice.

There are an increasing number of publications on the topic of Social Work in Europe. In general, they approach the topic either from the particular point of view of an individual or a small group of authors, serve as a collection of descriptions of the status quo of social work in specific countries or present a comparison of a number of national approaches to a particular practice issue. In this volume, the authors have sought to develop texts that combine both a description and analysis of their respective nation's welfare systems. As such, they allow for the identification of emergent themes and insights into not only their particular systems but into European-wide trends and processes. The work presented here will also serve as a background to the second volume of work by the authors that provides a developed and critical analysis of key dimensions and common concerns in social work across Europe.

It has not been possible to represent every country in Europe within such a volume. There is an imbalance in that the majority of countries are part of the European Union. This represents neither the narrow mindedness of the authors, nor a prejudice against Eastern and Central Europe, but more the practicalities of funding projects such as this under the European Union's Socrates Programme. Nonetheless, there has been a deliberate attempt to include examples of social work as practised in very different welfare regimes.

Editing principles

This book is published in English, since increasingly within Europe, English is the language of international communication. This places those for whom English is not a first language and who read this book at some disadvantage. With this in mind, the editors have sought to avoid unnecessary complexity of language and to provide explanations, within the text, wherever this seems to be helpful.

Translation from other languages into English in a specialised field such as social work is problematic. There are many terms that have no direct and meaningful translation. According to Cooper and Pitts, (1993), within the field of European social work there are a number of different vocabularies, each internally consistent and where terms derive meaning by virtue of reference to other terms. This presents enormous difficulties in translating *meaning* rather than words. We have tried to provide explanations for such terms but also have tended to leave these translated words to stand for themselves (for example, the term 'activitation'—see below). Hence, we hope that the book will introduce both new terms and ideas into the specialised language of social work as expressed in English.

Those who write English as a second language bring an additional richness and vitality to the language, often introducing ideas and modes of expression that reflect their own linguistic background. We have tried to preserve this richness in the material included in this book while also ensuring grammatical consistency and correctness.

The English language presents other problems. For example, it is difficult to refer to both men and women in an all-inclusive way when using the single pronoun. Using *he/she* or *(s) he* is clumsy, so we have tended wherever possible to use the plural form *they*—even if sometimes this strains the grammar.

There is anther vexed question—spelling. There are two kinds of English, the American and the British. This book contains both varieties; the use of either is common across Europe. If an author has used British spelling, we have retained it, likewise with those who have used American spelling.

The contents

In the course of eight seminars, each lasting several days, during which the group discussed and debated the ideas that came to form the content of these texts, a number of shared themes emerged that provided the basic premises underlying the work and shaped the construction of this book.

The over-arching view reached was that across Europe, the impact of global factors and processes have essentially undermined the capacity of Nation States to fulfil implicit aspirations and expectations of the concept of a Welfare State. As a result, the organising principles of social work are undergoing a profound reconstruction around issues of morality, rationality and capacity for promoting social inclusion and participation, as are the processes and procedures by which needs and problems are identified, defined, explained and response strategies developed.

From this perspective, the texts identify both the different and common dimensions of social work, highlighting the importance of the respective approach to the welfare regime, the regional structures, the level of reflexivity, the typical methods and the extent of professional identity in each European country. As such, the presentations of each system of social work in the different European States does not minimise the importance of the concrete political, social, economic and cultural differences of each country, but serve as a an orientation towards an understanding of how the nature and impact of global forces present a new and common challenge to all systems of social security.

The introduction, therefore, explores the impact of globalisation and modernisation processes in Europe, not only on the economic sector but also on the future of social policy, social security systems and social work practice. It argues that even though significant differences remain between welfare systems in Europe, variations in social work can be attributed to their common function as the specific response to social problems in each country. Besides the different dimensions of social work, such as the particular welfare regime or approach, location, organisation and actors in social work practice, a theoretical framework is presented which allows for a better understanding of the country specific texts. These country specific texts present the context and current situation of social work in the selected countries, based on a critical analysis of the historical and political background, both to the respective welfare regime, as well as the concrete construction of social work theory and practice. All the texts refer to the respective national social policy, social legislation, social security system, social work science, social work theory and practice, professional debate, ethical codes, social work education, social work organisations and offer a perspective on what could be an appropriate role and purpose for future social work practice. At the end of each country specific chapter we have included a series of questions for further consideration. These are designed to help students, practitioners and managers to consider the relevance of the material in relation to their own experience.

In conclusion, some ideas and commitments about European social work, which are shared by the author-group, are presented. Though social work practice in different European countries displays diversity within the different welfare systems, the emergent similarities in trends and challenges provide a basis for discussion, and outline the key dimensions of social work that are elaborated upon in the forthcoming volume by the author-group.

Chapter One

Introduction: The Challenge of Globalisation

Adrian Adams

The term 'globalisation' is now generally applied when referring to those processes of transformation that rapidly impact upon each location, sector, aspect and problem across and within Nation States (Giddens1994). Although initially associated with economic factors such as the free movement of capital, particularly following the break up of the European Eastern bloc, increasingly it is recognised that the flow of information and ideas as well as political and social activity occurs beyond and across national borders. As such they arise in and follow global trends to the extent that they now constitute a force that can no longer be controlled by any central authority (Kennedy 1996). In examining the impact of globalisation on world society, and in particular the countries of Europe, it is argued that national governments can no longer, either alone or jointly, control its effects, as it is within the separate functions of their subsystems, for example through the economy, scientific and technological developments and the legal system that the process of globalisation emerges, (Giddens, 1990). The price that has to be paid for this is that the benefits of 'progress' and 'development' increasingly flow directly into a global market and they no longer serve to augment tax revenue or to create jobs in the country where the activities originated. Thus, even the members of the European Community are competing with one another as global, economic and technical rivals and the effects of Globalisation are such that they simultaneously generate new opportunities for both competition and harmonisation across increasingly fragile national boundaries.

Across Europe the effects of globalisation processes have led to discussions on the future of the welfare state. Whereas traditional conceptions of the welfare state have assumed that it would be possible to maintain the unity of society to the satisfaction of the majority of people, despite all the complexity and highly differentiated pluralistic attitudes regarding 'social fairness' and 'liberty of the individual person' and the incorporation of basic values through politics, the assumption nowadays, increasingly, is that the antagonism between the implicit collective commitment of the modern welfare state and the right to follow ones own objectives represents an insoluble paradox, (Wilding, 1997).

One understanding of what is referred to by the term 'modern society', is that it constitutes 'a particular way of governing' and serves as the 'target and object' of national state government interventions, (Walters, 1997). From this perspective models of social welfare can be appreciated as deriving from dominant historically situated ideological forces. Thus in nineteenth century liberal capitalist society, 'poor laws' were directed towards the protection of the respectable from the dangerous classes and the control of labour. In the wake of the political consensus of post war reconstruction there emerged the 'welfare state', characterised as a community of citizens with equal status undivided by class, based on achievement rather than privilege. The project of a state, rather than liberal, capitalist regime to actively intervene in reconciling the contradictions of individual capitalist accumulation and societal legitimisation and the avoidance of economic malfunction and social conflicts through the insulation of the economic system and life-world through functional separation of tasks within the political administrative system has been exposed as contradictory, (Habermas, 1976; and Offe, 1984).

The paradox of the modern welfare state has been exposed as being that whilst its function is to ensure that all people are integrated into society, due to the developments in the global economy, it is evidently less and less capable of achieving this task, (Luhmann, 1997). Increasingly politicians no longer assume that the full inclusion of all people into society is possible; rather it now falls to citizens themselves, rather than the state, to take responsibility for achieving social integration.

Since the late 1970s substantial changes have occurred in production organisation. These have been characterised as a shift from a 'Fordist' mode, associated with post-war mass-production dependent on stable markets within a welfare state political economy; to a 'post-Fordist' mode of flexible specialisation, (Piore and Sabel, 1984), characterised by change and innovation, dependent upon automated production technology, flexible and efficient use of capital and labour and the reduction of waste in highly competitive markets. (For an examination of the relationship between 'post-Fordist' modes of production organisation and welfare organisation see Burrows and Loader, 1994.)

Constructions of contemporary society, whether characterised as high-, late- or post-modern are shaped by global forces and disruptions to the social systems such as:

- post-Fordist conditions of production and accumulation
- pluralism in moral politics
- diversity in individual and social identity.

The existance of these factors all challenge the presumptions of the possibility of improvement, development and realisation of ideals and goals in the following areas; the reliable foundations for generalisable knowledge; the primacy of scientific objectivity and instrumental rationalism. All challenging the Nation State as the unifying and directing form of social organisation.

Classifications of welfare

Classifications of welfare states in different countries have been developed primarily in respect of either their level of expenditure on social welfare, the level of 'decommodification', (Esping-Anderson, 1990), that is, the scale and manner of delivery of provision provided by the different welfare states, or by the 'coverage' of social protection schemes, that determine who receives welfare provision and the extent to which this is provided for by the state, (Ferrera, 1993). Recently, attempts have been made to classify welfare states according to both the quantity of welfare they provide and to where they stand within the 'ideal-types' of welfare regimes, i.e. social insurance or universal state provision, (Bonoli, 1997). Such classifications have led not only to the identification of four ideal-types of

welfare regime, that is, high and low spending universal systems financed primarily through taxation, and high or low spending systems financed through contributory earnings related pensions, but also to the existence of a number of mixed or difficult cases that include characteristics from more than one 'ideal-type' and that consequentially have the potential to evolve within a number of dimensions.

This multi-dimensional nature and consequent diversity amongst national welfare systems, deriving from the different cultural, ideological, political and socio-economic traditions, history and circumstances of nation states has implications for their potential convergence. The state welfare systems established during the early post-war years located social work within particular organisational contexts. All of these welfare regimes shared many common aims and objectives, most notably a concern with how best to combine the expansion of global economic markets with arrangements for domestic social stability and international peace. However, they are also characterised by their national diversity. Each State, whilst subject to the impact of global factors, has formulated its own response and social policies in the context of its particular history, traditions and legal and organisational frameworks. Therefore, the response of each state is mediated through its own welfare regime, which in itself generates its own unique formulation of social problems.

Whilst the consequences of globalisation are a common challenge to all European social welfare and social work systems, in both coping with the paradox of the modern welfare state, and avoiding social exclusion, each country has developed its own approach to dealing with these problems.

Global tendencies amongst welfare regimes

The impact of the Second World War and the emergence of welfare regimes based upon nationally specific traditions of corporatism, collectivism and other constructions of social responsibility within democratic systems, presented the nation states of Europe with the possibility of constructing the boundaries of and possibilities for social welfare services within the context of newly established state bureaucratic institutions, (Lorenz, 1994). The impact of global tendencies, for example, the influence of trans-national corporations and agencies, declining birth rates, the rise in the elderly population, the decrease in the working population and the dominance of world markets in shaping political ideologies through the relationships established between levels of economic development and levels of social expenditure, does not however imply that each nation state developed similar institutions. Nor have the persistent global problems (such as demographic changes and patterns in family types and household structures, with the increase in numbers of people living in poverty), implied that all nation states have responded by departing from the principles and structures of their existing arrangements in favour of a common 'global' system. However, even where significant differences remain between different European welfare regimes, with each state formulating its own response and social policies to the challenge of social problems in the context of its particular history, traditions and legal and organisational frameworks they can all be seen to follow a general process. Table 1.1 illustrates how common policy functions are located within welfare regimes; Figure 1.1 shows how nation states respond to the impact of global factors.

Table 1.1: The Location of Social Policy Functions within State Welfare Systems

Level	Policy Function
National Framework	Defining model or regime of social welfare and legislation
Regional	Strategic reconciliation and interpretation of duties and powers
Institutional	Organisation and administration of specific objectives
Professional	Implementation within practice regimes of technical expertise and codes of conduct.

Figure 1.1: State Responses to Global Factors

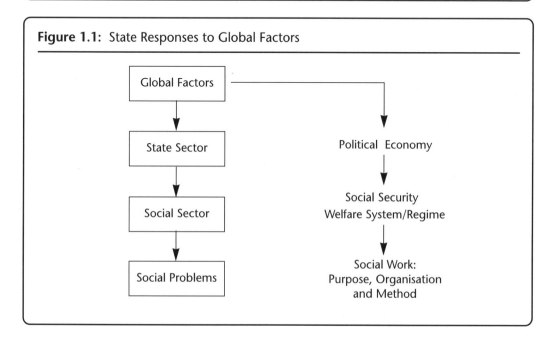

Variations in social work can therefore be attributed to their particular purpose as a specific response, rather than a solution, to the social problems arising within the particular approach to welfare as applied in different countries. One metaphor that has been used to illustrate differences in welfare approaches and the consequent role of social workers has been applied by van der Laan (this volume) to the Welfare Safety Net as being either a 'hammock', to support economically inactive citizens or a 'trampoline', that seeks to re-integrate them into economic activity. (Figure 1.2 below)

Whilst, as we shall see later, local variations amongst welfare regimes emerged and still persist, the current concern and central question for any model of a welfare state is, who pays for and who benefits from the welfare system and how can individual citizen's rights and liberties be reconciled with collective benefits and responsibilities? To this extent, the nature and extent of welfare arises from a process of negotiation between the state, representing the social collective, the market, representing the interests of capital and the individual citizen. (Figure 1.3 below)

One particular effect of globalisation that has impacted upon the welfare of individuals is the extent to which their status as citizens is determined through reference not only to the state but also increasingly the market. The notion of citizenship and the rights and responsibilities it confers is thus emerging as a concept determined by an individual's economic status and relationship to both the labour market, and increasingly their patterns of consumption of either private or public, that is, state funded commodities. (Figure 1.4 below)

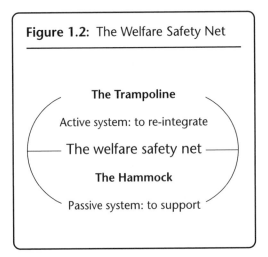

Figure 1.2: The Welfare Safety Net

Figure 1.4: Citizenship as Economic Status

Social Status	Economic Status
Child/dependent	Pre-active
Adult: Independent	Active: Employed— Wage earner
Welfare Dependent	Inactive: Unemployed/ Employable Unemployed/ Unemployable
Elderly	Post-active Independent State dependent

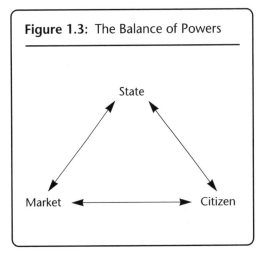

Figure 1.3: The Balance of Powers

Globalisation and its impact on social work systems

As a world-wide phenomena arising from the expansion of the capitalist world economy, globalisation impinges not only upon economic, technological, social and welfare institutions, but also upon understandings and experiences of the day-to-day transactions within them. Adopting a global perspective provides an understanding of not only convergence but also divergence in what constitutes social work in any country. Any adequate understanding of what essentially characterises social work requires that it is approached within the context of its relationship to the state and the community within which it is located.

The nature of globalisation and its relationship to and impact upon social work has been well documented and analysed (Trevillion, 1997; Dominelli and Hoogvelt, 1996). They argue that globalisation is embedded within the social work enterprise, in as much as it derives its traditions from: an international exchange and movement of ideas, which are central to the formulation of the purpose and characteristics of practice; its location within state welfare systems and its organisational delivery through bureaucratic agencies. In particular, the process of globalisation impacts upon understandings and constructions of client autonomy and the process and procedures of risk assessment and management in respect of vulnerable children and adults with regard to both shared and conflicting understandings of the concepts of free choice, informed choice, best interests, entitlement and preference.

The contributors to this book argue that globalisation has influenced the development of the philosophical grounding, professional identity, purpose, methodologies employed and the organisational context of social work practice. Understandings of social work can thus be best understood as being increasingly constructed through a global discourse on the forms and values of 'helping' and 'caring' that are contextually situated within localised, multi-dimensional complexes comprising:

- the public, political, bureaucratic institutions that are legitimised through social legislation and subject to periodical reconstitution;

- the personal, private, mediated and interpreted contexts in which social action occurs;

- the educational discourses and traditions based upon and within academic disciplines and institutions;

- the sets of particular skills that imply technical activity based upon the principles of scientific, empirical, naturalistic, positivist enquiry and action;

- the humanist endeavour or moral activity drawing upon universal principles, historical and cultural values and ethical codes.

Current constructions of social work practice are thus emergent through its activities relating to both 'caring about', the management and allocation of resources and 'caring for', the act of caring through the provision of services.

The tradition of social work

The global dimensions of social work practice emerged from, and are embodied in, the forms of social casework and social pedagogy, deriving from the cross fertilisation of mainly European and American practitioners and educators initially in the late 1920s and again in the context of emergent welfare states following the post-war period of national reconstruction.

In its initial formulation, social casework drew particularly upon the traditions of both The Society for Organising Charitable Relief and Repressing Mendacity (The COS) and the Settlement Movement, representing notions of Christian charity and humanitarian philanthropy through community action and reform in the UK (Younghusband, 1981) and the development of the social diagnostic approach through the work of Mary Richmond in the USA (Richmond, 1917). Social casework, underpinned by the application of psychoanalytic and sociological theory, presented itself as providing a scientific basis for social work and its claim to professional status.

In continental Europe the pedagogic tradition, encompassing educational, social and spiritual dimensions, impacted upon social work practice in the forms of social pedagogy and animation. Whilst drawing upon a common foundation of Christian morality and humanitarian philanthropy to that of the casework model, the pedagogical approach and its derivatives emphasise the learning process of the individual within a particular social context.

These two approaches, whilst sharing a common heritage, yet diverging in respect of the academic traditions and discourses through which they were articulated, emerged as the predominant forms of social work practice across Europe. Whilst both sought to acknowledge and locate individuals within a social context, in practice they have tended to operate at the level of individual interventions. Both approaches have, particularly since the late 1970s, been increasingly subject to challenge from within state welfare agencies.

However, in spite of the pressure from welfare agencies to re-shape professional practice, many of the essential principles that define the nature of relationship between 'practitioners' and 'clients' have remained remarkably robust across and within the range of activities that constitute social work practice.

> *Social workers' practice is mediated on the premise that individuals have troubles that warrant intervention. For social workers, the task-at-hand is that something, (resources, resolution, placation etc.) has to be done with some individuals, groups or communities. Social workers see as problematic not their practice but the organisation or resources available to them as well as their clients.*
>
> (Camilleri, 1996: p 89)

Variation in social work practice

According to Howe, social work:

> *...does not exist discretely, independent of its organisation and political context. What social workers think and do can be understood only in relation to the intellectual, ideological, and material surroundings in which they find themselves.*
>
> (Howe, 1991b: p 204)

In Sibeon's sociological analysis of social work, variation within social work derives from the malleability and instability of social work materials, i.e. anything pertaining to social work and their subsequent transformation between different social work sites by a variety of actors. He argues that social work material in local sites is shaped by and in turn shapes materials in other sites and that the process by which actors within and across sites interpret and manipulate material, whilst not 'insulated from larger patterns of general cultural and political meanings and practices', is not structurally determined, but is the product of actors 'strategies to achieve *self-formulated* interests'.

> *This means that the shape of social policy and social work is potentially highly variable and shifting: the shape of major social work materials at any moment in time is not a 'necessary effect' of any hypothetical 'needs' of social structure, but an emergent product of interaction among social actors who strategically disseminate material across sites and who interact and negotiate with each other (sometimes co-operatively, sometimes competitively) in pursuance of their perspectives and self-formulated interests and objectives.*
>
> (Sibeon, 1991: p 43)

Global concerns, within a European context at least, and particularly with regard to the issue of social inclusion and exclusion, have led to calls for European-wide standards for social care and the formulation of treaties on social rights that include clauses on anti-discrimination and equal opportunities, and the production of pan European codes of ethics for social work (e.g. International Federation of Social Workers, 1997). However, the principle of subsidiarity, and in particular the dualistic structure of the English legal system, leave the implementation of social policy and actions within the jurisdiction and interpretation of different national systems.

The variety of responses to common problems across European states highlights the structural differences between welfare regimes in respect of their arrangements for addressing the insurance/assistance divide, their capacity for decentralisation, promoting user participation and their dependency upon the provision of informal/invisible care. Such differences, arising from existing arrangements for funding and autonomous decision making at central, regional and local tiers of the state, in turn gives rise to the relative constraints and opportunities to social work practice.

Whilst it is true that social work, in its location and its interrelationship with post-war state welfare systems has been subject to fundamental problems, arguments and struggles over centralised or local and specialist or generic models and arrangements, at a European level, where welfare regimes differ, variation creates even greater tensions. For example, as Ruxton comments:

> *The provision and organisation of child protection services across member states varies enormously, and there is no guarantee that an abused child would*

receive a common response, even at a basic level, in different countries. For example, some states have established specific child protection agencies, whilst others are reliant on police and health services to ensure children's protection and welfare.

(Ruxton, 1996: p 7)

Purpose in social work

Howe has argued that the social work enterprise is primarily moral in its purpose in that it seeks to realise:

> ...humanism with a scientific face: ...to recover or isolate those who are in danger of becoming a social and economic liability.   (Howe, 1991a: p 149)

However, in his analysis of the construction in England of a unified family service in the early 1970s, he identified 'a critical association between the family and the maintenance of the state' (ibid: p 152) which reinforced the purpose of social work practice as being the social management of the family through supervision (surveillance) and intervention (education and treatment) achieved through an alliance between the courts and social work, (see also Donzelot, 1980).

Organisation of social work

This increasing emphasis within welfare regimes upon regulation has essentially defined the 'social' as that which emerges between the private and the public, a domain defined by both welfare and legal judgements within which interpersonal concerns are played out before a political audience. Historical accounts of the emergence of modern social work attribute its formation to the possibilities presented by the opening up of a new social space (Philp, 1979). This space arose from the bourgeois project to claim for itself the enlightenment ideal of the liberation of the individual from the constraints and domination of natural and sovereign law. An aspiration made possible through the powerful alliance of science, medicine, law and capital within the organising and regulatory administrative system of the democratic liberal nation state (Donzelot 1984). The 'social' became that:

> ...area where the state penetrates the world of private relations insofar as what takes place in those relationships concerns the rest of society, with those who work in this arena being defined as social workers.   (Howe, 1994: p 17)

As Howe observed, the nature of the alliance between social workers and their clientele has, due to the pressing need to reduce uncertainty, given rise to 'justice replacing welfare as social work's conceptual guide', with a 'legal partnership' replacing the traditional 'therapeutic alliance'. Social workers now:

> ...embrace both the judicial and the therapeutic in single acts of intervention—they judge and they treat; they control and they cure.   (ibid: p 517)

Clients and their behaviour are defined in terms of legal and, increasingly, economic consumption conceptualisations.

> The social worker's practices are more likely to be task-oriented and performance related, quantifiable and measurable, product-minded and subject to quality controls.   (ibid: p 529)

Additionally the 'post-fordist' organisation of social work agencies has created a starker division between strategy and operation through the:

> ...establishment of a tight core of senior, strategic managers at the centre, and of staff grouped into cost centres with managers at the operational level.

(Lloyd, 1998: p 713)

whereby,

> More work is devolved, but there is less flexibility in working conditions and limited decision-making power.   (ibid: p 717)

The increased separation within the welfare system between the functions of assessment of need, purchase and provision of service, allied to a return to specialist practices and teams has led to an increased degree of differentiation between welfare recipients. Increasingly, access to services is dependent upon the service categorisation or classification of whether the individual is someone who is a problem, often by reference to legal definitions or as someone who has a problem, that is, the vulnerable and distressed.

Conclusion

The contributions in this volume are premised on the acceptance that the processes of globalisation have indeed penetrated the fabric of societies and have effectively undermined the capacity of individual nation states to maintain a coherent welfare regime. As a result the role, functions and indeed identity of social work practice has been essentially challenged.

In order to address this challenge, those who are concerned with maintaining the continued presence of a valid form and role for social work in contemporary society need to broaden their understanding beyond the immediate horizons of national welfare regimes. The following chapters will examine how social work practice emerged in the context of different European countries and its prospects for future development.

Chapter Two

Social Policy and Social Work in the Czech Republic

Oldřich Chytil and Radka Popelková

Introduction

November 1989 represents a landmark in the development of Czechoslovakia with the beginning of the transition from communism, under the so-called 'Velvet Revolution'. Since that date Czechoslovakia, and especially from 1993 when Czechoslovakia split into two countries the Czech Republic and Slovakia, the Czech Republic has been undergoing a complete transformation in society comprising two major strands. Firstly, an economic transformation from a centrally controlled economy to a market economy. Secondly, a political transition from a totalitarian to a democratic regime. Both of these transitions have, as a consequence, led to social reform. Currently the Czech Republic is a society that has developed a market economy based on ownership and property but with substantial state intervention. As a result, social inequalities have arisen which might otherwise have been prevented or reduced. Czech society is not yet being formed through the long-term functioning of market and democratic mechanisms and subsequent social-political systems, (Machonin, 1998: p 5). These changes have also been accompanied by a transformation of the legal system. The Document of Basic Rights and Freedoms was approved, becoming part of the constitution of the Czech Republic after the break from Slovakia in 1993. New laws have been enacted since the start of this transformation but they do not always reflect the current state of society and lag behind the economic transformation.

The economic transformation was characterised by the restitution of property and by privatisation. Property confiscated after 1948 was returned to the former owners or transferred to municipalities. Socialist co-operative societies became private co-operatives or private companies. Some 22,000 shops, restaurants and service businesses were sold by auction and large and medium sized companies were privatised. The total value of the property thus privatised was some 1,900 billion Czech Crowns, (Potůček, 1997: pp 106–107). Part of this transformation resulted in a change for many from relative wealth to poverty. There was higher unemployment and an increase in the cost of living—the cost of food, consumer goods, rent, heating, electricity and public transport were all constantly rising. In particular, the cost of flats in some areas reached a level of a hundred times the average salary. In contrast, there was a significant decrease in incomes—real incomes are still below their level in 1989. This sudden decrease in real income, together with the increase in prices in 1990/91, was accepted by most people as necessary to achieve the change to a market economy. People anticipated that future economic prosperity would be the result of such changes (Machonin and Tuček, 1996: p 18; Tomeš, 1996: p 175).

Most of the population supported these changes in the first half of the 1990s and thus supported the neo-liberal political parties. However, by 1994 this position had begun to change. Public opinion surveys carried out in 1995 showed a growing discontent with existing policies. Almost half of those surveyed said that their standard of living was better in 1989 than in the mid-90s. The majority of the population were no longer satisfied with the economic and social policies of the conservative neo-liberals (mainly represented by the Civic Democratic Party led by Václav Klaus). Growing feelings of social injustice and the suspicion that the newly formed wealthy class had used illegal means to obtain their wealth appeared in the results of the surveys (Machonin, 1999: p 5). The disadvantageous economic development and the growth of economic crime contributed to the growing strength of the main opposition party, the Czech Social Democratic Party which strengthened its position in the 1996 elections and gained power in 1998.

The Consequences of the Transformation of Society

There was a continuous decrease in the gross domestic product during the 1990s, with the exception of the period from 1994–1996, and also in the second half of the nineties considerable economic problems arose. Apart from the GDP falling below the level of 1989 there was a deficit in foreign trade due to the poor management of the banks. By the first half of 1998, the cost to the state of saving the banking system had reached 160 billion Czech Crowns (Matocha 1998: p 11). The problems with the banking system resulted from subsidies to poorly performing companies where the state was a major share-owner, the failure of wages and salaries to keep pace with increased costs (health and education are amongst the areas showing the largest fall in real incomes) and from the failure of many companies where the owners were only interested in their own enrichment. These difficulties have led to a situation where employees may not be paid for several months, and legislation to prevent this is only now being prepared. Moreover, the many changes in society have resulted in more social problems, including increased poverty, unemployment and a rise in crime.

Poverty

Today, even the nature of poverty has changed. Before 1989, poverty had generally been temporary and associated with the family life cycle. Social policies were introduced to counter the effects of 'life cycle' poverty such as tax allowances for families with children, child allowance and paid maternity leave. Now a new area of poverty has arisen as a result of a shrinking labour market, i.e. discrimination and families who have not adapted to the new conditions. Whole new areas of the economy have been struck by poverty, since economic changes have limited the macro-economic actions which had traditionally supported sectors and areas of poor economic performance (Možný and Mareš, 1995: pp 17–25). It is mainly those families with children who have been worst affected. In 1997 the net monthly income per employed family member with children was

5419 Czech Crowns. This figure was 4195 Czech Crowns less than for those without children and even 221 Czech Crowns less than for pensioners (Zpráva, 1999: p 5).

Due to the poor economic conditions and the increased probability of poverty occurring as a result of unemployment, attempts have been made to alleviate this situation through the approval of the Law on Minimum Wage and the Law on Subsistence Minimum. According to these laws, 'subsistence minimum' is that level of a citizen's income below which a state of material need exists. If income falls below this minimum and cannot be increased because of age, health or other serious reasons then the state provides help through social care benefits. In February, 1991, the level of the minimum wage was set at approximately 50 per cent of the average wage and this was 6 per cent higher than the minimum subsistence level established in November 1991. By 1998 the real purchasing power of the minimum wage had fallen to 60 per cent of that in 1991 and this led to the complete collapse of the minimum wage, both due to its collapse as a protective social function and its misuse in the grey economy for tax and insurance evasion (Zpráva, 1999: p 6). The purchasing power of the subsistence minimum had also fallen, reducing the standard of living of those families with children relying on state benefits. The purchasing power of the subsistence minimum is now 25 per cent less than in 1989 and 12 per cent less than when it was set in November 1991. Consequently, it now only provides temporary protection from material need, and then only at the lowest levels of poverty which are still acceptable to maintain some human dignity, (Zpráva, 1999: p 6–7).

Unemployment

For several generations, unemployment had not been a significant factor in Czech society. During the first years of economic transformation unemployment was very low, averaging about 3 per cent. Apart from the development of service industries, a reduction in the number of people of pensionable age still working, extending maternity leave from two to three years, providing parental benefit until a child was four years old and extending holiday entitlement by one week all played a significant role in maintaining a high level of employment. However, the manner in which privatisation was achieved in the Czech Republic has influenced levels of unemployment. Companies were not restructured prior to privatisation. This was left to the new owners, who were required to restructure and down size the workforce in the unfavourable economic conditions following direct ownership, (Národní, 1999: p 1).

The level of unemployment has been gradually increasing. In 1996 the figure was 3.1 per cent, in 1997, 4.3 per cent and in 1998, 6 per cent. In January 1999 the level of unemployment in the Czech Republic had reached 8.1 per cent, and 419,000 people were out of work. By March that year the figure was 8.3 per cent, (Důležité, 1999: pp 30–31). The higher the level of unemployment, the lower the number of vacancies. There are 50 people for every vacancy in some areas and even more in others. There is a significant difference between areas—the lowest being in Prague and the highest, about 15 per cent, in areas where heavy industry, mainly mining, was once dominant. Young people without training, women with small children, those with low-level qualifications and the physically and mentally handicapped are amongst the groups most at risk, (Národní, 1999: p 1). The largest area of unemployment involves young people, and approximately 40 per cent of those recorded as unemployed are under 30 with the highest level amongst those under 19. Young people are considered to be of less use to employers because of military service or starting a family. Older age groups are less affected, partly due to early retirement, (Zpráva, 1999: p 2).

Crime

The transformation of society has been accompanied by a high increase in crime. In 1990 the number of recorded crimes was 216,852, by 1998 the figure had doubled to 425,930. Similarly, in 1989, a total of 71,069 people were prosecuted for criminal acts, by 1998 the figure was 129,271. The increase in criminal behaviour amongst children and teenagers is particularly significant. In 1990 the level of recorded crimes committed by children in the Czech Republic stood at 4,091, by 1998

this had risen to 11,999. In 1990 the level for teenagers stood at 11,167, by 1996 this had risen to a figure of 22,719. Additionally, investigations indicated an increase in the violence of all types of criminal activity amongst children and teenagers, (Kriminální statistiky, 1999).

Demographic change

In the Czech Republic, as in other countries, there have been significant demographic changes. These changes amplify the effects of the economic, political and social transitions. The major demographic change in the Czech Republic is to be found in the change of the distribution of age groupings within the population, as the average life-span increases. It has been estimated that by the year 2000 some 17.5 per cent of the population will be over 60 and that this will have increased to 20.6 per cent by 2010 and to 22.7 per cent by 2020. The average life-span has been gradually increasing during the 1990s (Průša, 1996: pp 7–8). Between 1990 and 1997 the average life-span of men increased from 67.5 years to 70.5 and for women from 76 to 77.5 years. Since 1989 there has been a decrease in the number of marriages, the average age of engaged couples has increased by 2.6 years between 1990 and 1994 and there has also been an increase in the number of unmarried couples. The birth rate has been falling and the age at which mothers have their first child has been increasing. As a result of the decrease in birth rate alone, the population of the Czech Republic has decreased since 1995, (Kokta, 1999: pp 1–7).

Attempts to Explain the Current State of Czech Society

Few sociologists have attempted to explain the current state of Czech society. However, Machonin writes that the Czech Republic's current social structure differs significantly from those of the developed western countries since neither a clearly defined economic elite nor a cultural elite, capable of responding to the needs of a modern society, has yet been established. He sees this lack of an elite as a major cause of the slow progress of the modernisation processes within society in the areas of information technology, business development, availability of a basic range of cheap goods, science, education, health care, ecology protection and democracy, (Machonin and Tuček, 1996: pp 335–336). While, Potůček writes that seven years after the fall of communism, the Czech Republic is characterised by deformed relationships, tension and imbalance between the market, state and civil sectors. The emphasis on private ownership and market principles occurred whilst the state and its authorities still acted in an outdated, centralist manner, (Potůček, 1997: p 176). Similarly, Večerník also sees the problems of Czech society arising from a lack of social stratification, unlike the situation in the west where the middle classes are dominant both numerically and in the socio-political sense. According to him, the transformation of society can be successfully completed only by a transfer of 'class hegemony' from the working classes to the middle classes. The latter support a balanced 'social cover' of the market economy through their economic and public market ambivalence and the democratic change of governments through their political ambivalence, (Večerník, 1997: p 267, pp 269–270). These opinions illustrate the impotence of contemporary Czech sociologists to understand the current problems of their society in the context of the problems brought about by globalization, and this impotence is reflected in such ideological phrases as 'modernisation', 'realism', 'responsibility', and 'the unavoidable character of development', (Hekrdla, 1998: p 6). The philosopher Kosík is perhaps the one writer who attempts to explain the problems of Czech society other than as a result of a poor introduction of the market economy. Hence, he believes that the problems result from two factors: the introduction of the primitive capitalism of the 19th century followed by the sophisticated neo-capitalism of the present. Kosík also assumes that there is no liberating alternative from the capitalist paradigm, (Kosík, 1997: pp 22–28).

Developments in Social Policy Since 1989

Social policy also had to react to the changing economic and social conditions and thus there have been major changes in policy affecting social security, employment, housing, health, education and the family. Social reform has become an inseparable part of the transformation process. The main social policy aims being to transfer to individuals and families the responsibility for their social situation, to liberate decision making on working conditions and pay, to increase the forms and subjects of social policy and to put in place autonomy and self-government in the social field. The original document on social reform was produced by the government of CSFR (Czech and Slovak Federal Republic) in 1990 and included 'safety net' provisions. These reforms were intended to provide the following:

- Active involvement in employment policy, to create the pre-conditions to allow employees to return to active economic activity and to provide a minimal level of income for the unemployed.

- Ensure a minimal level of income to those in work through a so-called minimum wage.

- Guarantee a minimal level of income for individuals and families with children in need by establishing a minimal level of old age pension, establishing a minimum subsistence level etc.

- Some assistance with accommodation for those in need through a contribution to accommodation costs, (Žižková, 1994: pp 10–11).

Social security policy

From the beginning of its existence in 1989, the government of CSFR produced draft proposals for the social security policy it intended to introduce. These policies included social insurance, state social support and social help. The first two of these have already been introduced, and, together, the three aspects of the policy are based on the different social problems they aim to solve.

Social insurance

Social insurance is a preventative policy, in that it aims to put in place financial measures to solve problems that people may face in the future. It includes unemployment insurance, sickness insurance and obligatory pension insurance (in this context the word pension has a wide meaning here and does not only refer to pensions given to older people—the narrow meaning of the term). Social insurance is financed through contributions from employees, employers and the state, and in 1993 became separate from the normal tax system. Old age, disability, widows', widowers' and orphans' pensions are provided through the pensions insurance scheme. Additional voluntary insurance, with a contribution from the state, has also been introduced together with a gradual increase in the retirement age. Since 1990 pensions have become effectively devalued as consumer prices have increased by 5 per cent per year. An increase in the retirement age for men to 62 years and for women to 61 years has been approved. Sickness benefits are based on income, with a top limit, giving 50 per cent of gross daily salary for the first three days and 69 per cent thereafter. Discussion on the total reform of the pension system has now begun as the costs are constantly increasing, whilst there is insufficient income from a reduced workforce to meet them. This discussion centres upon the types of pension, how they should be financed and how responsibility should be divided between the state, employers and individuals. A first step should certainly be to separate the pension fund from the state budget.

State social support

State social support is provided in a variety of areas, for example, in respect of maternity benefits and children's education. Two overall types of benefit are provided. The first are those which depend on the level of income such as child allowance, social supplement, housing allowance and transport allowance; these were introduced in January 1996. Second, those which are provided to all, including parental allowance, provision allowance, foster fathers care benefits, maternity grant and funeral benefit, which were introduced in October 1995. Two additional benefits—heating allowance and accommodation allowance—were introduced in July 1997 as separate benefits, payable for a limited period of four years. With the adoption of the law governing state social support, social

benefits have been unified under one set of regulations and new benefits introduced. The social problems and level of income of families are taken into account much more than in the previous system. Finance for this is provided from the state, related to the minimum subsistence level, which is established and validated through government regulations, (Základní, 1997: p 8 and 18). The declared aims of introducing a system based on need was to reduce benefits for richer families and thus provide more funds to aid those most in need. This latter aim has not been achieved, however, as the percentage of GDP allocated to this has been falling since 1991: from 2.7 per cent to 1.7 per cent by 1998. In real terms, benefits in 1998 were 39 per cent lower than in 1990, (Zpráva, 1999: p 6).

Social help

This system, which currently is no more than a proposal, is intended to ensure the basic living requirements for those who are in a condition of material or social poverty. It includes preventative activities, legal assistance in cases of material and social poverty and providing for special needs. Preventative activities are to be concentrated on the prevention of criminality, drug addiction, xenophobia, racism and violence. Legal assistance is to be provided to those unable to act for themselves because of old age, poor health or low mental ability. A person is deemed to be in a state of material poverty where their income is below the subsistence minimum and cannot be increased because of age, health or other major factors: this would result in an additional living allowance, possibly in the form of a loan. A person is deemed to be in a state of social poverty when they cannot provide their basic needs through being a minor, the loss of self-sufficiency, illness or poor health, family dysfunction, endangered rights or other major factors. Social care services (e.g. community care, sheltered accommodation, institutional accommodation, etc.) and social intervention services (social counselling, social fieldwork socio-therapy, crisis help) are intended as the solutions for social poverty. Social work is the initial source of social help, to be provided by the state, municipal authorities and private organisations, (Návrh, 1997).

Employment policy

In 1991, employment legislation was passed which formed the basis for creating employment offices whose objectives are to help people to find jobs, provide unemployment benefit, counselling, make analyses of the employment market and to be active in employment policy (creating new jobs and retraining schemes). Initially, unemployment benefit was available for a period of one year, now reduced to six months. It is paid at 50 per cent of an average net income for the first three months and 40 per cent for the subsequent three months. After six months, the unemployed move to social care benefits based on the subsistence minimum. The current legal minimum wage is less than the subsistence minimum for an adult and thus does not provide motivation for a return to work. Until December 1998 the minimum wage was 2,650 Czech Crowns and was increased to 3,250 Czech Crowns in January 1999, whereas the subsistence minimum for an adult is 3,430 Czech Crowns.

Housing policy

The intention in transforming housing policy was to transfer responsibility away from the state to the individual, to minimise the role of the state, transfer control to the local level, and to maximise the involvement of the private sector. However, the Czech government failed to create the environment in which this could take place, (Radičová and Potůček, 1998: p 136). The transfer of responsibility from the state to the municipalities was carried out too quickly and without the necessary preparation. This process created a variety of problems. For example, the capability of municipalities to assume this responsibility was overestimated, municipal housing funds were treated as a source of profit, and rents were deregulated and new building ceased, (ibid: pp 138–139). Although the state attempted to make individuals take responsibility for their own housing, this was impracticable due to a shortage of flats and the large gap between incomes and the cost of housing, (ibid: pp 138–139). There is now no real policy on housing: the only solution adopted by the government to the housing problem has been

to deregulate rents. Thus, if public pronouncements are to be believed, creating a market for flats. The housing problem is increasing, as there has been a complete halt in new building. In the second half of the 1980s some 50 to 60,000 flats were built each year, whilst from 1991 to 1994 the annual average was less than 10,000, (Večerník 1998: p 143).

Health policy

As with housing policy, the major development has been towards the privatisation of health services. Regional and District Health Centres, which formed the supporting framework for the existing health system, have been gradually closed. The formation of private health insurance companies has been an important change in health policy as these companies have been made responsible for operating the new compulsory health insurance scheme. Employees have to pay 4.5 per cent of their salaries for health insurance and employers contribute 9 per cent, whilst the state pays for non-earners. The health insurance companies have begun to finance separate health centres. Thus the first non-state health centres have gradually been developed and the first private medical practices have been formed, mainly involving outpatient care—both general practice and specialists, (Potůček, 1995: pp 125–126). Currently, the transformation of the health service is proceeding slowly and uncertainly, due to continual changes in policy, mainly in the area of finance. The financial means required are not available, due both to the worldwide trend of increasing costs for medical care and also poor management of both health centres and insurance companies. The state has attempted to solve these financial difficulties by closing hospitals, limiting the cover provided through health insurance and transferring the financial burden to the patients themselves.

Education policy

Since 1989, an employment market has gradually been created and simultaneously considerable changes have been made in the education system. The state monopoly on the provision of both basic and secondary education no longer exists, and a wide variety of different types of private schools has developed. In particular, technical colleges and grammar schools, which have attempted to be more flexible in meeting the needs of the labour market. Several new universities have been founded and changes made in subject areas and content. The programme for Optimisation of Secondary Schools provides an example of the lack of a clear and consistent policy adopted by the Ministry of Education. The aim of this 'optimisation' programme is to reduce the number of secondary schools, yet, paradoxically, the ministry has recently approved an increase in the number of such schools. Although the changes in the education system have been introduced in an attempt to provide for the real needs of the employment market, the desired results will take time to achieve. Retraining schemes are achieving more success in the current environment than the changes in the education system, (Potůček, 1995: pp 126–127). As a result of the state's poor economic situation, finance for education has been limited to such an extent that a reduction in the quality of the education provided has occurred where, for example, qualified teachers at all levels have been leaving. The Czech Republic spends a smaller proportion of its gross domestic product on education than any other European country.

Family policy

In the field of family policy the emphasis has been on supporting the family throughout its entire life cycle. The legislation on State Social Support in 1995 became the cornerstone of family policy, providing child allowance, housing allowance, etc. The right to benefits is conditional on an individual's or family income not exceeding the specified minimum subsistence level. Families with children but without means are not necessarily supported. Only those whose income is below the defined level receive support. The principle of solidarity between the rich and the poor takes precedence over that which pertains between families who do and families who do not support their children, (Potůček, 1999: pp 110–111).

Developments in Social Work Since 1989

Although there is a long tradition of social work within the Czech Republic, the first attempts to define social work legally did not occur until after 1989. As part of the restructuring of the social insurance system, the term 'social work' appears in the draft proposals concerning social help, where 'social work' is defined as a method for providing social help. This section will address the organisational arrangements, methods of practice and education for social work in the Republic after 1989.

Social work organisation

In practice, social work has continued more or less unchanged since 1989. Social work activities, in the second half of the 1990s, are still aimed at the same groups as before 1989, and include families, children and teenagers, sick people, older people, those requiring special help (e.g. unemployed people), ex-prisoners, homeless people, alcoholics and drug addicts. Social workers are still mainly employed by municipal councils and, at district offices, by the state, (Zákon č. 100/1988 Sb., 114/1988 Sb.). As was the case before 1989, social workers are also employed in the health services, including hospitals, baby care and mental homes, in the education system, for example in counselling institutions, children's homes and approved schools, in the prison service and in social care institutions, such as pensioners' homes and homes for disabled people. Since 1989, private organisations providing social care have become established, among the largest being Charity, Diakony and the Salvation Army. There are also many smaller organisations existing at a local level. These organisations provide services to cover homeless people, ex-prisoners, mothers, abused mothers and children, alcoholics and drug addicts as well as family counselling. As a result of the increasing level of social problems the number of social workers has increased. For example, in Ostrava, with 325,000 inhabitants, the number of social workers involved with families and children has increased from 17 in 1990 to 90 in 1996, (Roční, 1996).

Table 2.1: Social Workers' Qualifications

Qualification Status of Social Workers	% of employed social workers
University qualifications in social work	0.7%
Non-university qualifications in social work	29.5%
University qualifications not specific to social work	6.6%
Other qualifications not specific to social work	63.2%

This increase in the number of social workers has been accompanied by an increase in the number of those without qualifications. Research carried out by the Department of Sociology at Palacky University in Olomouc on the qualifications of social workers at municipal and district level gave the results in Table 2.1 as reported by Klimentová, (1997: pp 13–15).

There are several reasons for the large number of unqualified social workers, including:

- Insufficient numbers of qualified social workers available to meet the demand.

- Unqualified workers have few opportunities to gain qualifications through part time study.

- Employers' reluctance to replace unqualified social workers by qualified ones (e.g. of 12 recent graduates in social work from Palacky University at Olomouc only 3 obtained jobs in the social work field).

- Methods of social work employed in practice relate directly to the qualifications of those involved.

Social work methods

It is mainly the medical or diagnostic method of social work that is used in the Czech Republic. The social worker both defines the client's problems and either solves them or directs the client in how to solve them. The primary aim of social work is to solve clients' material problems. However, in some areas of social work practice, a task-centred approach is

adopted, whereby the client defines their social problems and possible means for solution in co-operation with the social worker. Consequently, client and social worker work together to achieve the solution. In social work involving families, group social work methods are used, run by social workers with a university level qualification.

Social work education system

Unlike the practice of social work, which has failed to react adequately to new problems, social work education has been developed intensively. Social work can now be studied at three distinct levels:

- social work academies (three years)

- bachelors degree at university (three years)

- masters degree at university (five years)

There are now eleven social work academies, six universities awarding bachelors degrees and six universities awarding masters degrees. The Association of Schools of Social Work was founded in 1993 with the aim of achieving a continuing improvement in the quality of studies. The members of the Association have adopted minimum standards for education in social work (in co-operation with schools in Great Britain, Holland and the USA). They evaluate the knowledge and abilities of graduates in social work to ensure that theses minimum standards are maintained. Nine schools are full members of the Association and a further four are associate members, (Havrdová, 1997: pp 8–10).

The History of Social Policy and Social Work in the Czech Republic

To understand the current state of social policy and social work in the Czech Republic it is necessary to review the developments in two important periods—from 1918 to 1938 and from 1945 to 1989. This section will address the construction of Czechoslovak social policy and social work in these two periods, the first, up until the Second World War, and the second, the post war period of the communist regime.

Social policy from 1918 to 1938

The Czechoslovak Republic was formed in 1918 at the end of the First World War. Many problems were carried over from the Austro-Hungarian Empire which the country had been part of for many years. It was also necessary to react to the new problems arising from the War. In particular, coping with those suffering as a result of the war, the war-disabled and their surviving dependants, and to react to the high level of unemployment. High levels of unemployment persisted for the next twenty years with little change. Social policy during this period evolved in both theory and practice. Karel Engliš and Josef Macek both played an important role in the development of officially sanctioned social policies as well as influencing social practice, (Houser, 1968: p 5). The establishment of the Ministry of Social Care in November, 1918 was an important step towards establishing a practical social policy. Initially, the new state retained the existing legislation from the old imperial system, but the government was anxious to put into place new legislation as soon as possible. This Ministry of Social Care was principally concerned with the care of teenagers and physically or mentally handicapped people, building and maintenance of housing, labour laws, care of the unemployed, job centres, trade unions, working class accident insurance, health insurance, a pension scheme and care for the war-disabled. The passing of the law concerning the eight-hour working day in December, 1918 was also highly significant. This law also tightened existing rules concerning night work for working class teenagers.

After the war the level of unemployment was high, averaging 8 per cent, (Deyl, 1985:

p 43), the worst period being during the Depression. The worldwide economic crisis quickly affected the country and the consequences of this crisis persisted until the mid 1930s. A law providing for state unemployment benefits was passed in December, 1918, and the aim of this was to provide a state benefit equivalent to the sickness benefit—for those who were, through no fault of their own, without any source of income, (Sociální, 1928: p 10). In 1925 this state benefit was replaced by state grants, which were in addition to unemployment benefits provided by trade unions under the so-called Gents system. One of the problems in Czechoslovakia was a serious housing shortage, and, in response, the government introduced the Tenant Protection Act to protect existing tenants from being given notice to quit and from rent increases. This Act also provided assistance for new building through subsidies and tax allowances. The Ministry of Social Care provided assistance for young people through financial assistance to existing youth care institutions and to enable new institutions to be formed. It also created a network of authorities providing youth care, (Sociální, 1928: p 11).

For the war-disabled, pensions were provided, together with additional treatment and training to enable them to return to work, (Sociální, 1928: p 12). Once the Czechoslovak Republic was established, it became separated from the insurance institutions of the former Austro-Hungarian Empire. The Republic attempted to establish and adapt the whole area of social insurance in a way appropriate to the changed economic conditions by adapting new constitutional laws to meet modern socio-political demands. This aim was achieved through the reform and gradual unification of existing laws governing pensions, sickness and accident insurance and by other legislative means. New laws covering pensions, insurance for employees and the self-employed to cover illness, disablement and old age, a working class accident insurance scheme and sickness insurance for public service employees were passed, (Sociální, 1928: p 12). The social care provided by the Ministry mainly covered those who lived in poverty, either in pre-economically-active (pre-school or school age) or post-economically-active age groups, who were thus unable to provide for themselves through working. One of the means of social care was through state charity providing necessary nutrition, accommodation, clothing and other basic needs. Essential medical care, usually for children, was sometimes included in this state charity. This was in addition to the state charity created by the 1863 law on the right of domicile that formed the basis for the Poverty Law of 1868. Care of those war-disabled relying on state help and protection also came within the field of social care, (Deyl, 1985: p 28).

Social work from 1918 to 1938

There is a long tradition of social work in the Czech Republic and its development has always been closely related to developments in education in this field. The formation of the Czechoslovakian Republic in 1918 was accompanied, in the same year, by the founding of the first school for social work in Prague, called the Higher School of Social Care. The length of study was four terms and a prerequisite for applicants was to be a minimum age of 20 and to have completed secondary education. The founding of this school was a reaction to the need for specialists able to create a modern social care system from the existing systems of care for those in poverty, youth care and the voluntary activities of various clubs. The Ministry of Social Care sought to integrate the state and voluntary social care systems, and an example of this process was the creation of the District Youth Care network which integrated state, club and private organisations involved in youth social care, (Sociální, 1928: pp 15–18).

Social workers in this period worked in municipal social care (care for those in poverty), youth care, social-pedagogical care (school care), vocational counselling, institutions caring for the physically disabled, mother and baby health care, care for tuberculosis sufferers and child health care. They also worked within the various voluntary clubs concerned with social care. They were the prime movers in the development of the system of social care, (Novotná and Schimmerlingová, 1995: pp 3–6). In 1925, a two-year school for social workers was established in Turcinsky st. Martin in Slovakia and a similar school in Brno, (Sociální, 1928: p 18). The demands of the practice of social work

required the creation of a university education in social work but this was not achieved until 1945. In 1935 the Higher School of Social Care in Prague was replaced by the Masaryk State School of Health and Social Care, where the course of studies lasted five terms and provided a higher professional qualification, (Novotná and Schimmerlingová, 1995: pp 3–6).

Social policy from 1945 to 1989

Until 1948, social policy in the post-war Czechoslovak Republic was a continuation of the pre-war policy. With the communist coup of 1948, the political and economic system was changed, with a consequent impact on both the instruments and interpretation of social policy. The nature and form of social policy in a socialist Czechoslovakia had to respond to the needs and interests of a state controlled economy, and so, therefore, the various benefits and services were changed in line with these ideological requirements. From 1948 to 1989 social policy was adjusted in line with both the political changes that occurred during this period and the development of the economy. Employment policy was based on full employment, and the right to work was accompanied by a duty to work that was obligatory by law. Where people did not work, without a reason that was acceptable to the state, they were considered to be parasites and were punished accordingly. State administration was mainly concerned with planning and worker placement. Unemployment as such was non-existent. On the contrary, there was a shortage of labour due to both the extensive development of the economy and low levels of productivity, (Tomeš, 1996: p 172). Wage policy was based on central wage regulation, since the state, the owner of all companies, determined both wages and productive stimuli. The state provided grants for areas of low productivity and those sectors employing mainly unskilled workers, such as mining, metallurgy, industrial building, heavy engineering and, later, agriculture. Those involved in physical work were given preferential treatment and male wages were higher than those for women. White-collar workers were at a disadvantage, as wages for the 'non-productive' workers in science and technology were substantially lower than those in industry, (Tomeš, 1996: pp 172–173; Kalinová, 1993: p 4).

Family policy was aimed at supporting the birth rate. During the 1970s, social measures to this end included extending maternity leave and the provision of loans to those with young families. Throughout the whole period of the communist regime the numbers of women in employment increased, as the state needed labour and families needed more than one income. Families received family allowances to supplement their income. There was also a programme of extensive subsidies for goods, services and rents to maintain low prices, and thus everyone received a supplement to their income from salaries and other social benefits, (Tomeš, 1996: pp 173–175). Housing policy was based on the control of rents, with subsidies for rents of state flats, while the state aimed for a large construction programme of new flats to solve the chronic post-war housing shortage. In the 1950s the development of co-operative house building began, offering loans at very low interest rates. Similarly, private house building was subsidised through offering building sites free or at a low price, on favourable and long-term credit terms. In spite of this policy the demand for flats was never fully satisfied. Health policy was based on the provision of a free health service, since there was no private practice, only the state health service. Part of health care included a free spa service, that is, the opportunity to spend time at a sanatorium or health resort, for both children and adults. Preventative care was also provided and well organised with great emphasis on mother and child care, as well as a hygiene service, health and safety at work and the organisation of curative stays in recreational facilities for children from industrial areas, (Zákon č. 20/1966 Sb.). Education policy was related solely to the needs of the state, which did not regard education as being of great importance. Obtaining a high level of education and qualifications did not result in the achievement of a better position within society nor did it guarantee a high standard of living. Instead, emphasis was placed on apprenticeships in those areas of industry involving demanding physical work, and 50 per cent of the population completed such apprenticeships. The tradition of advanced specialised schools remained, with research in spring 1993 showing that 76 per cent of the population had a secondary education, 34 per cent had school leaving certificates and more than 34 per cent were apprentices. Of those in the economically active group, 10.7 per cent had received a university education, while for the age group 24 to 29 the figure was 12.7 per cent (Malinová, 1994: pp 1–3).

Social security policy was gradually developed. In 1948 national insurance legislation was approved, unifying various existing insurance systems covering a variety of risks. The Central National Insurance Company was established on a funded basis. In the early 1950s the finances for social security were found from the state budget and a separate office for pensions and sickness insurance was established. In 1957 the national insurance system was further reformed with pensions based on salary and length of service but differed depending on occupation, (Potůček 1995: p 26). In 1968, further legislation added the provision of social care to that of pensions and sickness insurance. Social care provided additional assistance to those who had inadequate income from work, pensions or sickness insurance or experienced other difficulties, (Zákon č. 121/1975 Sb.). In the field of social care the state provided counselling and education as well as allowances, pensioners homes for sick and disabled people, homes for lone mothers with children under three, village SOSs (foster care groups) etc. (Vyhláška, MPSV CR č. 130/1975 Sb.).

Social work from 1945 to 1989

In 1945 the Political and Social College with a Social faculty was founded in Prague, and in 1947 the Social College in Brno, both providing a university education in social work lasting for eight terms. In 1953 both colleges were closed, as, according to the communist regime, there could be no social problems in the new era of socialism and thus no need for social workers. From 1953 to 1989 the only education for social work consisted of two years post-school education in social-legal schools. In the 1950s and early 1960s the only areas in which social workers were employed were in child and youth care and in institutions for sick and elderly people. The demise of real social work had occurred.

An important step in the development of social work in Czechoslovakia occurred in 1968. One outcome of the Prague Spring was the admission that social problems existed even in the era of socialism. This resulted in a reformation of social policy. The Ministry of Work and Social Affairs was re-instated. Programmes for work with families, sick and elderly, ex-prisoners and homeless people were drafted, based on the experience gained in West European countries. Social work was developed in companies, schools, the health system, prisons and social care institutions. Many people with university education, teachers, psychologists, sociologists and lawyers, had been forced to resign after the occupation of Czechoslovakia and during the political oppression of the early 1970s. Many of these now became social workers, making a great impact on the development of social work. They brought abilities into this field that made the new social programmes feasible—the ability to introduce new methods and the ability to carry out research, (Chytil 1996: pp 1–3).

An illustrative example of social work practice in Czechoslovakia during the 1970s and the 1980s concerns work with those recently 'released from prison' in the city of Ostrava (325,000 inhabitants). Specialised social workers began work with ex-prisoners and in 1973 the first social work centre in this field was established in Ostrava with a staff of eight social workers assisted by four psychologists and two external lawyers. In 1975 a psychologist joined the centre staff. The work of the centre was divided into five phases.

1. The preparatory phase: collection of information by social workers from staff inside the prison, prisoners' families and the prisoners themselves.

2. The relationship forming phase: emphasis on gaining the clients' trust by persuading them through words and actions that their problems were understood and that their future was a matter of real concern. The main social problems encountered were: unfavourable interpersonal relationships (broken family relationships); problems in finding work (lack of qualifications, illness); housing problems; health problems; financial problems.

3. Diagnosis and planning phase: this phase had two parts. Firstly, to produce a socio-therapeutic plan concentrating on a solution to the basic problems and achieving the clients' stabilisation. Secondly, a strategic plan concentrating on achieving changes in values, improving interpersonal relationships and teaching new behaviour patterns.

4. Implementing the plan: using a modified version of Glasser's therapy of reality.

5. Completion and evaluation of the therapy.

Achieving solutions to clients' social problems required co-ordination of the work of various institutions. Various commissions were set up with representatives of the prisons, courts, prosecutor's office, police, health services, trades unions, employers and social workers. This system proved effective and included the provision of a network of voluntary workers co-operating with social workers and based mainly in the workplace. In Ostrava there were more than 1200 such voluntary workers and a special magazine was published for them, (Chytil, 1991: p 57).

Contemporary Theoretical Discussion on Social Policy and Social Work

Current discussion of social policy centres on criticism of the social policies adopted during the socialist period in Czechoslovakia and on the need to establish a coherent social doctrine for the Czech Republic formed in 1993. There are two basic theories concerning the practice of social work in the Czech Republic: the androgogical theory and theory of communicative behaviour.

Social policy

Current writers in this field all agree that the social policy of socialist Czechoslovakia proved to be both dysfunctional and inefficient. This period was characterised by the central position of the state, with the state's paternalistic role and absolute monopoly in the formulation and provision of social policy and finally by state 'directivism'. Hence, the state was authoritative concerning all social problems. Individuals were not responsible for their conditions, economic and civic activities were inhibited. Social policy provided wide-ranging social security but paid little attention to the differing social needs of the individual. This presented problems due to the limited financial resources available. The mechanism for allocating resources was inefficient, so there was no link between what the individual gave to the state in the form of taxes and what was received from the state. Social security was provided as part of the state budget, leading to the false impression that services were provided free of charge as a gift from the state, (Žižková, 1994: p 10).

Similarly, there is agreement that social policy has until now fulfilled two main roles, that is, the protection of vulnerable groups during the economic transformation and providing a model for social security, (Sociální, 1997: pp 7–8). In 1997, discussion intensified on the need for a 'social doctrine' covering the main areas of social concern in society, including: health, education and health care, housing, social equality, social protection, minorities and so on. This notion of formulating a 'social doctrine' was first raised in 1990–1991, when some sociologists and specialists involved with social policy called for this approach as a possible continuation of the basic efforts (mainly aimed at creating a social rescue network) in this field. These first initiatives were unsuccessful due to their emphasis on the neo-liberal model of residual social policy that aimed at only meeting the individual or family needs of those in significant difficulty. Hence, the function of social policy was seen partly as to improve the oppressive social impact of a short-sighted economic policy. There is presently little agreement among individual authors concerning the development of such a 'social doctrine'. Currently, there is an emphasis on one-sided measures leading more towards solving an acute fiscal imbalance than to an emphasis on the generally held principles of social justice. Hence, the move for a nation-wide consensus on social policy is receding into the background, (Machonin, 1998: p 6).

Social work

Discussion of social work theory was, and still is, linked to the development of the education system for social workers. Pre-war social work was oriented towards a psychoanalytical theory of social work. The psycho-educational theory of social work first appeared at the Higher Political and Social School between 1946 and 1949. Krakešová, the author of this theory, believes that the main cause of personal problems in life is to be found in the non-satisfaction of the basic human needs. Thus, the aim of social work should be to identify the causes of failure and on that basis select the most suitable psycho-educational influence. A social worker's relationship with a client is based on trust and respect and the aim of social work is to create new educational opportunities to remove bad habits gained by a negative influence in the past, (Krakešová, 1973). This theory remained influential in social work within the Czech Republic until the early 1990s. At the beginning of the 1990s, Jochmann looked towards androgogy for a theoretical basis of social work. According to Jochmann, the notion of 'androgogy' can be understood using three care elements: care, education and culture. 'Care' means establishing those conditions, mainly social and psychological, necessary to achieve one's satisfaction with life in general, and the performance of one's social role and involvement in culture. 'Education' means establishing a personality, personalisation and socialisation mainly in the sense of developing a sense of social direction and taking a socio-directive role in culture. 'Culture' means transmitting and gaining knowledge, abilities and habits which are needed to perform social roles as well as adapting an individual to the cultural system. Jochmann considers institutions that offer extra-curricular activities, for example, the employee's company, social work (care), cultural and educational institutions, to be the field of action for androgogy, (Jochmann, 1992: pp 11–21).

In 1992, Chytil and Hubík tried to establish the theoretical basis for social work in the Czech Republic. Their ideas came from the paradigmatic change in social sciences based on work by Bachtin and Habermas. They have attempted, based on criticism of the present subject-object schema in social sciences, to develop a communicative basis for those disciplines of social science, which have arisen from the subject-subject schematic. The theory of communicative approaches, according to

Hubík and Chytil, allows us to resolve many questions which could not previously be adequately resolved, mainly in the links with social sciences. They class social work as a social science, as a dialogical communicative activity which leads them to see clients as unique individuals participating in life through a particular communicative association. Thus social work should be oriented towards communication rather than as an understanding of reality, (Hubík and Chytil 1992: pp 41–46). The systematic approach is now having a significant impact on both the theory and practice of social work in the Czech Republic.

What constitutes good practice in Czech social work in the future?

Co-operation between state and non-state institutions is necessary if the future aims of Czech social work are to be met. This co-operation has already begun, as can be seen most strongly in the case of social work with children and young people. Delinquency and other anti-social phenomena amongst children and young people are greatly influenced by the way they spend leisure time. Problems resulting from delinquency are often worst in large residential areas. Children and youngsters wander around bored, destroying property, committing petty crime or gather in flats experimenting with drugs and sex. Such places need more youth clubs and centres to offer free and attractive activities of the young people's own choosing. Another factor feeding this anti-social behaviour is teenage unemployment. Annual analyses have shown that one third of young delinquents are jobless. In the past, high-risk youth came mainly from malfunctioning and incomplete families of low social standing who lacked material possessions. Today, the social standing of parents, poverty and social grouping seem to play no role at all.

Social workers who work in District Authorities Social Departments specialising in juvenile delinquency and disturbed behaviour often suffer both from excessive bureaucracy and too many clients. Sometimes they are not seen to be available to their clients either due to geographical or social barriers or because the pressure of their work keeps them off the streets. Neither do other more traditional institutions (e.g. educational and psychological advisors who assist pre-school and schoolchildren), meet the needs of problem young people. Thus there is a need for new types of social service to focus on these groups, with the emphasis on prevention. A 1994 Government Decree stated that 'reclamation centres' should be established in areas of high juvenile delinquency to offer preventative care to children and the young people vulnerable to anti-social phenomena. The centres can be state owned or private, residential or non-residential or a combination of both. They provide advisors, therapy programmes, hobby groups, clubs, discos, tutorials, weekend programmes, holiday programmes and space for individual programmes and streetwork.

'Streetwork' began in the Czech Republic in 1993. The purpose of streetwork is to reach those who have failed to get help from other social and educational institutions. Typical target groups for streetwork are street children, young female and young male prostitutes and homeless children. In a broader sense, the target group for streetwork comprises children and teenagers who spend their free time in the streets, are prone to anti-social behaviour and are in social need or in crisis. The different types of streetwork, according to the Ministry of Labour and Social Affairs, are 'direct streetwork', 'indirect streetwork' and 'extended street work'. Direct streetwork consists of working in the streets, monitoring, searching, attendance, making contacts, crisis intervention and harm reduction. Individual and group work takes place both outside and in low barrier (open-to-all centres), youth clubs and community centres. Indirect work includes paperwork, institutional proceedings, project work, presentations and public relations. Extended work includes method advisors, education and supervision.

An example of streetwork

Social Work at Frýdek-Místek is a specific example of social work with problem groups of children and young people. The town centre consists mainly of high-rise residential areas inhabited mainly by miners with a high level of unemployment. This system is considered to be a good example of social work in the Czech Republic. The model described below has been initiated by lay people and is based mainly on personal relationships although some necessary formal structures have been established.

Streetwork with young people under the age of 12

This is located in Slezská drop-in (a cellar room at Frýdek) for high-school age kids. The work is organised by four social assistants and peer assistant teams of up to 20 young people of high-school age, recruited by the social assistants. Activities on offer include regular meetings at the drop-in, and regular weekend activities and summer camps. These activities are led by peer assistants who have prepared the main parts of the programme.

Streetwork with young people aged 12–18

This is located at Klicperka drop-in (a cellar room at Frýdek) for gangs and gang members from social problem areas, who are growing-up in the streets, prone to alcohol and drug abuse (many junkies), with basic school (sometimes not completed) education, jobless, criminal and behavioural problems. For these young people, group activities such as regular meetings with discussion, games, tea, programme planning, indoor sports on a daily basis (soccer, basketball, etc.), sports tournaments with food awards, one-day trips (walking, biking tours), cinema, museum, car stunt show, etc., monthly experience weekend in the mountains (cooking together, social psychological games, sports) are all provided.

Harm reduction streetwork

Also based at Frýdek, and staffed by three social assistants and peer assistance groups but supported by an 'ethopedist', (roughly translated as a person who has received specific training in work with young people), a doctor, and a private psychologist and psychotherapist. The target group is young people under the age of 21 at risk from drug abuse. The services on offer, in the form of a semi-open centre, are a regular music club, pub visits, new exchange, medical services and general advice and assistance.

Conclusion: Future Aims of Czech Social Policy and Social Work

In the future, the aims of any social policy must be to solve those problems arising from a high level of unemployment, an ageing population, unequal distribution of health services and an increasing disparity in incomes. The most topical problems that have to be solved are those resulting from the transformation of the state health services and those caused by the lack of a housing policy. The formulation of a Czech 'social doctrine' has been considered to be the main task in the field of social policy, (Sociální, 1997: pp 1–8).

In the field of social work, the establishment of a professional profile of social work, with a consequent profile for education, has been seen as a priority by the Association of Social Workers, their teachers and employers. The aim is to define social work relative to other care professions in terms of the qualifications required. Shifting the orientation of social work towards a non-medical and non-paternalistic approach, accepting clients as partners who can solve their own problems with help from the social worker as required. Improvement of the qualification structure for social workers, including proposals for part-time study, is also required. Priority also needs to be given to supporting non-state organisations involved in social work and the need to substitute outpatient services for institutional care. The culmination of the discussion on social ethics, which began after 1989, was the approval of the Ethical Code of Social Workers for the Czech Republic by the Society of Social Workers of the Czech Republic. In view of the fact that compliance with the code is not required by the employer's organisations, Czech social work aims to ensure that adherence to this code is maintained. A possible means to achieve this is through the establishment of a Chamber of Social Workers, membership being conditional on compliance with the code.

The rapid transformation of the economic and political systems imposed upon Czech society that occurred in 1948 and again in 1989 created a level of disequilibrium between the state, the market and citizens that has disrupted the processes of structuration, (Giddens, 1993). For both members and observers of Czech society, the reciprocal interplay between action and structure that legitimises the cognitive and moral order has been de-stabilised to the extent that the mutual knowledge within society is proving inadequate to address contemporary social problems. The formulation of the 'new social doctrine', and the re-orientation of social work practice as a 'communicative activity' exemplify the attempts to reinstate stability into the processes of production and reproduction of social life.

Questions for Further Consideration

- The development of social work practice in the Czech Republic provides a graphic illustration of the power of the state to construct the form and nature of social work. How does the Czech experience compare with the experience in your home country?

- How different is the response in your country to delinquency and the problems of troubled young people? What could be learned from the Czech experience and response, and how might this be applied in your country?

- Czech social work is searching for new models of social work practice to move from approaches to social work where the social worker is dominant. What can be learned from the Czech response to this problem? How does it compare or contrast with the situation in your home country?

Chapter Three

Social Policy and Social Work in Finland

Juha Hämäläinen and Pauli Niemelä

The Development of Finnish Society after the Second World War

In comparison to other Nordic countries, the change from an agrarian to an industrial society and the subsequent development of social policy, social legislation and a welfare state took place relatively late in Finland, with agriculture and the rural population remaining important to the political economy until as late as the 1960s (Tuori, 1995: pp 66–67). The term Nordic welfare state model is used to characterize a particular form of social welfare that is to be found typically in the Nordic countries—the constituents of this model are explained in this chapter.

Throughout the 1950s, in spite of the cost of post-war reconstruction, a period of rapid development in heavy industries took place and the country became increasingly affluent. This rapid industrialisation, economic growth and modernisation of society provided the foundations for the establishment of a Nordic welfare state model and the implementation of a social security system during the 1960s. The system of national insurance and welfare services expanded and diversified during the 1970s and the 1980s. During this period, the economic, political and theoretical dimensions of the Nordic model were embedded in Finland, as were the theoretical and practice elements of professional social work. During the years of economic growth, political decisions were taken and policies introduced that assumed a continuing growth in the national product and wealth.

However, at the beginning of the 1990s, Finnish society experienced a deep economic depression, which resulted in a financial crisis for the extensive social security system that had by then been established, which threatened both the economic and political viability of the Nordic model, and this crisis was compounded by the globalisation of the world economy which presented further challenges to the Finish economy. By the beginning of the 1990s, the rate of unemployment had risen to 20 per cent. Both central government's and municipalities' tax revenue had decreased, and public expenditure increased, especially in the welfare sector, placing great strain on the Nordic model of social security. Because of the high unemployment rate, there was a dramatic increase in the number of people needing economic and psycho-social support, i.e. clients of social work, at a time when central government and the municipalities were obliged to trim and cut welfare services. The shortage of the resources necessary for maintaining the welfare system, and the resulting reduction in the provision of preventative services and supports, gave rise to an increase in psycho-social problems. This led to an increased demand for correctional, i.e. social work, services which experienced considerable pressure and strain in the 1990s.

At the end of the 1990s, the financial preconditions for maintaining the Nordic model seem to be returning once more. In 1997, the growth in the Finnish GNP was 6.3 per cent. From 1997 to 1999 this was 5 per cent. In 1999 the GNP was 29.8 per cent greater than in 1993, the worst year of the recession. Despite difficult economic problems, the Nordic model has managed to survive in Finland even during the worst years of the depression. Although its basic structure remains almost unchanged, the processes of globalisation have placed limits on the government's ability to influence income distribution through taxation and income transfer policies. This will change the economic preconditions for a state-centred social policy and has required that the system be modified in many respects.

The Nordic model of social welfare is dependent upon the taxation and income transfer measures carried out by the state, as not only social insurance, but also the system of social services organised by the municipalities are financed by taxation. The global market forces that are directing the

Finnish state-centred system of social policy towards a market-based system of social policy prevent the state from controlling the processes of income transfer, which in turn may mean an increase in income disparity. Despite this trend Finnish society remains an example of a society based on the Nordic welfare model with a substantial middle class.

The Development of Social Welfare and Social Security in Finland

In Finland, social political discussion proper began in the 1870s, following general patterns across Europe. Concerns about the living conditions of workers and their children in the industrial areas led to the first steps in developing legislative social care, protection and social insurance for workers along with increasing demands for developing the poor relief system. In 1879, influenced by the reforms in Great Britain, a Poor Law was introduced that defined relief of the poor as the responsibility of the municipalities. Around this period, the social insurance system was also developed but social welfare legislation was minimal, (Jaakkola, 1994: pp 110–117; and Tuori, 1995: pp 67–71). Aside from public poor relief a variety of philanthropic activities of social movements and forms of organised self help among workers for the relief of social and moral problems emerged, (e.g. Jaakkola, 1994: pp 149–158) these diverse activities all called for increases in public responsibilities and legislative reforms.

Immediately after independence in 1917, many social political reforms were made in Finland. By 1922 most of the legislative plans in social policy from before independence were completed and a new Poor Law was also enacted in 1922. In the period between the First and Second world wars, social policy and social legislation were characterised by an individualised approach to care of the poor, based upon relief of only the most acute needs. The Poor Law enacted in 1922 replaced the earlier poor statute of 1879, but the changes were not significant. Poor relief was still the task of the municipalities and recipients were liable for repayment. The Poor Law was complemented by the laws of special care enacted in 1937. These laws covered the protection of children as well as the care of

vagrants and alcoholics. A national pension law was enacted in 1937. The purpose of this law was to provide for every Finnish worker in case of old age and incapacity for work. A maternity allowance was also introduced in 1937. During and following the war the system of family allowances was developed, with Child Benefit being the most significant form of aid.

The period following the Second World War is known as the reconstruction period in the history of Finland, heralding a new era in social policy and social security and in which social work became 'professionalised' and institutionalised and characterised by:

> *...governing people through standards and norms for everyday life becoming a central strategy of modern professional intervention.*   (Satka, 1995)

Repairing the damage caused by the war gave rise to the organisation of social security as a national project. This was the origin of the Finnish welfare state in which both the economic and political basis of the welfare state were created. In legislation social assistance replaced the Poor Law in 1956, the national pension system was renewed in the 1950s, and in the early 1960s the work pension system based upon personal earnings was regulated. The social insurance system was also renewed in the beginning of the 1960s as a universal national insurance. In the late 1960s a universal family pension system was developed on the basis of personal earnings. The legislative basis of social security for all citizens was created step by step in the 1950s, the 1960s and the 1970s, (Tuori, 1995: pp 79–86).

Through various national insurance schemes, (insurance of old-age pension, work pension and health insurance), and by organising social services as an extension of income transfers, the prosperity and health of people was assured by the government. The development of the welfare state continued in the 1980s through legislative fine-tuning until the period of economic depression and large-scale unemployment in the 1990s, (Urponen, 1994: pp 204–260; Satka, 1995: pp 301–335). In the 1970s the focus of reforms was moved from income transfer to services, especially to social and health care. In 1972 the national health law was passed, making the municipalities responsible for the availability of health care services in their region. Only minor reforms were initially made in the legislation for social care. The crucial reforms were made during the 1960s, the 1970s and up until the middle 1980s. The new legislation on social care departed from the tradition of care of the poor, where care was exclusively aimed at the disadvantaged members of society (Tuori, 1995: pp 86–92). This offered a basis for the extension and diversification of the social service system and created a unified social service.

The rise of the Finnish welfare state in the 1960s and 1970s meant an enormous expansion of the social and health care system. New forms of, and organisations for, social and health services were created and new professions were born. Social work became professionalized and institutionalised based on high professional qualifications and expertise that can be achieved only through a relatively exacting education. Since the 1980s social work has been defined as a social service given by social workers as distinct from other social services given by other skilled personnel. In this way social work became established as an institution of the social security system of the welfare state. Although preventive measures are also involved in social work - according to the ideology of the Finnish welfare state - its main role is to serve as an ultimate shelter in the social security and welfare service system. During the 1990s norm-based strategies have decreased but a juridical-administrative approach still applies to the institution and methods of social work.

Child Care in Finland

At the end of the 19th century, concern about working class children's problems and demands for organised child welfare led to activity in the area of child care law. In spite of progressive proposals concerning child care legislation, there was no legislative break-through in this area. Public child care developed as a part of the common poor relief under the Poor Law. In addition to public child care organised primarily by municipalities and backed up by the government, philanthropic charities played an important role in the field of child protection, (Pulma, 1987: pp 64–122).

At the turn of the century, child care activities such as kindergartens, children's

homes etc. were established in the biggest towns in spite of a lack of specific legislation. A new specialist vocation arose from these developments for working in, administrating, co-ordinating and developing the network of public and private institutions for the social care of children. Together with other forms of poor relief, the development of organized child care activities are the origin of professional social work in Finland. The legislative reforms of the early 1920s didn't include significant changes in child care due to a belief that a new law would shortly be enacted. In any case, the forms and principles of child care were included in the Poor Law of 1922 but a specific child care law was not enacted until 1936, as part of a comprehensive reform of the social care legislation. Between the world wars non-profit making activities and in particular child care and child protection services were developed in close connection with the public sector under the patronage of the government, (Pulma, 1987: pp 161–194; Satka, 1994: pp 272–294).

Following the end of the Second World War many important developments occurred in both the theory and practice of social care of children. The field of child care expanded and diversified, especially in the terms of preventive services. A new Child Welfare Law was enacted in 1984, based on the principle of the 'best interest of the child'. A child was seen as an individual with his or her own rights. Family-centred principles and methods as well as multi-professional collaboration are emphasised in child welfare. The field of child welfare is seen as a multi-professional system including a multitude of institutions. Social workers are seen as central to these activities, (Mikkola and Helminen, 1994). In the 1980s and 1990s, juvenile legislation and juvenile policies were developed in the spirit of international agreements and declarations concerning children's rights.

According to the general agreement about children's rights, the primary right of a child is to live with his or her biological parents. The biological parents are the child's educators and have the responsibility to take care of the child. According to Finnish legislation, the authorities have responsibilities to support parents in all levels of care. The legislation primarily emphasises that the caretaker of a child must ensure the child's general development and welfare, and that the caretaker is the one who makes the decisions about the child's education and other personal needs. The essential goal of juvenile legislation is that the child is in the care of those persons who have the best qualifications for this task and that the child has a solid and permanent relationship with those persons. According to the law the child has his or her own rights; the parents or other caretakers do not have unlimited power over the child. The legislation is based on the principle of a child's individuality.

Child welfare is aimed at the balanced development and welfare of a child as well as securing his or her close relationships with the biological parents. In particular it emphasises: the guarantee of good care and the necessary control of a child in regard to the child's age and stage of development; that the child must receive understanding, safety and affection; the child shall not be neglected, punished physically or subject to any other form of abuse and that the child's development into a state of independence, responsibility and adulthood is to be supported.

The child is considered to be not only a member of the family but also as an independent subject of justice. From this point of view, a child's personal wishes and opinions are judicially significant. The law underlines that a child who is able to form his or her own opinion must be allowed to express feelings and opinions freely. The child is to be heard in all administrative and legal procedures concerning him or her. Both the parents and the authorities shall take the child's opinions into account. For example, at 12 years of age a child cannot be placed in care against his or her will. These principles, particularly concerning the child's individuality, may sometimes conflict with the protection of the child and the protection of the family. There is a clear principle in law: that of the child's best interest. This principle of the child's best interest is crucial in compulsory measures of child protection, in which the parents' and the child's needs, wishes and interests may be in conflict.

The child has a right to know his or her own biological parents and be in contact with them even if they live apart. The child's needs are also taken into account in cases where the termination of state care is under consideration

with a view to returning the child to the biological parents. The right to meet the biological parents is not, however, unlimited, e.g. if there is a danger to, or threat against, the child's best interests. The essential principle of the general agreement on child rights is that the state shall guarantee the child protection and care, taking into account situations where the child's circumstances for one reason or another could endanger his or her development and health. In Finland, this is a special area of child welfare, in which social work plays a central role.

The Organisation and Practice of Social Work

In most Western European countries, since the end of the Second World War, social work has become a legitimated professional institution within society. This institutionalisation and legitimisation of social work is closely connected with the development of the social policy and ideology of the welfare state in its different forms. The expansion and differentiation of social work as an institution arises from the formulation of the responsibility of the state for its citizens' well-being, (Compton and Galaway, 1989). The development of social work and social work education are closely inter-related with, and dependent upon, emergent trends in social policy.

The specialised features of social work in Finland can only be understood if they are examined in the light of the Nordic model of the welfare state. Social work is considered to be a part of the welfare state system, the aim of which is to create comprehensive social security for all citizens. Social security is a basic principle of Finnish society, and social work's position, aims and tasks are closely linked to this. To a great extent, social work is understood as the final safety net in the social security system. In addition to its role and function in relation to the solution to social problems, social work is also seen as fulfilling tasks relating to the prevention of problems, in co-operation with other professional groups in the social field.

In the Nordic countries, the emphasis on public employment has led to a high rate of participation by women in the job market, particularly within the social services and day-care services for children. This means that social workers enjoy a relatively high status in society, although not to the same extent as that of health services workers. Municipal autonomy is an intrinsic part of Finnish public administration. Local authorities have taxation rights, i.e. the right to collect taxes from the local population and organisations within the municipality. By collecting tax revenues, the municipalities maintain the public administration and other infrastructures necessary to society. Even though the state does both finance and impose certain duties upon them, the municipalities are largely independent, both administratively and financially. The common aim of the municipalities is to provide for the welfare of the citizens through provision of the most important welfare services, such as social, health, education and leisure services. At the same time, the municipality acts as a pivotal employer in the welfare service sector.

Particularly in Finland and Sweden but also in other Nordic countries, social work serves as an instrument of public welfare policy and is defined as a public service with most social workers' salaries paid by the municipality, i.e. social workers are public servants. However, private social welfare associations and enterprises have begun to play an increasingly important role in the recent attempts to rationalise and restructure the social and health service system.

The Nordic system of social security, health and welfare, places great emphasis on the integration and joint administrative and legislative co-ordination and co-operation between social and health care institutions and services. Social work has been seen as part of a multi-professional network, with social workers working increasingly as members of multi-professional teams. Special aspects of social work in public health have played an important role in the development of social work theory and practice in a system where social and health services are administratively bound together.

In Finland, the main task of social work is to complement the other instruments of social and health policy, i.e. other services of the social and health care system. However, social work cannot be understood only as an instrument and an institution of the welfare state. The basic role of social work is to protect people against the state, not vice versa, (Rose and Black, 1985). It has been emphasised that as an institution of the welfare state, social work is in a critical relationship with the political and economic structures of power. The economic and political crisis of the social welfare system has on the one hand threatened the identity of social work as an institution of the welfare state with respect to its role in responding to the problems that arise as a result of the state's and municipalities' economic policies, yet on the other hand its value as a social institution has become clearer through its role of representing clients against the public system.

In Finnish society, the municipalities are legally required to provide income support, that is, social assistance, to those persons whose income does not allow them to fully support themselves. In practice, social workers assess the need for this support and make the decisions as to how this is allotted, based on standards laid down by the Council of State. Those who reside permanently in Finland have the subjective right to income support if they fulfil all the criteria. In addition, the social worker may use his or her discretion in the allocation of income support. In this allocation, the household income is viewed in relation to everyday costs (e.g. rent, food, clothing, health costs, television licence, etc.). Since the beginning of the second half of the 1980s, the number of those receiving income support in Finland has doubled, (Ritakallio, 1997), although the number of social workers allocating income support has remained the same.

In the 1990s a significant increase in the number of people in need of economic and psycho-social support has changed social work practice in the social centres of municipalities. Generally, social workers have been meeting new problems with old instruments and with staff resources that are far too small. This has encouraged Finnish social work to seek and find new orientations and strategies. For example, evaluative research methods into the quality of social work have been developed. During the 1970s the main reason for needing income support was still illness: today it is unemployment. In the 1990s social workers discussed the problems and life history of income support clients more than they did during the 1970s; and they collaborate at a much earlier stage of their work with other officials, (Ritakallio, 1997). Most of the working hours of those social workers employed in the municipal social work offices are spent dealing with matters related to income support.

For the most part, the work of a Finnish social worker takes place in the office. A significant amount of the worker's time is taken up with administrative tasks. The provision of social work is statutory and there is a great deal of legislation that directs the nature of the work that can be undertaken, although as yet actual legislation for regulating professionals is only now under development. The municipal system of social services includes a wide range of people belonging to different professional groups including social workers with a university education, social educators, advisors and counsellors for the mentally handicapped who have a college level education, and social carers who have school-level qualifications. A polytechnic system was created in Finland in the 1990s that is also responsible for educating workers in the social field. Those who have a degree in the social field from an institute of higher education are not yet recognised as having a valid qualification for social work; however, for the most part, they are normally employed within the social service system. In addition, there are workers within the system of social services other than those who have an actual professional degree in the social field, for example, psychologists, public-health nurses and doctors.

Since the beginning of the 1970s increasing emphasis has been placed on collaboration between those under different administrations, with particular emphasis on collaboration with workers in health care. In the 1990s, municipal social and health activities have been administratively combined. Over a quarter of social workers in Finland already work in health care organisations. As a result of this combination, the boundary between social and health services has become less clear than previously. Professional co-operation, i.e. inter-professional networking and teamwork in various forms are beginning to receive more emphasis, in both the practice and theoretical basis of social work and education.

Non-governmental, non-profit organisations have traditionally had a proportionately small role to play in the Finnish welfare state as providers of welfare services and as organisers of social work. Of the 4,000 or so social workers in Finland, over half are employed in municipal offices and about a quarter work in hospitals, which are also mainly owned and maintained by the municipality.

The particular areas in which social work is conducted are municipal child guidance and family counselling, A-clinics (addiction clinics) and mental health clinics. In addition to social workers, psychologists and doctors are also employed in these centres, as well as public health nurses. In addition, social professionals without social worker status (professionals qualified at polytechnic or college level) are primarily located in state institutions maintained by municipalities.

Since 1999 social professionals who have studied in polytechnics are referred to by the title 'socionomist'. In spite of a common title there are, however, differences in the programmes of study within the polytechnics. Some programmes are for example more pedagogically and culturally orientated, others emphasise social administration or health models. In the international context it should be emphasised that Finnish 'socionomists' do not share the same professional status and role of social workers.

Theoretical Approaches to Social Work

There are two dominant competing traditions in the Finnish interpretation of social work: a welfare tradition that emphasises the therapeutic nature of the work and spiritual support, and an administrative and legislative tradition that emphasises the provision of material support. Current debates focus on the necessity of combining these two approaches, (Louhelainen, 1985: p 24).

Whilst it could also be argued that these traditions are more diverse than they are similar, and that within their respective histories two different approaches have developed, in actual fact, the differences between them relate to on the one hand the legitimisation of the professional nature of social work, and the other, the legitimisation of a universal social security (social security policy). Hence the focus of the municipal social work office is on the distribution of income support to those who need it, whilst hospital social work adopts a more therapeutic orientation. Increasingly, then, these two traditions have grown closer to each other in many ways, and together they form a certain area of 'social' development. Alongside the administrative and therapeutic work, the pedagogic approach has, since the early 1990s, begun to be adopted in Finnish social work.

Nowadays, social work is characterised by methodological pluralism. The methods of social work, as do the content and tasks, vary depending on the environment in which it operates. In general, the methods of social work are traditionally divided into individual, group and community social work with the majority of the work being individual-focused and family-related. Whilst there is a strong tradition of settlement work in Finland around which community work has developed, this work is not regarded as 'professional' social work. In the 1990s, various projects have multiplied in the social field, something that has strengthened the position of the community in social work.

In Finland, the extent of private, voluntary and charitable work has always been fairly small, with responsibility for social work being located within the overall role of the state. At the parish level, responsibility for care has been passed to the municipality and the community and the church's social ethical tenets have become subsumed into state social legislation. At the same time the professionalization of social work practice has defined the work as done by someone who has an education in social work.

Although social work in Finland has now become institutionalised within the state apparatus, it is very important to acknowledge that its origins can be found in the philanthropic movement and a collective sense of social responsibility. The significance of this is that the tradition of social work is closely associated with the concepts of altruism and voluntary activity. When regarded from this point of view, the origin of social work is deeply ethical, drawing from both the Christian principle of love for one's neighbour, and also from rational deontological categorical imperatives.

The administrative tradition that is associated with the Nordic approach to social work, and which closely resembles its German counterpart, (Louhelainen, 1985: p 24), can be understood as one that is embedded within a tradition of social security policy. Whilst all welfare regimes establish a legislative base for the provision of social work and an administrative framework for its practice, it is a matter of increasing debate as to whether social work does indeed require such a structure in order to fulfil its wider social function.

The legislation that led to voluntary and temporary aid becoming an official, systematic operation, serves as the unifying factor between the philanthropic and administrative orientations of social work and the subsequent economic determinants of the care system as it evolved into a centralised state system of subsistence security. Descriptions of the move from relief work in 1879, to official relief for the poor, 1922, and later to social assistance, 1956, and then social welfare in 1982, show a tradition in which the economic support of citizens became a collective responsibility of society. With the passing of time, official legislation was drafted which affected the security of subsistence, i.e. the final stage of social security which has become the essential feature of the present system and operations.

Since 1937, official care in Finland has included child welfare as well as the care of those with alcohol problems and vagrants/prostitutes. The latter was abolished in 1986 and the law on alcohol was changed to a law against the abuse of intoxicants in the 1960s and was again changed in 1986. In this way the official system of social welfare with its legislation and administration has taken over responsibility for a wide range of tasks, which had previously been the concern of individuals, charitable organisations or the parish.

Descriptions of the move from relief work to relief for the poor and later to social assistance and then social welfare nevertheless often omit something of great relevance. Namely, the move towards security of subsistence in the form of a universal national insurance, in contrast to social insurance based on work, these developments occured initially in 1937, again in 1956 and especially in the 1980s. Needs-based social welfare is first and foremost the origin of universal social security that has developed into a universal right that includes protection from some forms of risk to the whole population. The Finnish welfare system, which incorporates both a subsistence support system and a welfare support system provides a comprehensive model of social security.

It is one thing to recognise the administration of social work as the process by which social work is carried out in social offices, and quite another to consider social administration as social work. This confusion arises from the fact that in Finland, social work and social policy are often treated as being one and the same. Nevertheless, a distinction must be made between the professionalisation of social work and legislation that authorises social work. Social security is a particular system that is administered at local level as municipal social welfare, at the organisational level as social insurance based on work and at the national level as universal insurance comprising social security as well as social insurance.

However, let us return and examine municipal social welfare. One relevant consequence of the institutionalisation of social welfare has been the creation of officials, civil servants and bureaucrats. There has been criticism that these officials have come to dominate the welfare system, and that social work carried out in the social office is considered to be in need of reform, (Development of the Social Office, 1981). Before the creation of a salaried work force, trustees were responsible for the administration of welfare tasks; indeed the municipal social committee is still responsible for many issues that arguably would be better dealt with by professionals.

The organisation of income support (the former relief for the poor) is the responsibility of the social administration at municipal level. Its objective is seen as beginning the complex process of meeting and developing the individual's welfare, security and employment needs and capacities. In all, with the addition of social work, the juridical-administrative tradition is first and foremost a tradition of social security. The development from an individual needs-based benefit system to a collective evaluation of benefits is specifically the development of social security/social policy. The tendency of the previous forms of benefit to persist, although often in a quite changed form, is part and parcel of the process

of evolution from a model of relief for the poor, to income support, and finally to universal social insurance.

In the period immediately following the Second World War, the universal care policy for both responsibility for the poor and the disabled, and the control of social deviance emerged gradually, through the efforts of public authorities, the state and local authorities. The position of social work within this Nordic model can be understood as one profession among many other professions in the complex institutionalised and legalised system of social and health care services; social work is essential to act as a support to, and representative of, or advocate on behalf of, the individual within the welfare system.

Modern phase in Finland

Until the beginning of the 1980s professional social work education was largely at bachelor's degree level. From 1984 this has advanced to master's level. Master's programmes in social work were historically developed within universities' Departments of Political Science with social policy as a major area of study. At the end of the 1980s some universities students studying social work could also study social psychology, sociology or public law as a major. Since the 1990s, those who have a master's in social sciences or education have had the opportunity to take courses in social work to acquire the qualifications necessary for professional social work practice. During the 1990s, social work developed as an increasingly independent field of study, and at the same time, to become a major in the master's degree in social sciences. Nowadays, the knowledge base for social work is considered to be multidisciplinary, but social work is also seeking to establish itself as a discipline in its own right in relation to traditional social sciences.

The development of the professionalism of social work in the twentieth century has mainly occurred outside of state social offices. Medical social work in health care, the churches, 'family counselling social work' and other organisations, in particular social work therapy clinics for alcohol-related problems, have all been involved in developing social work theories and practice models that focus on direct work with clients.

One of the key features of social work is its focus on the subjective welfare needs and experiences of individuals, the client-worker relationship and the particular knowledge and skills of the practitioner applied in practice. This approach is in contrast to that of social welfare administration which is blatantly organisation centred and concerned with social problems based upon the legislative framework and which require more administrative activities and social administration. Social work thus serves as a support process whereas social welfare is an administrative service or agency, through which the administration of social work is usually, but not always, effected.

Finnish social welfare law provides a clear distinction between social welfare and social work both conceptually and contextually. According to Section 1 of the law, social welfare is understood as being some form of organisation that provides social services, income support, social responsibilities or activities linked to these, the aims of which are to promote and support public social security and the functional capacity of the individual and the family. In contrast, Section 18 of the law, refers to social work as a form of professional guidance, counselling, solution to social problems of the individual, as well as other support activities which support and promote the security, coping or function of either the individual or the family. Therefore, social work is defined, quite correctly in our view, as a professional activity that occurs within a particular social welfare environment.

In Finland, social work education has increasingly separated from the science of social policy. Its own theoretical basis as a science has been developed through theoretical debate together with diverse empirical research; in particular qualitative research methods have been used. This has not, however, meant that social work as an institution and a profession has had to loosen its connection with, and reduce its functions in, the Finnish social security system.

Traditionally, Finnish social work theory is influenced by the Nordic social welfare model and Anglo-American constructions of social work, with the tasks and functions of social work arising from these two sources. Theories of social work and about social work, i.e. the theories concerning the reasons for social work,

have been especially connected with the Nordic model of social policy whilst theories of how to 'do' social work, 'second order theories', are mostly influenced by the Anglo-American tradition.

Social policy as a discipline and social political theories played a role in social work education until the end of the 1980s. In the modern interpretation of Finnish social work, the concept of the social problem is a central one. The tasks of social work are largely defined theoretically around the concept of the social problem. This has linked the theory of social work to research about social problems and the social political intervention linked to these and social policy theories. During the 1990s, attention has also increasingly been focused on new types of social work paradigms, such as eco-social, eco-psychological and psycho-social. In Finland, social work is largely researched empirically. However, this form of research, at present, mainly consists of collecting separate fragments of information rather than a systematic development of the theory of social work. Actual discussion on theory with regard to social work is mainly conducted through the concepts of social policy, but this is also fragmentary and localised.

Since the 1960s debate and research about social work and indeed social policy in Finland has been partly influenced by radical sociology. Attention is paid to the structural factors of society, both as the causes of and solutions to social problems, (Satka, 1994: pp 326–327). Marxist political and economic theory inspired the development of so-called constructive methods in social work. Criticism of official social work raised the issue of alternative social work through the encouragement of self-help. Traditionally, professional discussion on social work has primarily focused on the tension between administrative and therapeutic work. Increasingly, and particularly within the academic domain and within masters level programmes, there is discussion on a wider range of issues. These relate to the tasks and the nature of social work, the appropriate qualifications and legislation necessary for practising professionals, the ethical basis of social work and the professional development of social work, especially as to whether social work is a profession or a semi-profession. The relatively low status of the profession, in conjunction with low salary levels as well as the political dimension to social work have also naturally been among the topics of discussion.

The Finnish Union of Professional Social Workers issued a manifesto in 1991 with guidance on the professional ethics of social work. This manifesto resembles other equivalent social work codes of ethics, and emphasises democracy and human rights, the preservation of human dignity, social justice, respect of the individual's independence and workers' confidentiality, eradicating exclusion, the right of self determination, the right of the individual to participate in the handling of matters affecting them, as well as the social worker's personal responsibility for making ethical judgements with regard to his or her practice.

Social work education emphasises the concept of public service rather than specialisation in any one sector of social work. However, the subjects of educational establishments, and choice of studies and assessed work allow the student to direct his or her studies towards a particular area of social work. A relatively wide and complex knowledge of social legislation and the social security system, which enables the social worker to act as a 'social advocate', are emphasised as a prerequisite to becoming a professional. In particular, emphasis is given to the development of skills that relate to co-operation, counselling, communication, service planning, administration management, report writing and a capacity for reflection, a general knowledge of the social sciences, as well as the ability to analyse and utilise research, the overall aim of which is to equip the future practitioner for 'enquiring social work'.

Speculations on the Future Development of Social Policy and Social Work in Finland

As a result of national economic problems in the Nordic countries, with the exception of Norway, the state-centred model of social policy has been strongly criticised in recent years. Due to the rapid rise in unemployment, the costs of the overall system of social insurance have increased dramatically since the beginning of the 1990s. Although the recent economic boom will hopefully lead to a decrease in unemployment, a high rate of unemployment

seems to be a relatively permanent state of affairs in the Nordic countries.

Both the liberalisation of world trade and the economic integration of Europe threaten the Nordic model in as much as the high levels of taxation upon which it depends can no longer be sustained. As a result, services can no longer be made available freely or cheaply to all in accordance with the universal social policy principle, (Sipilä, 1999: p 11). Ultimately, the future of the Nordic model of 'universal' provision depends upon the availability of the necessary financial and political preconditions, (Hämäläinen, 1998: p 78). Because of economic, political and cultural globalisation, increasingly both of these preconditions are slipping from the grasp of the state.

Political commitment has been the mainstay of the welfare state model in Finland. Attempts have been made to resolve social problems primarily at macro level by creating a social security system that, as comprehensively as possible, prevents the occurrence or deterioration of social problems. As a result of the economic crisis of the 1990s the system not only suffered setbacks but at the same time experienced calls for its dismantling from neo-liberal political activists and commentators. The result of this has been an increase in various psycho-social problems and complications at micro level as well as an increasing shift of attention to intervention at the macro level which has reinforced the position of professional social work and increased its significance. Furthermore, in the education system, the position of social policy as a subject and an area of study has become weaker, while the position of social work has become stronger.

Contemporaneously with the financial problems of the social insurance system, neo-liberal demands for moving away from the Nordic model of the welfare state have increased in all the Nordic countries. In the 1990s, the questions of prioritising as well as privatisation of health and social services have been increasingly raised in political and scientific discussion as:

> ...the mass unemployment of the 1990s fits poorly with the Scandinavian social care service model.
>
> (Sipilä et al., 1997: p 44)

Unemployment undermines the foundations of funding the system and cannot be resolved through social care.

In the future, there is an obvious need to reform the financial and administrative system of health and social services in the Nordic countries. Changes are probably not going to happen suddenly, but rather step by step, through economies in the programmes of public health organisations, social insurance and services. In the next few years, the development of the system of social work will be connected with these reforms in the Nordic countries.

In Finland, as in the rest of the world, the development of social policy and social work is increasingly shaped by a global economy and international organisations. This will increase the effect of inter- and supra-national factors on national social policies and social work practice, (Deacon *et al.*, 1997: pp 2–3). Global economic competition tends to erode social security provisions by the introduction of models of flexible labour and the tendency to casualize and marginalize labour in the developed countries, (Deacon, 1998: p 12). Thus, the economic and political circumstances of the Finnish welfare state arise from global economic, political and cultural processes.

The economic and political crisis of the welfare state has also resulted in a crisis for the institution of social work. Over the past few years, this theme has coloured discussion of social work in the Nordic countries. As problems in the national economy have grown more serious, the question of prioritising social services has become more pressing. For the first time since the Second World War, all Nordic states are suffering from widespread unemployment, which has caused a huge wave of social problems, for example alcoholism and drug abuse, or various kinds of mental health problems.

The future of the Nordic model of social policy and social work depends primarily on the development of the national economy of the Scandinavian societies, which together with the financial preconditions, also brings ideological demands. These are connected with the political attitudes of the middle classes, which form the majority of the population in the Nordic countries. At present, there is a relatively wide political consensus for the policy which is based on the principles of the Nordic welfare state model, although in recent discussion, not only the conservative parties but also most of the social democratic parties in all Scandinavian countries are stressing reduction and cutbacks in public spending and the privatisation of some public activities, (Hanssen, 1997: p 127).

The Nordic model 'to develop personal social services as a public universal utility' is under pressure in two ways: from the globalisation of the economy (particularly the movement towards European Economic and Monetary Union) and from the international similarity in political solutions to social problems, (Abrahamson, 1997: pp 173–174). In the Nordic countries, except for Norway and Iceland which are not members of the European Union, the future of the social and health policy systems is closely connected with the economic and political development of the European Union.

The Nordic and the Continental social policy models are probably going to converge within the EU countries. The ideas of active social policy and universal social rights of citizens are stressed in the European Union. However, there is obviously increasing political interest in seeking new inspiration from the Anglo-American model of residual care policy both in the Nordic and in the Central European countries. In Finland, social work has achieved significant autonomy as a discipline in the 1990s. Through continuous empirical research, which develops context based theory and methods, the autonomy of social work will still increase. Discussion concerning the philosophical basis of social work will aid social work in becoming increasingly independent as a discipline. The emphasis on research and development of social work theory and practice depend, of course, on changes in society and its social problems. In Finland, the fundamental issue for the future of social work, its tasks and content as an institution and a profession focusses upon the extent to which the Nordic welfare model can be maintained.

Questions for Further Consideration

- Implicit within the principles of the 'Nordic Model' of social policy is the notion that social welfare should be universal, need-based and prevention-oriented. Therefore, in Finland, social services are based on taxation and income transfer and are mostly provided by municipalities. What are the aims of social policy in your home country and what role does the state play in delivering social services to people?

- One function of social work in Finland is to maintain an appearance of legitimacy for the state by presenting a caring image to society. What is the function of social work in your home country and what kind of relationship exists between state and social work? What kind of relationship between the state and social work do you think might be the best for your home country or more broadly across Europe?

- For the most part, the work of Finnish social workers takes place in the office where they complete administrative tasks (e.g. assessing needs, allocating financial support, organising services, evaluating outcomes, etc.). What is the major role of the social worker in your home country? What proportion of their working hours do social workers spend engaged in administrative tasks and what do they feel about this?

Chapter Four

Social Protection and Social Work in France

Emmanuel Jovelin and Evelyne Tully

Introduction

This discussion of the nature of social work in France begins with a consideration of some basic information about France.

The French population

As of March 1995, the total population of France comprised 58.5 million people. Of these 26 per cent were under 20, 59 per cent were between 20 and 64, 20 per cent were over 60, and 15 per cent over 65 some 7.4 per cent of the total population were immigrants from abroad. As regards the population of children and young people, two million were under three and therefore did not yet attend school. Of the 14.5 million over the age of three who attended school, 17 per cent were in nursery schools (kindergartens), 27.5 per cent in primary schools, 41 per cent in secondary schools and 14.5 per cent in higher education. The working population, those either in or seeking employment, comprised 22.5 million people. The remainder of the 16 million adult population included retired people and other non-working people (mothers at home and handicapped adults). In total 70 per cent of women were in work, a number that decreased significantly following the birth of a third child. Living as a couple was still the norm; 62 per cent of people aged 15 and over lived as couples, 27 per cent of whom lived with children and 35 per cent were childless. Life expectancy was 74 years for men and 82 years for women. The index of fertility was 1.7 per woman, the rate of the replacement of generations being 2.1. The infant death-rate was 4.9 per thousand, (INSEE National Survey, March, 1995).

The administrative system

Metropolitan France is divided geographically and administratively into 22 regions, sub-divided into 95 departments and further divided into about 38,000 districts. In 1982, two major laws were passed defining the delegation of responsibilities as between districts, departments, regions and the state in relation to town planning, vocational training, apprenticeship, education, social work, environment, culture, ports and rivers, and public transport.

The Social Security System

Although a law providing workers with some protection in respect of industrial accidents had existed since 1898, and another in respect of retirement for workmen and farmers since 1910, it was not until 1930 that a social insurance system was established for wage-earners. This was nearly 20 years after such a system was first introduced in the United Kingdom and almost 50 years after a similar system in Germany.

The current system of social security in France was established in 1945, when Pierre Laroque was invited by the then Temporary Government to prepare a comprehensive plan for social security. This system was aimed at providing all citizens with the means of livelihood whenever they were unable to earn their own living through work. The system was to be administered both by representatives of those who were insured through the scheme and of the state. Laroque's approach to social security combined three different policies:

- an economic policy aimed at full-employment;

- a health policy organised by the medical profession and associated agencies;

- an income redistribution policy aimed at modifying the division of wealth resulting from unregulated market forces.

The assumed link between social protection and full employment was so great that the 1945 system did not provide any insurance measure in the event of unemployment, an omission that was only redressed in 1958. This approach adopted by Laroque had broad similarities to that proposed by Beveridge in the UK (see page 125), and was intended to insure the whole population against social risks and provide each individual with their basic minimum needs, thus helping to generate and ensure a sense of national solidarity. Moreover, the scheme also sought to unite in one general social security system, the different arrangements and agencies that already existed.

However, these objectives were never achieved, as some categories of wage-earners retained their existing, more advantageous pensions and self-employed people were excluded. Employers often preferred autonomous institutions, run by themselves or even jointly with the wage-earners, where they could decide upon the level of coverage as opposed to a compulsory, unified social insurance, decided by and under the authority of the state.

The result was a system that was a compromise between the demands of competing political and social groups and incorporated aspects of social protection from both the German (Bismarck) (see page 52) and UK (Beveridge) (see page 125) systems. The co-existence of aspects of these two models accounts for the ambiguity that surrounds French rights of entitlement to social security benefits. With, on the one hand, social rights that each individual citizen has claim to by virtue of *being* a citizen and on the other, rights that the individual acquires through working and making compulsory contributions from those earnings.

Following the end of the Second World War, social security was extended by providing allowances to a larger proportion of the population. The effect of economic growth allowed for an increase in personal contributions without simultaneously inhibiting an increase in net salaries. However, by the mid 1970s, as economic growth slowed down, unemployment grew and earnings contributions declined. The resulting levels of poverty created a demand for new measures, such as the *minimum integration* income, to be financed through general taxation rather than by earnings related contributions. Additionally, the state was obliged to improve and extend coverage to neglected groups through

measures such as the provision of universal family allowances, an increase in the minimum income for older people and a new allowance for handicapped adults.

The resulting decrease in earnings related contributions coupled with the increase in state expenditure on health, old age pensions and family support imposed an unacceptable burden on the system. Consequently, steps were taken to salvage the system including the calculation of contributions on full rather than part salaries and, from 1991, the introduction of a new measure called *generalised social contribution* which was applied to other sources of personal income. Patient contributions to health care were increased, family allowances were no longer given to those with an income above a certain level and the contribution period for a full pension was extended from 37.5 to 40 years.

More recently, the state has included in the national budget more and more exemptions from contributions in order to encourage the creation of jobs. However, in spite of all these measures the costs of social security to employers acts as an obstacle. Table 4.1 illustrates the dependence of the French social security system on earnings related contributions, and the consequent effects of high levels of unemployment.

Table 4.1: Financing of Social Security (Based on 1994 Data)

Origin of contribution	Percentage of contribution
Employers contributions	50.2
Employees contributions	22.6
State contributions	14.1
Self-employed contributions	4.5
Service contributions	0.7
Affected taxation	7.9
Total	**100**

Employment and income distribution

Government statistics for the end of February, 1998 show 3.33 million people, i.e. almost 13 per cent of the population eligible to work, as unemployed and seeking work. The unemployed are distributed unequally amongst the population in respect of age, sex, qualifications and the length of time being unemployed. Along with people aged 50 and over, young people are particularly vulnerable to unemployment. Of the 8 million young people aged between 15 and 24, 70 per cent continue studying or go on a training course after school. Nearly 25 per cent of men and 33 per cent of women in active life in this age bracket are out of work. Far more than age, possessing vocational training recognised and accredited by a diploma is a deciding factor in being able to obtain employment. The priority given to people with such a diploma who apply for employment results in a large number of employed people being over-qualified for the jobs they occupy.

Unemployment represents one, but not the only, cause of poverty. The minimum legal salary is 5,280FF (about 800 Euros). Almost six million people live on less than 3,000FF a month (about 460 Euros). Two thirds of these benefit from *social minima 1* (different minima are set for different social groups), mainly for old age and *minimum integration income*. These *minima* represent state payments of 12.5 thousand million Euros per year to provide income support. The state also pays rent allowances and personal contributions to health insurance (Alternatives Economiques no.30).

The provision of social security has been in decline for the last 15 years. The rate of reimbursement for health consultations and medicines has decreased and now represents about 60 per cent of the actual costs. Supplementary mutual insurance companies have raised their contributions and also their tariffs. After being reimbursed by their mutual insurance companies, families still have to bear about 14 per cent of their health expenses. Moreover, 17 per cent of the population cannot afford supplementary mutual insurance. This often effects the most vulnerable groups e.g. elderly people and unqualified workers.

There is also unequal access to medical care between different social and economic classes,

and between urban and rural areas. There are differences between regions, as regards facilities and staff levels. For instance, the Nord Pas de Calais region receives only 5.9 per cent of the total annual budget granted to hospitals by the national office of health insurance, and yet it represents 7 per cent of the French population with four million inhabitants.

At the beginning of 1998, there were eight *social minima* in place for different population groups: the elderly, handicapped people, isolated people, the jobless, and people with low incomes. These take the form of either a *contributory minimum* for those who have contributed in the past, or a *solidarity minimum* for those who have not contributed enough. Altogether, there are 3,180,000 beneficiaries of one or the other of these minima. Rates of benefit to these different groups vary, ranging from the lowest of 1,311FF per month to 3,471FF for old age or disability pensions, to 3,881FF per month for lone pregnant women, (Liasons Sociales, 1998).

Table 4.2: The Budget Disbursement in 1996

Area of spending	Percentage of budget
Old age pensions	41.9
Health	33.3
Family benefits	15.2
Employment	8.0
Measures against poverty	1.6
Total	**100**

Towards equality of opportunity

The French social security system was intended to serve as a safety net for those, who by virtue of illness or old age, were unable to work. However, the aim of achieving universal social protection through full employment, as envisaged by Laroque, has proved to be unachievable. Whilst workers benefit from health care, compensation in case of illness and unemployment and retirement pensions based upon their own and employers' contributions, the situation is quite different for unemployed people. Neither unity, uniformity, nor universality have resulted from the contributory based social insurance system. Additional forms of social assistance have meant that the social insurance system is not sufficient to meet the needs of the population.

The assistance minima created in the 1980s were settled at levels far lower than those of previous allowances and the relative level of these minima has decreased by 15 per cent in comparison with the average standard of living, leaving many recipients' living standards below the 'poverty line'. The overall sum allocated to assistance measures has remained steady since 1983, about 1 per cent of the GDP (Gross Domestic Product), but the number of beneficiaries has increased by 70 per cent. The consequent inequalities that have resulted from the social security (contributory) and social assistance (non-contributory) elements that comprise the general social protection system in France, are a continuing source of public dissatisfaction.

The principle argument against raising the minima is to maintain a gap between the minima and the minimum salary. The adoption by France of the common European Currency prohibits any increase in public debt. Although it does not prevent an internal redistribution of wealth, and many beneficiaries of assistance would prefer employment to an allowance, it is argued that this would require a reduction in the levels of compulsory contributions, which in turn would lead to an increase in public expenditure and a budget deficit.

Successive governments have sought to address this dilemma, yet in the 1990s inequalities have increased; poverty and regional variations persist, social ties are loosened and there has been an increase in the incidence of violent crime and the abuse of drugs. As the guarantor of social cohesion, the State exercises its responsibility through the formulation and co-ordination of social policies, the provision of public services and by ensuring respect to the fundamental principle of human rights and equality before the law. Recently, a fundamental change has occurred in the conceptualisation of poverty and social exclusion. Hence, for example, social exclusion is now conceived not in terms of particular categories of people but through a calculation of the degree of severity of social risk, threat, destabilisation, collapse and exclusion.

The increase in both the numbers of unemployed and the average period of unemployment, particularly amongst young people, has been identified as central to the genesis of social problems. Accordingly, 400,000 jobs for young people are being created, mainly within the national education and public transport sector. These jobs are offered with a five-year contract and may lead either to vocational training or a permanent job. A law to promote social cohesion has been in preparation for several years and is aimed at solving the crises in unemployment, homelessness and family debt. This legislation, proposed by the Ministry of Employment and Solidarity, will, over a period of three years, devote 7–8 million Euros to a programme of social reconstruction.

Other measures have also been proposed. Health coverage is to be extended; a social inclusion/personal support project for young people without formal qualifications (TRACE: Trajet d'Acces a I'Emploi) is proposed; apartments in and around Paris, if left vacant for at least two years, would be subject to a tax in order to encourage the owners to rent them; social minima would be indexed to prices, and the lowest of them increased by 29 per cent. Another proposal is to encourage the beneficiaries of social minima back to work by allowing them to add their allowance to the whole of their half-time salary for three months, to half of it for six months and to a quarter of it for the next three months. One particular initiative is representative of the new approach to combating social exclusion, that of the new urban policy.

Urban renewal and social development policy

France has 361 urban areas, housing 75 per cent of the population and where 80 per cent of employment opportunities are provided. Following the housing shortage after the Second World War, between 1950 and 1970, a major building programme took place. Many large apartment blocks were built on the outskirts of towns where land property prices were cheap. The inhabitants in these high-rise flats initially comprised a social mix of predominately younger people. The drawbacks for the inhabitants soon became apparent, since the properties were built to poor quality standards, mainly as regards soundproofing, and there was also a lack of social and commercial amenities and adequate means of transport to the town centres. The economic and industrial crises that occurred between 1975 and the early 1980s, particularly in the former industrial areas of the North and East of France led to these areas being characterised by high unemployment levels. In addition, in a considerable number of council owned properties, there was a high proportion of large families and also of foreign residents; both of which factors further gave to these dormitory settlements a sense of isolation from the mainstream.

In 1977, an inter-ministerial board was established with responsibility for financially supporting agreements between the districts, owners of collective flats, and the state. In particular, this board sought to development some 50 selected sites on the outskirts of big cities. The approach that was developed, *'Housing and Social Life'*, was innovative in as much as it sought the active participation of local residents in the process of social development. Between 1981–1982, this approach was further developed in the form of *'Social Development'* with the support of the Ministry of Education which established these sites as priority education areas. Between 1984 and 1993, 400 sites in 21 of the 22 regions in France and three million people were affected, with no less than 14 different ministries involved in the project. In 1990, a law was passed concerning the implementation of a right to housing and in 1991, a law which established *financial solidarity* between districts.

By 1997 urban social development was designated a 'partnership' policy, led by the State and the localities, in order to combat exclusion in urban areas, and to promote employment and social and cultural inclusion of people living in deprived areas. However, the number of locations concerned fell from 1,300 to 1,034, these were divided into three problem 'categories', with 50 different measures of assistance offered according to the category in which a locality was placed. Despite attempts to improve housing conditions for over 30 years, housing shortages persist and waiting lists have doubled.

The Development of the Social Professions within the French Social Welfare System

Social welfare services in France emerged during the late nineteenth century. Their development was influenced by three primary sources. First, the French constitution of 1793. Second, emergent feminist ideas such as those of Marie Maugeret, founder of a Christian feminist magazine, whose aim was to raise women's consciousness of their 'right to rights'—in particular their right to work. Third, concepts of social solidarity aimed at the eradication of class differences, regeneration of the people, and a reconciliation between the poor and the rich and the combating of social unrest.

However, with the exception of laws intended to prevent imminent social disorder such as, for example: 1811, support to children; 1838, assistance to insane persons; and 1851, free hospitalisation for the sick and elderly, it was not until the International Congress of Assistance of 1889 in Paris that a general framework of public assistance that reflected the principles of the Constitution was developed (see below). Following the Congress, laws were established for the provision of free medical care (July 1893), care for tuberculosis (1902), care for older people, disabled and chronically sick people (July 1905), care for expectant women (June 1913) and care to large families (July 1924).

The nature of the social welfare system in France derives from the particular relationship and responsibility of the state towards those in need of social support. On this issue, the Constitution of 1793 is clear. It defines public welfare towards those people who are unable to work as a *'sacred debt'*, in as much as poverty is understood as an insult to the *'sacred ideal'* of citizenship. It is the state's responsibility to support its citizens in their right to obtain the means to exercise fully their citizenship, and the legitimacy and authority of the state rests upon the satisfactory exercise of this duty. Thus, access to public welfare is established as a right of citizens. Unfortunately, these principles have never been fully realised, due to the lack of resources allocated to the measures that have been introduced by successive governments.

The general purpose of welfare intervention, as expressed at the 1889 Congress, emerged from an alliance between the Church, bourgeoisie and aristocratic classes, whose interests and attachments were to traditions opposed to both the Republic, and the aims and objectives of National, Republican and International Socialist ideals and aspirations. In practice, the particular forms of social work intervention specific to France arose from the historical interplay and connections between three principle disciplines: Social Assistants (who provide support for all of the family), Specialist Educators (who provide education for maladjusted youth) and Social Animators (socio-cultural educators). Together they comprise the traditional range of practitioners working within the overall social welfare system.

The 'social assistants'

Around 1896, under the leadership of Marie Gahery, a number of middle class women were recruited to open an office in the eleventh district in Paris. The aims of this group were similar to those of the settlement movement in England. Between 1900–1910, a number of 'social houses and social centres' were opened under the general term of *Infantile Maternal Protection*. The purpose of these houses and centres was to educate and support children, to assist mothers and to find jobs for the unemployed. In 1912, a branch of the *National Council of Women* established groups within schools in Paris, with the intention of addressing children's cleanliness and hygiene within their home and also to combat alcoholism and tuberculosis, (Guerrand and Rupp, 1978: p 59). This model of help epitomised early forms of social support as being auxiliary to middle class professional and charitable interventions.

In 1914, the association of *Visiting Nurses of France* was established, as was the *School of Superintendents*. The creation of compensation funds and social assurance offices in Paris, and social aid in the forms of visiting nurses, factory superintendents, visiting controllers and family aids, produced a comprehensive range of functionaries who exerted surveillance and social control over the material, physical and moral conditions and behaviour of the working class in both their domestic and work settings. By the end of the war, these visitors and superintendents were

an established feature of social life and the workplace.

In 1907, Gahery established a practical two-year course of study in social training for women. Whilst this was to have only a short existence, there soon followed a free private school to train new 'visitors', established by a priest, Jean Viollet. This training introduced the principle of social inquiry and provided courses on political economics, social legislation, applied psychology, hygiene and home economics along with training periods in the field. In 1911, a social training school for Catholics opened, followed by a school for Protestants. By 1927, both schools had become experimental centres of training and offered diplomas to their graduates.

Contact with America during the First World War brought new methods of social investigation and classification, especially the method of social casework. Among the promoters of these new methods was the Rockfeller Mission which established a methodical form of social intervention, developed a specialised social service for children and collaborated in the establishment of the first juvenile court in Paris. After the war, some women established themselves as *social assistants*, so distinguishing themselves from charity workers and in particular from visiting nurses. This professional identity of the emergent profession was further consolidated at the first International Congress of Social Service in Paris in July, 1928. By 1932, the Diploma in Social Assistance was established and by 1938, the role of the visiting nurse was abolished.

The Second World War saw a diversification and extension of the social assistant's role and tasks. These tasks included those associated with providing 'social and sanitary protection' in the home through the provision of services to the family, support to pregnant women, nursing mothers, infants, pre-school age and school age children. They were also responsible for the organisation of free anti-tubercular clinics, the combating of venereal diseases, the prevention of family breakdown due to alcoholism, advice to families regarding social rights, providing aid to poor people, disabled people and the protection of children, (Guerrand and Rupp, 1978: p 121).

Following the formation in 1944 of the National Association of Social Assistants, new arrangements allowed greater access to the profession by women who had been previously working without formal qualifications. In 1946, legislation formalised the range of tasks to be carried out by Social Assistants and by 1950, a professional code of ethics was established. In 1951, a ministerial decree stipulated that nobody may use the title of *assistant de service social*, or any similar title that it could be confused with or take on a job in the public or private sector, without having the (1932) State Diploma.

During the 1950s, the adoption of American models of case work epitomised the approach taken by social assistants who applied an individualised, client centred and psycho-analytic orientation in their practice. By the end of this period, social assistants had formalised their professional base, acquired primary responsibility for the implementation of social policy and established themselves at the centre of a state directed system of social service. In 1965, a circular was issued regarding the constitution of those services operating under the authority of the Department of Health and Social Services. Subsequent circulars confirmed the nature of formal organisations for social assistants, the function and the range of social services to be provided and their professional role in respect of three spheres of activity:

- by location: i.e. those services to be offered within a geographically defined area;

- by category, i.e. services provided within a particular organisation, for instance to employees and their families in industry, or within schools, health services, ministries, and so on;

- by specialisation, i.e. the social aid to a class of people who have special difficulties, for instance children, teenagers, adults within institutions such as hospitals, homes for older people, etc.

The specialist educators

Specialist education derives from the law of 1850 concerned with the education and care of juvenile offenders who, whilst acquitted in accordance with article 66 of the Penal Code, were not returned to their parents but were taken to a penal settlement for 'discipline and work'. The role of the specialist educator developed from the work of those who had responsibility for these young people. Originally, those with such responsibilities would have been either former non-commissioned officers or young men of 'good moral character'.

By 1912, with the introduction of juvenile courts, young offenders were increasingly being returned to their families or to foster care and there was a decline in the use of penal colonies, (Pinatel, 1986). By 1927, the remaining colonies became 'Houses of Supervised Education' and the warders became instructors. Further, by 1930, regulations were established that defined the term Supervised Education.

The term 'specialist educator' was coined under the Vichy regime during the period of German occupation, when the concept of 'maladjustment' in childhood was adopted. The Vichy government promoted an ideology of 'regeneration' through youth sites and movements such as the *Companions of France*. The aims of the ideology were to teach young people the virtue of work, and develop moral qualities in the context of group living.

The first school for specialist educators, directed by Jean Pinaud, was created near Paris in Montesson. By 1943, four training centres had been established in Montpellier, Lyons, Toulouse and Montesson. In 1947, the National Association for Education of Young Maladjusted was established. By 1950, fourteen training centres were registered and by 1970, twenty-nine schools existed. A State Diploma in Specialist Education was created in 1967.

Today, specialist education agencies provide a range of services including specialised family placements, 'medico-psycho-educational' centres that offer assessments, treatments, consultations and follow-up services. They also provide probation and supervision services, monitoring of state benefits paid to families, and homes for young, unmarried mothers and their children. Specialist educators work in a range of establishments including children's homes, reception and observation centres run by either public agencies or private organisations, secure homes, medico-professional institutes, regional establishments for adapted education and national establishments of the young deaf or blind and psychotherapeutic centres. The range of agencies, establishments and services that are categorised under the term specialised education are not all governed by the same set regulations, and specialist educators are not the only social workers to intervene in these establishments.

Social animators

The range of activities encompassed by the term 'animation' is much broader than those relating to the activities of the social assistant or specialist educator. The origins of socio-cultural animation are closely related to the idea of mass education, which developed from the time of the French Revolution and later during 19th century industrialisation and the adult and working men's educational movement. Concerning children, socio-cultural animation relates especially to the organisation of activities outside school as represented by the tradition of youth clubs that sought to guide and re-educate through socially acceptable leisure activities. The movement represents the ideal of the development of a public conscience and liberation as represented by the Condorcet Report of 1792.

Three main influences contributed to the evolution of socio-cultural animation, each with its own specific framework of reference. First, that of the Church in the form of Christian charitable work with poor people, second, the secular movement aimed at creating a more equal society, and third, the trade unions and the formation of popular universities. Examples of these are the 'teaching league' founded in 1866 by Jean Mace which became the French League of Teaching and Permanent Education that sought to combat social ignorance and intolerance, (Besnard, 1980) and charities such as 'Leo Lagrange' which still play an important role in the field of training. Under the leadership of Pelloutier in 1886, work grants were established from which developed an educational trend that culminated in the establishment of 'Popular Universities'. These universities were created to promote the intellectual potential and promote the cultural education of the 'people' through contact with intellectuals. More recently, socio-cultural animation enjoyed a popular revival in a France during the 1950s and '60s as illustrated

by the introduction of 'specialised prevention clubs', and the 1959 programme of 'preventive social action for families'.

A diploma of 'educator animator' was first offered by the National Institute for the Professional Training for Community Animators in 1963. Professional animators work in a wide and diverse range of social settings and in a variety of roles. The work includes cultural activity and promotional work with individuals or groups, for example, with theatre groups. In the 'socio-cultural' arena, animation centres around the development of work opportunities and apprenticeships in the fields of artistic expression, crafts and sports. In the 'socio-educative' arena, animation is centred on structured educational and leisure activities for children, young workers and older people.

The generic role of the socio-cultural animator is to promote communication and act as an informant and educator in various fields, providing information about health, in health shops, about leisure activities and work, through youth information centres, and about justice, in law shops. More specifically, animators can be distinguished as either *general animators*, who essentially have administrative or managerial functions or *specialist animators*, working with either children, young people, old people, or immigrants, or specialist by virtue of working in particular settings such as theatre, plastic arts, music or the craft industry. In the specialist areas there are 'instructors' who have the State Certificate of Sports Educator or the Aptitude Certificate to the Animation Functions.

This diversity of work environments led the Ministry of Youth and Social Affairs to set up in 1978 the *DEFA*, a training programme for future animators. This diploma is composed of five separate units, a practical period of twelve months and a report. It may be completed over a period of between three and six years after registration. Access to the programme does not, as is usual at this level, require the *Baccalaureat* (High School Diploma). Informal community 'leaders', who may not have the *Baccalaureat* have been encouraged to follow these programmes. In addition, several university programmes exist in the field of animation. These include a 'licence' (the name of one level of university qualification), Degrees in Scientific and Technical University

Studies, and a Master's degree in animation. There are also a variety of Diplomas and a State Certificate of Technical Animator of Popular Education and Youth.

The New Social Professions

The erosion of traditional forms of social work

By the end of the nineteenth century, the target group for social intervention had been clearly established as the worker and his family, and increasingly his children, in the newly industrialised urban context where working and living conditions were particularly hard. Their purpose of social intervention was to provide the necessary regulation, assistance and control, through a variety of educational measures, for social adjustment utilising a case work method within a broadly humanistic approach, (Aballea, 1996: p 11).

Chopart, (1996) has argued that social work has traditionally operated outside the realities of the economic and productive sphere. Thus, whilst working class families may have been the principle targets of social welfare interventions, it has been assumed that their wages derived through industrial work were adequate as a means for escaping poverty. Accordingly, social work intervention has placed more emphasis upon the individual client's personal and moral character than on clients' collective working conditions. Consequently, the primary locus for social work intervention has been focused upon domestic and social life in the community. However, the economic and social crises of the 1970s and '80s have challenged such forms of social work practice with regard to the purpose, targets, institutions, and relationship of social work to other social institutions that support social ties and community life such as the family, school, industry, police, and the judiciary.

The possibility and probability of success in social work projects has always presumed that the numbers of people on the margins of society were reasonably low and the means for their reintegration reasonably sufficient. However, the economic crises of the 1970s and '80s have shifted attention to the economic spheres of production and consumption as

increasing numbers of often qualified, able and willing young men and women became jobless. During this period social security benefits proved insufficient to meet the material needs of the unemployed. This failure of the social security system was also attended by a progressive decline in the provision of collective facilities, e.g. social housing and publicly funded facilities for the promotion of community health, culture and participation.

The social problems of the 1980s and '90s, large scale and long-term unemployment, increased violence towards children and young people, insufficient housing, debt and widespread social exclusion, have given rise to a new approach to the implementation of social welfare policy. This approach is characterised by initiatives that are based on partnership between several agencies, are regionally or locally focused, project based and subject to a rigorous evaluation of their effectiveness. These 'new' services are increasingly subject to competition and are developed as a shared responsibility with either the private or voluntary sector. Many practitioners are already working in new organisations and agencies. However, most of them still work in the traditional field of child and family care.

In 1988, a new right, *the minima integration income* was established within the principle of subsidiarity. However, the provision of this right has been accompanied by the imposition of a responsibility. Beneficiaries are expected to achieve a level of independence that is commensurate with the level of assistance they receive. Accordingly, the social work task has become that of promoting self-sufficiency and the social re-integration of individuals within this newly defined social 'contract'. However, the dilemma remains as to how social integration can be achieved without the availability of adequate employment opportunities.

It is now suggested that these developments have created an essential division within social work practice that brings into question the coherence of its practice aims, methods and target groups, (Mission Recherche— Experimentation, 1996). What is argued is that the 'new' services require skills and 'competences' which are different from those associated with traditional social work practice. The new preoccupation with a procedurally led approach, task centred work and crisis management coupled with the lack of importance now attached to the psycho-social model of intervention has weakened the foundations of social work, (Santelmann, 1995 and 1998).

The creation of new jobs to fit new social policies

The increasing focus upon regional social policy that emerged during the 1980s gave rise to the introduction of new practices and management agendas directed at the local context. This approach has challenged the traditional autonomy and general competence of social workers, many of whom have been replaced in favour of a new and heterogeneous group of semi-professionals specialising in emergent local problems, services, politics and networks. In particular there is a growing cadre of generic middle managers whose expertise in financial and project management is considered to be of equal importance to traditional social work knowledge and skills, (Bailleau, 1988).

Decentralisation and the application of market principles to social welfare administration has created a plethora of new agencies, practices and jobs in response to the changing patterns of need and problems and the composition of welfare clientele, (Ion, 1992 and 1993). These changes have occurred within both the third sector and in statutory public services, which are increasingly adopting a positivist, empirically justified, cost-efficiency culture.

This diversification and proliferation of new jobs in the field of social welfare has been accompanied by a multitude of training programmes at university level—outside of the diploma of social work. Several universities have introduced specialised programmes, such as master's degrees and diplomas in social intervention, administration and policy development. The diversity in and de-regulation of social work practice has led to a similar process within the professional and semi-professional groups engaged in the field of social welfare. This in turn has given rise to a loss of discrete focus as to the purpose and nature of social work and the particular requirements, knowledge, skills and values of those in practice, (Tricart, 1992; Richez-Battesti, 1994).

Towards a redefinition of social work

In November, 1994, the French National Organisation of Social Workers redrafted its code of ethics and reformulated the definition and responsibilities of social work. The sources from which this new definition drew inspiration were, The Universal Declaration of Human Rights (1948); The United Nations' Convention on Children's Rights (1989) (and their integration within French legislation); the definitions of social work drawn up by the United Nations—Division of Social Affairs (1959) and the General Assembly of the International Federation of Social Workers in Sri Lanka (1994).

This new French code of ethics for social work defines and identifies the purposes of social work as being to:

- support the individual in society, through interventions that ensure the autonomy of individuals, groups and communities;

- develop and promote the potential of individuals' responsibility for themselves, their personal and social relationships.

According to the code, social work practice contributes to social development through preventative action that improves the quality of life. Therefore, social workers have a responsibility towards:

- those who are the object of their interventions;

- the laws that regulate their profession;

- the institutions within which they are employed;

- their own continuing professional education and development.

The code asserts that social workers share a commitment to:

- combat poverty and exclusion;

- repair injustice;

- help clients realise their rights;

- recognise and facilitate the increase of individual autonomy and social responsibility.

In addition, the code reaffirms that the professional values and principles of social work, that is, respect for others regardless of race, religion, culture, gender or age and the right to self-determination and so on, should be applied in the context of whatever problems clients experience or changes to social policy and legislation are implemented. It also recognises that as the three professional groupings that constitute traditional social work have sought to consolidate and modernise and as new practices and approaches in the social arena have developed, a range of other jobs has proliferated in the field and that these additional categories of workers have achieved a level of prominence that requires recognition. These include general and managerial domicillary and support workers, medico-social professions i.e. psychiatrists, general practitioners, nurses, psychologists, occupational therapists, physiotherapy, speech therapists and chiropractitioners along with youth careers advisors, early-years educators and a range of specialist and ancillary workers in nursery schools.

Geng (1977) has distinguished two main categories of workers in the social domain. First, there are the academically qualified or professional groups, comprising the social assistants, specialist educators, including educators of supervised education, female educators of young children, advisers in social economics and delegates to guardianship, and socio-cultural animators. Second, there are the family aids and workers, instructor/educators (IE), and mental health helpers (MPH). However, Verdes-Leroux, (1981), and Thevenet and Designaux, (1985), distinguish three categories. First, those professions centred on the family: aids of social service, advisers in social and family economics, family workers, conjugal and family advisers, maternal aids, delegates to guardianship with social benefits. Second, the educational professions: specialised educators, instructors-educators, technical-specialised educators, educators of young children, school educators, specialised school educators and mental health helpers. Third, there are those professionals in charge of animation, which fall under the purview of the Ministries of Social Affairs, Health and Solidarity and Youth and Sports.

Conclusion

The development and changes in social security and social welfare policy in France during the twentieth century have allowed for both the creation and subsequent restructuring and categorisation of the social professions. Traditionally, social workers have served to legitimate the actions of the state in response to emergent social processes and needs. These responses developed into a complex judicial, administrative and professional framework of regulations, structures and services that mirrored the complexity of the situation it sought to address. Within this framework, social workers established a central role for themselves amongst the myriad of other professional groupings and voluntary workers.

The economic crisis of the 1970s exposed an essential flaw in the social security system, namely, that it could not assure the necessary means of subsistence for its citizens. As a consequence of this economic crisis of welfare, new forms of social exclusion were identified, as well as the extent of imminent social risks to the general population and their potential impact upon a wide range of classes within society. These factors have posed a fundamental challenge to the social professions who are charged with the development and implementation of new measures and interventions appropriate to the new conditions.

However, as Ion, (1993), has observed, the call for the development of new forms of practice has coincided with a period of increased rigidity, i.e. a procedural approach to practice, reductions in allocation of resources and the 'freezing' of posts. All the social professions, but especially educators and animators have been affected by the uncertainty that has arisen in respect of their roles, function and the methods that they should apply. Many have expressed a sense of exclusion from the processes of debate and decision-making around the formation of new social policies and the re-structuring of their role and tasks. Concerns have also been expressed over the increase in the employment of unqualified people in social education centres, mental health services and special schools.

The increase in long term unemployment and social exclusion, coupled with the deregulation and decentralisation of services have required that social professionals adapt to new and uncertain conditions. As Demailly, (1991), has observed, with respect to the teaching profession, social workers are now caught in a similar crisis of professional identity, in as much as they experience a sense of powerless with regard to their capacity to respond to the circumstances of clients, public expectations of them and in securing their own future employment.

Questions for Further Consideration

- In France, access to public welfare is a right of citizenship. This contrasts with the situation in other states such as the UK where access to services is based upon eligibility within locally determined criteria. How is access to welfare services determined in your country, and to what extent does the means of access to a service pre-determine the role and function of social workers?

- The historical relationship of three principle social professions in France, (social assistants, specialist educators and social animators), has allowed for the development of a range of specialist services designed to address both the social and individual needs of different client groups. What are the consequences, beneficial or otherwise, of a welfare model within which there are a range of specialist practitioners with different traditions and functions, rather than one in which there is a generic form of social work education and practice?

- In reformulating the definition and responsibilities of social work in 1994, the French National Organisation of Social Workers recognised that along with the three traditional professional groupings that constitute social work a range of other jobs and categories of workers now require recognition. To what extent is this process of recognising people and practices outside of traditional social work occurring in your country and is it likely to lead to the enrichment or erosion of professional practice?

Chapter Five

Social Policy, Social Security and Social Work in Germany

Peter Erath, Wolfgang Klug and Horst Sing

Introduction

This outline of the history and nature of social policy and social work in Germany takes as its starting point the reunification of the East and West German states in 1990, when the division of Germany following the Second World War, a decision regarded by most Germans as inhumane and that had lasted 40 years, was reversed. The reunified Germany became a new political entity, but in so doing it inherited different economic and social structures from the former separate states and these had created a different set of expectations and aspirations amongst the citizens of the former states. Three factors in particular exerted a major influence on the reunified Germany. First, the political instability and economic collapse of the former Soviet republics had led to the collapse of the traditional markets for the industry of the former East Germany. As a consequence, greater financial assistance and transfer of resources from the West to East within Germany than had been anticipated became necessary. Second, economic globalisation was increasingly challenging and mitigating against the highly developed and successful industry in West Germany. Third, the impact of global economic conditions were further compounded by the Maastricht Treaties and the process of European unification which imposed limitations on national politics in Europe, in particular the capacity of national governments to compensate for the social and political consequences of market forces by means of Keynesian type policies.

All these factors have called into question the traditional system of social security in Germany, as established by Bismarck in the late nineteenth century. Current debate centres around the question of whether it will be possible to develop a 'third way' between restoration of the former system or an inevitable reduction of resources and a decline in the provision of social welfare. The historically evolved system of social policy, social security systems and social work in Germany, when compared to other European systems, is characterised by the following key features:

- The solution to the nineteenth century 'social question' of a social insurance model, upon which Bismarck's system was based, was essentially a reactionary or conservative approach to social problems.

- The Nazi regime in Germany demonstrated that the fundamental aim of a social security system could be reversed and that dealing with social problems is not only a matter of providing for individual needs but also essentially a question of democracy and the achievement of social cohesion.

- The institutionalisation of civil rights, a constitutional state, a strong Federal Constitutional Court and the strengthening of the social security system and social work through charitable organisations led to the development of a corporatist approach that assumed a functional model of society, (Luhmann, 1972; Baecker, 1994). This system rests on the premise that it would provide services that other systems cannot provide, for the purpose of integrating people in especially difficult circumstances and preventing exclusion from society.

- The training of social workers in Germany, which predominantly takes place at 'Fachhochschulen', higher educational institutions that provide professional as opposed to purely academic education. They are regarded as being 'of equal value but of different kind' to universities, which has led to a practical and professional orientation which is particularly valued by charitable organisations. The high status of social workers in Germany is also reflected by their relatively high salaries in comparison with other European countries.

The Impact of Modernisation and Globalisation Processes on the Future of the Welfare State in Germany in the Context of German Reunification

Global economic and political developments as well as national social problems and policy aims have increasingly highlighted and contributed to the essential paradox of the welfare state, i.e. that more and more people expect the state to both grant them extensive rights of individual liberty and, at the same time, provide comprehensive social security. The achievement of both these aims has become increasingly impracticable due to the general economic situation of the Federal Republic of Germany.

The social situation in Germany since 1990: increasing problems and needs

Within the context of general trends in Western European countries, such as increasing competition in all economically relevant sectors, continuation of change to a service and a 'self-help economy', rising numbers of elderly people within society, increasing processes of individualisation, constant immigration pressure, etc., the social state model in Germany is increasingly subject to external pressures and internal tensions. Particularly since 1990, when reunification took place, we can identify a clear increase in social problems, such as:

- a drastic rise in unemployment, leading to an increasingly high demand for financial assistance (unemployment relief) from both the federal and local administration. At present there are four million people without a job, with the figures in the new states of the former East Germany twice as high as in the former West Germany;

- a clear fall in birth-rates, especially in the new states, and increasing life expectancy creating increased demand on pensions and the health care system;

- a very high number of foreign workers, civil war refugees, immigrants, asylum seekers and 'guest workers' are resident in Germany. However, immigration policy is very unpredictable and often creates new problems;

- a constant increase in the number of relatively poor people. The general criterion for determining poverty in Germany is that a person who has less than half the average income is considered poor.

The definition of poverty adopted by the European Union is that poor persons are individuals, families or groups of persons whose financial, cultural, and social means are such that they are excluded from the minimal standard of living of that country which means their household budget is below 50 per cent of the national average. It is estimated that approximately 10 per cent of the population in Germany (and 15 per cent in Europe) are currently living below this level and that the number is growing.

(Abrahamson and Hansen, 1996: p 12)

This in turn has led to the emergence of 'sub-cultural differentiation', a new phenomenon in German history. More and more young people are growing up in very poor conditions and receiving no vocational training so that they are likely to be socially excluded. At the same time, there is a huge increase in juvenile delinquency and violence as well as a decline in the capacity of families to help themselves.

Cuts in social benefits

The increase in such problems has been accompanied by a reduction in social benefits in the respect of pensions, health and unemployment insurance. Additionally, there are government proposals that the employed should make a greater contribution to the costs of social security benefits through private payments. People who are dependent on welfare and not able to contribute will only receive minimal standards of state support. These proposed measures are considered necessary due to on the one hand the high rate of structural unemployment, which reduces the number of taxpayers and consequently the state revenues for financing social services and on the other, an increasing number of people who are dependent on welfare benefits. These problems create a chronic budget deficit that challenges the viability of current social policies. Additionally, there has been the introduction of tax incentives for potential investors in the new states of the former East Germany. The resultant loss of state revenue has coincided with a decrease in tax revenue from entrepreneurs and taxpayers who are transferring their profits to foreign countries, whilst declaring their losses in Germany, i.e. tax evasion. Present policy aimed at reducing the high social security contributions from both employers and employees, thus reducing the cost of labour in order to create new jobs has not proved a success. In effect this has only achieved an increase in so-called 'McJobs', i.e. low-paid jobs. This increase in part-time jobs, for which no 'social security contributions' are payable has led to a situation whereby, as no contributions are made, no benefits in the form of old age pensions or unemployment benefits are available. The consequence is that even some of the employed population, will become at some stage in their lives dependent upon communal 'poor relief' thereby increasing the costs of state funded assistance.

A vicious circle is developing in which fewer and fewer people with a job have to pay higher rates of taxes for more and more people in need. The basic premises of the Bismarck system of social security are now being questioned as more flexible models of employment take hold and the economy and the labour market have become increasingly independent from each other. One of the negative results of this vicious circle is the popular debate over the alleged misuse of the welfare system. The 'social climate' is thus deteriorating, with people from the former West categorising their compatriots from the former East as 'social parasites' and xenophobia in both East and West clearly on the increase. Consequently, this situation is an ideal basis for agitation from extreme right-wing groups.

Reunification as a turning point in recent German history

Although the reunification of the two German states had been the declared objective of all political forces in the Federal Republic of Germany for decades, the realization of this project still came as a surprise to all Germans and to the world. In 1990, it was finally

decided to chose Article 23 of the Basic Constitutional Law as the quickest of the available ways to achieve the reunification of the two German states.

This Basic (Constitutional) Law was at this point applied to the (West German) states of Baden, Bavaria, Bremen, Greater Berlin, Hamburg, Hesse, Lower Saxony, Northrhine-Westphalia, Rhineland-Palatinate, Schleswig-Holstein, Wurttemberg-Baden, and Wurttemberg-Hohenzollern, and was to be subsequently applied to other parts of (East) Germany as soon as they joined the federation (Article 23). Through the application of this measure Germany was reunited under a treaty of unification in which the German Democratic Republic basically took over the law of the German Federal Republic and avoided the necessity (following Article 141 of the Basic Law) of devising a new joint constitution.

This approach did not, however, solve the social and economic consequences of reunification. Whilst it was recognised that both German states had developed very different social and economic structures during the years of division and that there would be striking disparities in all socially relevant sectors in a reunited Germany, such was the enthusiasm for reunification, that critical analyses of the quality, scope and consequences of such disparities were at first generally dismissed. In particular, not enough attention was paid to the fact that modernising the East German economic and social structure had to be achieved under an enormous time pressure. In particular the following economic factors were neglected:

- the problematic transformation of socialist enterprises into capitalist ones;

- the rapid loss of the markets of Eastern Europe for East German companies;

- the fact that East German products could not compete on an open, world-wide market;

- the fact that East German companies were not even able to sell their products in their own region since competitors from the West with whom they were unable to compete effectively entered this new market.

Consequently, it was only a matter of a few months until not only had the enthusiasm for the benefits of reunification been exhausted, but also almost all companies in the East were bankrupt. At the same time a reunified Germany, and especially the population in the East, had to face the common problems of all Western industrial countries including growing unemployment rates, public budget deficits, an increasing strain on social security systems, structural changes in the industrial society and immigration pressures.

The historical event of reunification and the emergence of economic and social burdens may have aggravated the social situation in Germany, but a second, more profound explanation of the crisis in the welfare system and specifically the future of the welfare state in Germany is offered by an appreciation of the process of globalisation. The present German welfare state, developed from its origins in the nineteenth century, was based upon bourgeois and socialist ideologies whose basic tenet was the amelioration of social problems. In its present form as a 'social-constitutional state', enshrined within the German Basic Constitutional Law, the present German welfare state has become inadequate in the context of late 20th century global conditions. It has become clear that the so-called 'economic miracle' of the post-war era could only conceal for a short time the fact that social problems will continually challenge social and economic systems.

The Development and Status of Social Welfare Policy in Germany

The establishment of social security systems and of professional social work is closely linked to the formation of the nation state, in particular in connection with its interpretation as a social and welfare state. According to Ritter:

> The Welfare State is an answer to the growing demand for regulation as a consequence of the ever more complicated social and economic conditions effected by industrialisation and urbanisation. It is also a reaction to the decreased importance of traditional provisional systems such as the family in particular. Last but not least it is a reaction to class antagonism having become more acute. It is the aim of the welfare state to integrate the population by social security, increased equality, and socio-political participation. This way existing political, social, and economic systems are to be stabilised and at the same time changed in an evolutionary manner by a process of constant adaptation.   (Ritter, 1991: p 20)

While, according to Kaufmann, (1997: p 1), the successful development of the welfare state in the Western democracies was mainly based on the dynamic interaction between the following factors:

- A strong state, i.e. a state able to reach, implement and control decision making.
- A market economy which allows free decision for companies and continuously increasing their productivity.
- The development of a social sector stabilising the subsequent problems of economic dynamics and the living conditions of the total population.
- The contributions of private households, in particular of families.

Bismarck's social reforms and the creation of the social security system

The replacement of the system of poor relief developed in the Middle Ages by a modern system of social security in Germany is generally equated and associated with the name of Bismarck, following the introduction of legislation in the 1880s governing the safety of employees against the life jeopardising risks associated with illness, accident, invalidity and old age. Three main factors, at this time, contributed to identifying the necessities of life and their general implementation through the mechanisms of the nation state across Europe and in Germany in particular.

1. The economic and social changes, including a change in values, which rapidly occurred in this period and which impacted on the constitution and the actions of political parties. These changes are represented by the loss of the importance of land as a source of wealth and income; the family as a productive community and source of security to its members in times of need; and the increase in importance of capitalist forms of production and labour markets; the mass migration of workers and the urbanisation of society and consequently the dissolution of traditional social relations and forms of mutual help.

2. Constructions of and provisions for minimum, basic standards of living,

unlike the situation in the most advanced industrialised nations, such as Great Britain, Belgium, Switzerland, France and the Netherlands, did not arise in Germany where trade unions were less developed than those in Great Britain, but developed from political forces outside the workers movement. However, the introduction of social insurance demonstrates that both the national and conservative forces in Germany accepted that the social and economic order needed to be reformed and that, in spite of a lack of awareness and current problems, they were able to make the necessary, political decisions. One consequence of this was that the 'social question' in Germany was directed into a 'revisionist channel' and therefore did not result in a general revolution as happened in 1917 in Russia. An extract from the so-called, 'Emperor's Memorandum' from 1883 illustrates this approach:

> *Already in February of this year we have had our conviction expressed that the cure for social harms will not exclusively lie in repressing social-democratic insurrection, but rather and to the same extent in the positive fostering of the workers welfare... We would look back on all successes with even greater satisfaction if We should be able to have created the consciousness that We have left the fatherland a new and lasting legacy of inner peace and greater security and effective help for the needy, which they deserve.*
>
> (Extract from the so-called, 'Emperor's Memorandum', in Reidegeld, 1996: p 150)

3. Along with an acknowledgement that the state also has to find solutions for social problems and with the acceptance of a collective self-commitment to 'a nationally organised, comprehensive, obligatory, joint and several community of employees, employers and state', (Ritter, 1991: p 62), wealthy citizens had to give up their idea that poverty, with the exception of acts of fate such as in the case of severe disability, was usually caused through an individual's personal negligence. Therefore, as a consequence those concerned should have no legal claim for support. Thus, in the intention of its authors and supporters, Bismarck's social reforms moved from 'a social welfare policy to a social insurance policy'

which was established not only without the consent of the workers' movement but also in contradiction to the 'targets of the workers' movement, namely emancipation, separation, accession to power, establishment of solidarity', (Reidegeld, 1996: p 242). Targets that were not achieved.

The three social insurance laws of the Bismarck era—the 'Sickness Insurance Act' of June 15, 1883, the 'Industrial Accidents Act' of July 6, 1884 and the 'Invalidity and Old-Age Insurance Act' of June 22, 1889, offered more social security to their beneficiaries among the wage-earners than had previously been available. However, in terms of the general economic and political order the real beneficiaries were those who supported the maintenance of the status quo by responding to the universal call for 'social reform' with a workers' insurance policy. Thus the 'social damage' of the highly capitalised industrial economy was compensated for but their underlying causes of this 'damage' were not addressed, (Reidegeld, 1996: p 245).

The objective of a great section of the workers' movement, i.e. to make the necessity for assistance of the poor obsolete, by adopting a system whose structures and measures were integrated within economic and political aims, was implicitly rejected from the very beginning by Bismarck's social reforms. He regarded such an objective as utopian. By focusing social welfare policy on a social insurance policy which enabled the 'welfare state' to force virtually the entire wage-dependent population into an insurance system, whose structures were fixed by the law-making body and whose transfer was supervised by the administrative authorities, the state achieved an incredible increase in power and tied a large section of the population to a direct and more complete dependency on the state.

Crisis of the welfare state in the Weimar Republic

In Germany, more than in those countries which were the victors in World War One, significant efforts in the form of social interventions by the state were made in the post-war era both to reduce the considerable potential for social unrest arising from the lost war, and also to prevent the creation of the new problems arising from mass unemployment caused by the change from a war economy to a defence economy, aggravated by anti-democratic mass movements such as the KP (Communist Party) and the NSDAP (National-Socialist German Workers' Party).

It is true that social insurance proved to be efficient, but developments in this field were inconsistent. On the one hand the restructuring of the Weimar Republic into a welfare state did not take place solely at the constitutional level, but was achieved through linking the idea of the welfare state to the concept of a modern, pluralistic society based on safeguarding the interests of organised social and economic forces as expressed in the constitution. On the other hand, the partial success that was achieved, at considerable effort, was largely destroyed by the world-wide economic crisis at the beginning of the 1930s and thereafter became an irrelevance in the ideological battle of political parties with totalitarian elements. The democratic parties and democracy as a system were increasingly accused of having caused the grave economic and social problems which facilitated the seizure of power by the national socialists. With the Act of Enablement, passed in 1933, and the rapid 'Gleichschaltung' (forcing into line) of the most important social changes intended by the Nazi regime, together with the changeover to a war economy in conjunction with the total control of the population under totalitarian rule, this period of development of the welfare state came to an absolute end.

Social security in the Nazi state

In the fields of social welfare policy, social security systems and social work, as in all other areas of society, National Socialism, in line with national socialist ideology and its machinery, sought to achieve an alteration and 'Gleichschaltung' of the old structures. Approaches and institutions of a pluralistic nature that had been initiated under the Weimar Republic were dismantled. This was achieved by destroying the trade unions and by forcing the workers' movement into line in the 'Deutsche Arbeitsfront' (German labour front): through the regulation of work relationships, the health care system and to some extent the informal sector of welfare. The

propagation and implementation of the social-Darwinist and racist ideology was manifested in policies such as 'negative eugenics', the forced sterilisation to prevent the reproduction of 'hereditary diseases', and the extermination of so-called 'unworthy life' (euthanasia). The expression of such Nazi philosophy is well expressed in an extract of a speech made by Goebbels:

> *The core of bourgeois social philosophy was the individual. Consequently, it is guided mainly by compassion, or mercy, or Christian charity, or similar convictions. Our socialist philosophy and practice differs completely from such notions. We do not consider the individual important, we do not agree with those that say: feed the hungry, relieve the thirsty and dress the naked—these are no motives for us. Our motives are of a completely different kind. They may be summed up most concisely in the following sentence: we must have a healthy people in order to assert ourselves in the world. And a healthy people is not only represented by arms, ideas, or convictions, a healthy people is also represented by the vigour of its body and the vigour of its soul. And the vigour of the body and the vigour of a people's soul need to be cared for, sustained, and particular provisions have to be taken: our socialism lies in the community.*

> (From a speech by Nazi propaganda minister Goebbels at an NSV-convention at the NS party rally in 1938, in Vorländer 1988: p 369)

The attempts of the Nazi regime to establish a social security system through the notion of the 'German labour front', which was to incorporate the entire population within its ideology and to further control virtually all 'national comrades' through its monopoly of 'welfare' (which of course included the elimination of 'anomic elements' or 'persons harmful to society'), more or less failed at the outset. However, the tendency to universalise and standardise social security in fact showed some similarities with the plans of William Beveridge for a British social system (see page 125), in particular the social security system and an adoption of a standard pension.

The Federal Republic of Germany as a 'social constitutional state' (Sozialer Rechtsstaat)

The catastrophe into which Germany was plunged by the Nazi regime was too great to allow a return to the point where the Weimar

Republic had ended. Not only had the consequences of National-Socialist rule to be overcome but also the reasons for the failure of the republic had to be analysed in order that conclusions for social welfare policy could be determined which would prevent a future failure of democracy within Germany. The new constitution was of great importance. Its premises were determined by the following four factors:

1. The foundation of the Federal Republic of Germany was a product of the Cold War; it took place in a divided country and was therefore approached by parliamentarians with mixed feelings. The new constitution and foundation for the state was regarded as a provisional measure.

2. The Parliamentary Counsel—the body that prepared the constitution—consisted of two equally strong blocks with 27 representatives of the CDU/CSU and 27 of the SPD, while the third strongest group, the FDP that was represented by 5 members, tipped the scales in decisive items.

3. This balance of power between the two strongest opposing blocks and the belief that the constitution was only a provisional measure facilitated, on both sides, acceptance of decisions which led to, amongst other things, the social and economic order not being clearly defined. Rather, only the constitutional basis, for arriving at a concept of the social and economic order and the subsequent development of the welfare state by the legislative body and other groups in society, was created by defining the state as a 'social constitutional state'.

4. The basic constitutional structures which were then incorporated into the development of social welfare policy, social security systems and social work in the Federal Republic of Germany had been drawn up with the objective of avoiding the deficiencies of a purely formal constitutional state by stipulating mainly positivist fundamental rights together with a highly effective safeguard against the infiltration of extremist efforts that might harm 'liberal fundamental order'.

Especially in the early years of reconstruction, constitutionality, democracy, a welfare state system and federalism, together with moral convictions such as the inviolability of human dignity, the importance but also the social responsibilities of private ownership, became part of a 'constitutional patriotism' which was accepted as the 'appropriate form of the collective identity' of German society, (Kaufmann, 1997: p 164). Despite existing political and ideological differences and increasing criticism from neo-Marxist commentators the 1960s, the interpretation of the state as a 'moral entity', which was quite common in the German history of ideas, was eventually expressed in a constitution containing both 'civil and religious characteristics', (Kaufmann, 1997: p 165). This stands as a complete contrast to the period of the Nazi state which represented the degeneration of state power through the absolute instrumentalisation of a misanthropic ideology.

Together with the success of the social market economy, full employment and personal affluence for all, this 'constitutional patriotism' created a lasting political climate which made it possible for social welfare policy, social security systems and social work to progress and develop well into the seventies. The success of this development in the Federal Republic of Germany had, to a large extent, hidden the paradox between the liberty of the individual and social equality, a paradox that all modern states have to face. In a climate of social and economic progress the indissolubility of this paradox seemed to be less and less worrying and was constitutionally embedded in the Basic Law through use of the term 'social constitutional state'. What has to be taken into account here is mainly the specific relationship between the 'social constitutional state' (*sozialer Rechtsstaat*) and the 'social market economy' (*soziale Marktwirtschaft*). It is possible to see this exclusively in the context of a competition of ideological systems, i.e. the former Federal Republic as a 'bulwark against the East'. The easing of the social hardships of laissez-faire capitalism by the welfare system may be seen in the context of the competing ideologies. Moreover, the exorbitant 'economic miracle' in post-war Germany caused an 'exhaustion' of the male German labour force so that socio-political measures became necessary (a policy to recruit guest workers, women's liberation and emancipation) to create a new labour force that would make a lasting contribution to the overall labour force.

The social problems that were recognised in the society of the 'economic miracle' were generally viewed as being resolvable through economic measures that contained them at a level that was acceptable to everyone by means of financial help in the form of social insurance benefits, especially as the social security systems included more and more people and offered growing support. All other forms of 'deviant behaviour' should be covered by social work which underwent a considerable development after the 1970s. However, by the 1980s, in particular following a review of the health care system and the discussion of the introduction of private nursing insurance, it became increasingly clear that the increasing growth of social problems demanded too much from the system in the long run. Another factor contributing to this was the relative over-population of Germany that rendered respective measures in the areas of labour programmes and the health system superfluous. Whilst the enthusiasm for German reunification delayed consideration of these issues for a short time, disillusionment followed with its inevitable outcome—the initiation of unprecedented, fundamental debates about the economic and social order.

The Social Security System in the Federal Republic of Germany

The system of social support in Germany consists of a differentiated network of various structures. There are three levels of support within the overall structure. The 'first' level of social security is to provide for the immediate needs of the people by means of material aid. The 'second' level is that of professional social work, the aim of which is to encourage people who cannot be assisted on a merely material basis to 'help them to help themselves' for a limited time, and the third level comprises honorary (assistant) and voluntary social help which is intended to prevent people from getting into a situation of need, and which is to provide help in every day situations.

Principles of the Social Security System

Acts of the welfare state are based on Article 20 of the Basic Law which stipulates: 'The Federal Republic is a democratic and social constitutional state'. The term 'social' is here understood to be an obligation of the state to provide public assistance for all sections of the population, but especially for groups in need, according to Eucken:

> *It is the first aim of government policy to make sure that there is no need for social security measures in the first place, and if there is any such need then it should be as limited as possible. Secondly, it has to be established whether situations of need that occur despite these attempts were caused by governmental intervention. In this case it would be useful if any action in the field of social policy would aim at the avoidance of any governmental measures with socially undesirable results. Only in the third place additional activities of social policies may become necessary in the form of measures of redistribution, and if so, side or future effects will have to be taken into account.*
>
> (Eucken, in Hamm, 1989: p 364)

This duty derives from the three principles of subsidiarity, solidarity and justice, which were decisive for the 'fathers' of the Basic Law, considered below:

1. The first principle of subsidiarity, in the context of human society, is that outside external support increases in its value when it encourages self-help. Consequently, the prime objective of state and social activity has to be the support of personal initiatives:

> *Whatever the individual can do him or herself is not to be taken over by activities of the community, for this would not be a help or improvement, but quite the reverse: impediment, damage, and limitation of the free development of the individual that is always dependent on the activation of his or her own energy…In any case, one has to ask whether the task in question can be fulfilled sufficiently, satisfactory, and without over-exertion by the closer community, which is also limited in space and competency, or whether it is necessary for the community in a wider sense, i.e. without the limitations of the closer community, to interfere in order to achieve good and satisfactory solutions.*
>
> (Nell-Breuning, 1957: p 220)

In the sector of social work this means that, in particular, family ties and obligations and 'Freie Wohlfahrtsverbände' (non-governmental and non-profit organisations) have important functions. Especially since and as a result of the failure of the 'Third Reich', direct state interventions into the interpersonal sector should be approached with caution and kept to a minimum.

2. The principle of solidarity recognises the fundamental dependence of the individual: no one can survive on his/her own, and that we are essentially mutually inter-dependent. This principle applies at both the individual and social level. From this inter-relatedness and mutual dependence in respect of our needs there follows a mutual responsibility to each other. Each member of society can thus claim solidarity with the all others as well claim that each individual identifies with the collective. Accordingly, the concept of solidarity requires the welfare state to develop a system of social measures to safeguard social advancement, to create social partnerships and to cover the essential needs of all sections of the community by means of collective public assistance and insurance against potential risks.

3. The principle of justice sets the welfare state the task of distributing all resources among the population in a just manner. This construction requires a recognition that the 'economic state' on its own cannot achieve social balance. In this respect the objective necessity for continuously modified intervention by the state into the social structure has become the leading principle of the welfare state as expressed in the Basic Law through granting a minimum of welfare facilities; eliminating social deficiencies by law and continuing to develop social structures.

The tasks and structures of the 'first' level of social security

Since the social security system as described above is the result of a long-lasting and complicated social process a variety of definitions have arisen. A simple definition, proposed by Lampert, is that the social security system is understood to be the:

> *…sum of all facilities and measures which aim to protect the citizen against risks associated with the temporary or permanent loss of income because of illness, maternity, old-age or unemployment; the death of the bread-winner (marriage partner or parents); unforeseen expenditure in the case of illness, maternity, accident or death.*
>
> (Lampert, 1996: p 220)

As such it comprises a number of insurance schemes against occupational disability and invalidity; old-age and retirement; accident; ill-health insurance and unemployment. Moreover, the social security system includes support for war victims, public assistance and other social transfers within the framework of housing policy, policy regarding the promotion of vocational training and policy on domestic relations. The core principles of these safeguards are insurance, provision and assistance, (Lampert, 1996: p 221).

Second level supports: the legitimisation of social work

Caring for the physical, mental and spiritual well-being of ill, handicapped, poor and vulnerable people has had a long tradition in Europe, the origins of which can be found in the Christian-Jewish system of values. Thus, Thomas Aquinas, (1224–1274), writes:

> *Since charity is a commandment it follows that it is necessary action for the realisation of the love of one's neighbour. It is, however, also part of charity that we not only wish our neighbour good, but that we also act accordingly…Accordingly in as much we act from the intention and seek to affect the well-being of another, it becomes necessary that we help him in times of need, through giving of alms. And this is why giving alms is a commandment.*
>
> (Thomas Aquinas, 1985: p 162)

In the modern state, traditional forms of assistance (almsgiving, feeding of the poor etc.) have been largely replaced by professional services; assistance to the poor is replaced by a system of legal rights to public assistance and of state guarantees, (Müller, 1988). This second level of social support is legitimised by the social constitutional state of Germany in three ways:

a) Through the principle of the 'social state based on the rule of law' in Article 281 of the Basic Constitutional Law and which serves as a formula to connect social and liberal thinking when drawing up the Basic Law.

b) By the interpretation of democracy laid down in the Basic Law.

c) By the provision of fundamental individual rights upon human rights.

Definitions of social work

Social work/social pedagogy (note: the social pedagogic approach is orientated towards education and the development of social skills rather than provision of material assistance (both terms are used synonymously in Germany) entails, according to Meyer, that:

> *...personal care be organised and performed within the framework of the social security system for individuals or groups who need care due to their age, their social status, their physical or spiritual well being. This applies, for example, to children, young people, old people, people without permanent residence, the homeless, handicapped people, persons in need of care, and delinquents.*
>
> (Meyer, 1978: p 150)

Thus, the range of work undertaken by social workers in Germany is very extensive:

> *Facilities and measures of social education accompany the life of babies, children, juveniles and young adults: prenatal counselling and baby care, crèches, nursery schools and day-nurseries, reform schools, leisure homes and facilities open to everybody, camps and recreation measures, support of youth organisations and international youth exchange programmes, monitoring of foster children and adoption programmes, public guardianship, juvenile court assistance and probation service.*
>
> (Kreft and Mielenz, 1988: p 482)

As a 'social response to social problems', (Staub-Bernasconi, 1996), social workers give assistance particularly when people experience a crisis during the course of their lives. This includes, for example, unemployed juveniles, single parents, foreign families, drug addicts, people suffering from chronic diseases and old people.

The aims of social work

Depending upon their particular professional role, social workers specifically aim to:

- offer support in the forms of personal and environmental assistance in order to enable individuals to become self determining;

- give concrete assistance to individuals and groups in overcoming obstacles in their social circumstances;

- offer guidance and exert influence over the environmental circumstances in order to maximise opportunities and human potential;

- develop a variety of mechanisms for the promotion of assistance.

Professional education, training, philosophy and ethos of social work

Normally, social workers are granted their diploma following eight semesters of advanced professional studies that including an integrated practical year (Diplom-Sozialpädagoge); or following eight semesters of purely theoretical university studies (Diplompädagoge). The purpose of the studies in social work is to ensure that social workers acquire the ability for independent professional action in the various areas of social work—on the basis of academic knowledge and methods. The development of a professional orientation towards the human being, the focus of social work, provides the rationale for the entire education. There are professional associations of social workers in Germany, but their position and influence are, compared with other European countries, rather marginal. The more social work has taken on the appearance of, or an approach of being a 'business', the more urgent have the calls become for social work to adopt a professional ethical code. The debate over ethical principles has already begun but as yet has not yielded any concrete results.

In many countries social, medical and juridical professional groups are only entitled to practice if their service is bound to the welfare of the public within an organisation that is subject to a professional code of ethics or code of conduct. A violation of those rules can lead to exclusion from the professional organisation and to prohibition from practice. This is justified on the grounds that society is conceding to these groups a monopoly for the fulfilment of a social task. In Germany we do not have such a professional body for social work. Nevertheless, professional organisations are trying to develop a binding ethical code that would provide the basis for an autonomous professional group.

Organisation of social work in Germany

The traditional system for the organisation of social work in Germany is distinguished by a dual system comprising government institutions (public welfare work) and independent supporting organisations (free charitable associations). Up to the present time these two organisational groups have had a monopoly within the sector. Under Articles 2 and 9 of the Basic Constitutional Law, overall responsibility for the planning and obligatory provision of services rests with the public institutions. The implementation of services is often then delegated to the independent charity organisations, these can decide, in turn, which methods to choose for the fulfilment of social tasks. Based on the principle of subsidiarity, the public authorities have an obligation to give preference to charity associations, to provide services that they can take on. Increasingly, charities can offer their services through fixed contracts. The importance of this way of financing can be seen from the fact that charities now finance 70 per cent of their work through fees for their services. This unusual position for charitable organisations was justified by the fact that on the one hand they are 'non-profit making', and on the other, they undertake tasks within the social system that otherwise should be provided by the state.

This division of responsibilities remained largely unchanged until the 1990s. Following EU policy on competitive contracting out of services, commercial profit-making organisations now also tender to provide services. The following illustrates how functions are divided between (1) public authorities, (2) charities and (3) private organisations:

1. Public authorities supporting social work include the following agencies

   - social security offices funding social insurance benefits

   - youth welfare departments funding youth work

   - housing offices funding housing assistance

   Their role is to meet the legal entitlements claimed by people in need, as stipulated within the Basic Law, and thus serve as legitimated public authorities fulfilling the duties of the state. Accordingly, social work, alongside other social roles, has a control function, for example when applying the right of custody (1666 Civil Code).

2. Charitable associations, as non-profit making agencies provide 'free welfare work' which is understood as being any social support offered on a free and non-profit making basis and in an organised form that is self determined by the agency as opposed to fulfilling statutory duties. Such 'free welfare work' is regulated under the provisions of Article 19, 34 of the Basic Law and differs from 'public assistance' in that agencies are accorded freedom of action to achieve self-determined targets. This is in contrast to public agencies acting with the authority of the state in the fulfilment of legal duties. The purpose of the charitable associations is to provide planned, direct, preventive support to people in need, which 'exceeds the objectives of a self-help organisation'. By common consent, a body can only be designated as an 'association' when it has nation-wide links and operates to a common policy. The 'umbrella associations' are understood to be those associations of free welfare work that are combined to form the Bundesarbeitsgemeinschaft der Freien Wohlfahrtspflege (Federal Working Association of Free Social Work). The following organisations are members: Arbeiterwohlfahrt, Deutscher Caritasverband, Diakonisches Werk Deutschland, Deutsches Rotes Kreuz, Deutscher Paritätischer Wohlfahrtsverband and Zentralverband der Juden.

   Charitable associations assume that in a number of areas of need neither the market nor the state supplied services are sufficient to provide all people with goods and services. In those situations, where market and state fail, it is the charitable associations that support people in need. The particular characteristic of charitable associations is that they belong to the non-profit sector, i.e. to organisations whose formal objective is not to make profits. Organisations such as churches, ecology groups and also sports clubs and parties belong to non-profit organisations (NPO) and the form of the charitable associations derives from this tradition. In most cases they are organised as non-profit associations pursuant to the law of associations at community, county, district, state and federal levels.

Welfare associations fulfil their task by providing their own professional services and by the use of volunteers. Welfare associations are represented in all fields of social work, for example, 40 per cent of all people treated in hospitals were treated in facilities run by welfare associations and 60 per cent of old people's homes and nursing homes and about 75 per cent of all social services are provided by welfare associations.

3. Increasingly, social work services are being offered by private organisations. These organisations comprise foundations, charitable societies and companies with limited liability or private enterprises based on the Civil Code or the Commercial Code. They offer services in traditional sectors of social work, for example, health and domiciliary services for elderly people. Social workers who cannot find a job on completion of their vocational training may establish a company to offer care under the care act. Besides these small-scale operations there are a number of large enterprises that have found the social sector to be a most profitable area for investment, especially in the sector of rehabilitation. Indications suggest that these businesses may in the long term threaten the financial viability of established charitable organisations.

Further development of organisational structures of social work

As in the rest of the European Union, arising from its four basic principles of free exchange

of goods, free capital market, free job market and free service market, an increasing emphasis on the role of a market rather than state led approach to welfare is gradually gaining ground in Germany. This is well illustrated by Oppl:

> *The rendering of social services is...a process of production like any other: in the social sector it is also important to be able to render or produce the necessary services and products. The services/products are offered in an open marketplace and they find or do not find, as may be the case, customers/purchasers.*   (Oppl, 1992: p 153)

For social work this means that not only will the state withdraw more and more from the position as guarantor of services, leaving an increasing number of services to the free play of market forces, but will, instead, finance only a minimum level of provision. But also in the long-term, as is already the case in nursing insurance, the individual will be given money so that he can 'buy' the appropriate social service on the free market. The classic division of all markets among the charitable organisations will thus gradually come to an end and its unusual position in the welfare state will be replaced by competition among numerous suppliers. This will ensure that clients are in a position to choose the supplier that offers the 'best' service at the most favourable price. Consequently, competition for customers gets tighter and tighter. This applies to both competition among the welfare associations, who have long since become rivals, and between welfare associations and private suppliers. This development poses an enormous challenge for social work because whilst seeking to meet a growing demand for social aid it simultaneously faces more and more problems in financing its services. Moreover, social work has to tackle the problem of the hitherto unknown phenomenon of competition among service suppliers.

Status quo and future perspectives of the practice of social work

The practice of social work in the 1970s was characterised by a considerable degree of freedom which allowed individual social workers autonomy in the manner in which they defined and implemented their role in completing the tasks of professional practice.

The primary objective was to establish a good relationship between the social worker and client rather than assistance being dependent upon or defined in terms of the provision of material or financial resources. Work was neither systematically documented nor evaluated and notions of quality were understood in terms of the personal commitment and the competence of the social worker.

Since the 1980s, and especially since the introduction of private nursing insurance, as the legal rights to assistance have increased whilst municipalities have faced budget restrictions forcing them to streamline their administration, new financial and procedural controls have been introduced. This has resulted in a decrease in the freedom of action allowed to the individual social worker. As a consequence the following tendencies have been strengthened:

- At a local level, 'improvements' in the social services have been made by ensuring optimum transparency, co-ordination, co-operation and full utilisation of all services available.

- Within individual organisations, the introduction of targeting services on certain specified client groups, coupled with the profiling of services, based on the specific expectations and needs of the 'customers', for the purpose of determining standards and measures for evaluation, quality management, assurance and control have been introduced, (Meinhold, 1997).

- At the level of the individual worker, there is an increased requirement to adhere to the achievement and implementation of facility-specific quality standards.

At the same time quality assurance methods are being adopted from the business community along with other approaches that have been in common use for decades in some other European countries. For example achieving certification in accordance with International Standard 9004 ff., cost consciousness is now a requirement of social workers; increased competition amongst a variety of service suppliers and the setting up of private agencies all indicate a greater orientation towards market principles. Together

these tendencies constitute a fundamental shift in approach, from one that is primarily orientated around the client relationship to one that is orientated towards cost effectiveness of the service. This is exemplified by the care management approach which seeks to match funded practical assistance to a defined legitimate category of need.

Perspectives on what Constitutes Appropriate Practice in Social Work

The focus of the current discussion on social politics in Germany today is the question of how society will be able to maintain a balance between 'social justice' and 'individual freedom' in the face of increasingly scarce financial support from the government. In the field of social services the proposed solution to this conflict between competing ideals is to promote 'more market—less state' and 'more voluntary—less professional' involvement. This solution has gained a general agreement amongst both politicians and citizens of a variety of political affiliations. However, the adoption of such an approach demands of social workers that they radically reassess both their methods and the efficiency of those methods. This may prove to be an opportunity for the development of social work practice if we manage to avoid the dangers arising from the imposition of hasty, ill-considered change.

Whilst the general population do not question the need to save money, it is the media who have particularly singled out weaknesses in the social services. All aspects of social policies and social work practice have come under scrutiny and are under pressure to resolve the dilemma of achieving more with less money. The introduction of privatisation and the deregulation of welfare services are aimed at both saving tax payers' money and releasing government from the direct responsibility for certain aspects of social services. In addition, new private competitors are forcing the suppliers of services to become more efficient and to improve their services, if they are to retain their viability within the welfare 'market'. In areas that do not permit total privatisation (drug counselling, help for the homeless, etc.) the introduction of 'quasi-markets' is affecting increased efficiency. In particular, the means that have been introduced into the state sector that characterise this approach are:

- the development of market-orientated strategies
- an orientation towards the 'customer'
- an emphasis on outputs rather than the input of the system
- state financial support being dependent on attaining successful outcomes

At first sight, these approaches appear quite reasonable, but considered more closely they turn out to be too simplistic. In particular, what is neglected is that social work intervention as a rule does not only deal with a single 'customer' but with a cluster of 'stakeholders': the client who expects sound treatment appropriate to his or her individual need; the government agency that finances the services and seeks an effective and permanent solution to the 'problem' and the taxpayer who expects that the measures chosen are as inexpensive as possible.

A new, appropriate form of social work will have to take into account a number of considerations, none of which in themselves will prove adequate, but taken collectively may provide an adequate model.

Firstly, in order to satisfy growing public mistrust of the nature and efficiency of social work, the process of social assistance must become more transparent to both the client and the funding agency. In order to achieve this, all components of the services provided will have to be identified; the aims, purpose and targets of the intervention made apparent and changes introduced for the appropriate supervision of the process of the work undertaken. In addition, both the process and the outcomes of the process of social assistance should be made subject to both internal and independent evaluation, including an evaluation from the service recipient.

Secondly, in order to ensure the responsible use of public money in the field of social work, it is necessary to establish that intervention in each individual case is justified and that the client/recipient/customer in question is committed to contribute to the process. The 'plans for help' are a means, in a form similar to that of a contract, to formally secure the client's duty to contribute to an agreed process of assistance that seeks to maximise the client's

own potential and capacity for change and personal responsibility.

Thirdly, an exclusive orientation of social work towards positive outcomes has to be considered in relative terms. The value of social work cannot only be measured by its output but, more importantly perhaps, by the quality of the process of intervention. Hence the establishment of quality standards that can be assured through quality management measures of process must be a long-term goal of social work practice.

Fourthly, the enormous costs generated by the provision of social work services can only be justified, in the long run, if a delegation of certain services to less expensive 'assistant professions' can be achieved and that those services undertaken by volunteers should be integrated wherever they prove beneficial. In Germany, there is still not enough co-operation between professional social workers and volunteers, or those that do not have official qualifications. Integrating such 'assistant labour' should not lead to a loss of quality, especially if social workers supervise them and promote their education and training.

Finally, we would argue that it is only if social workers make their work transparent, continually try to both respect the personal dignity of their clients and to improve the efficiency of their methods and measures, can they expect that their work will be respected and financed by the public; particularly as it is the case that social work cannot always be successful. By the same token, social work *can* be acknowledged as having a valid contribution to make to the functioning of modern society, and the public will increasingly acknowledge the credibility and competency of social work in the context and debates over questions of social politics.

Third sector and voluntary social help

Social help has also always been provided by people who are neither trained nor paid. Nonetheless, against the background of cuts in the social sector, a new debate around the issue of 'citizen involvement' has arisen relating to the question of voluntary forms of help, voluntary services, and self-help. The co-operation between social movements could both improve the situation of a locality, group or individuals, and in so doing save money for the community.

The essentials of such an engagement are: voluntary contributions, motivation based on a community of interest; co-operation with other individuals to reach a given social objective and self-management rather than the predominance of professional interventions. According to Huber the movement of citizen involvement arises from an alliance of 'people who are taking the initiative and join up with like-minded people to bring about something to achieve a shared aim', Huber, (1987: p 19), namely to improve their own or other people's situation.

> *In this sense citizen involvement has not only to be differentiated from paid employment and statutory work, but also from domestic work, work within the family, leisure time activities, moonlighting, etc. Citizen involvement does not primarily fulfil an economic or subsistence-economic purpose like outwork or the shadow economy, it is more related to political activity, produces 'community goods', serves 'common welfare', in a manner that is quite different from individual leisure time activities.*
> (Beck, in Kommission, 1997: p 147)

This new social movement is causing a gradual change in apparent values in Germany, particularly in the environmental sector, arising from a perceived need for greater participation and democratic activity. It is argued that experts should no longer decide which problem should be tackled in which particular way, rather this should be done by those who are directly concerned with or affected by these problems. Similarly, large organisations should no longer decide how to organise social work, rather this should be done by those who are the recipients of services and that anonymous institutions should no longer advocate on behalf of people in need but people in need should be able to represent themselves in the process of securing their rights.

As policy-makers discover 'citizen involvement', and it is used as an argument to justify cutting state funded social services, there is the danger that this may result in professional social work being considerably reduced. In order to develop a critical analysis of the problem of the relationship between social workers and 'honorary' social help and self-help activities we need to develop methods that will allow for the identification of what is appropriately located within the domain of professional social work and what could be appropriately left to the 'third sector'.

Concluding Remarks and Considerations

In today's Germany, people recognise that it is not possible to find an ultimate solution for social problems due to their complex character and the impact of the processes of modernisation and globalisation as outlined above. Although in the seventies the general opinion was that social problems could be solved by politicising social work, in the present situation it is accepted that problems such as poverty, drug addiction, propensity to violence, trafficking in human beings etc. are highly complex and partly worldwide phenomena which can at best be restricted. This realisation has created a challenge within the field of social work in respect of both its theoretical basis and its public status. The notion that problems could be solved by identifying and applying the correct theory is no longer accepted as it is now acknowledged that social problems are obviously too complex to be 'solved'.

Luhmann's statement relating to the educational system, that it sought to 'basically do something impossible, (Luhmann, 1987), applies equally in the field of social work. In other words, modern systems suffer from structural defects that cannot be eliminated even with the best intentions of the people involved. The structural defect of social work lies in the fact that a solution to an individual's problem cannot be achieved through outside help alone, the person involved also needs to help themselves. Therefore, only some aspects of the needs of the individual concerned can be fulfilled. Within the framework of the professional intervention the welfare worker can organise money, help to find a flat, discuss problems with his client etc., but social workers cannot achieve this without the co-operation of clients. Further doubts about the adequacy of the services provided by social work arise from three issues for concern that Baecker, (1994), describes as follows:

- concerns about the motivation of workers which suggest that all assistance helps the one who is providing rather than the one receiving help;

- concerns about stigmatisation which suggest that services are self-serving rather than focused on the needs of welfare recipients;

- concerns over efficiency which suggest that services impede rather than encourage the potential for self-help.

All of these issues re-emphasise the basic problematic nature of modern social systems; that they cannot reflect upon and monitor themselves and therefore develop 'blind spots', which, under certain social conditions, generate public doubts about their efficiency and rationale. As discussions on the future of the welfare state proliferate, they are of direct relevance to social work. Accordingly, we would argue for the need to generate a critical debate on the theoretical basis of social work practice, particularly within the context of the German situation, emphasising the question of how social workers should organise their work in order that they develop adequate methods of intervention.

Questions for Further Consideration

- A paradox highlighted in this chapter is that 'more people expect the state to both grant them extensive rights of individual liberty and at the same time, provide comprehensive social security'. How has this tension been resolved in your country and what are the implications for day-to-day social work practice? How does this resolution compare with the resolution of this tension between liberty and security in Germany?

- Changes in perceptions of economic well-being can have profound effects upon the development of forces such as racism or xenophobia. Are these phenomena linked in your country?

- The emergence of the 'market' in the provision of social welfare poses considerable challenges for the future development of social work. Are similar developments in progress in your country, what can be learned about both the practice and management of social work under such conditions by examining both the German system and also the system that exists in your own country?

Chapter Six

Social Work in Italy

Rino Fasol

Introduction

In order to reconstruct the evolution of social work in a country it is necessary to consider the interweaving of social policies, institutional structures and organisational models. The assumption behind this approach is that a continuum that extends from the macro-level of national systems, to the meso-level (which we can take to comprise the regional sphere) to the micro-level of local systems, exhibits the progressive shifts due to a combination of various factors. What I wish to emphasise as regards this continuous process of adaptation is the role of actors and their interests within the organisations that operate in the social and health welfare system. The aim is to identify the constraints on the action of practitioners and the margins of discretion that the organisations leave for the definition of the goals of social-welfare work, for the choice of models and instruments of intervention, for the construction of organisational models, and for the development of work styles.

My main concern is to highlight the congruities and incongruities among social policy directions as they are defined at the central or local level, the design of institutional structures, and the planning of organisational models that should enable implementation of the policies and achievement of their aims. The most interesting level at which to examine these gaps is that of the services which operate in direct contact with communities and citizens.

At this level, social work becomes the production of services as a concrete response to the real needs of the community. Consequently, on the one hand the system of rules, and on the other the capacity to interpret the role of the social worker, come into play. Influencing this capacity are the constraints of organisations, their cultures, the degree to which the available technologies have been developed, but also the outcome of constant confrontation among actors, a confrontation in which professional identities count for a great deal.

The Recent Development of the Welfare System in Italy

Thorough assessment of the problems now confronting the Italian system of social and health services first requires a brief survey of the most significant recent developments in Italy's welfare system as regards social policies, institutional structures, and organisational models.

The situation in the 1960s

Until the 1960s, according to Olivetti Manoukian:

> ...from a legal and institutional point of view, the public health and social welfare system in Italy...was still essentially the one that arose during the twenty years of Fascism. It was characterised by the strong centralisation of measures delivered by national agencies operating through formal classifications of various types of need and various types of user, and at the same time by the marked fragmentation of facilities and services.
>
> (Manoukian, 1988: pp 11–12)

The guiding principles of social policies went no further than the reparation of damage—that is to say, intervention to remedy the consequences of a disadvantage or disability already evident and recognised. This partly explains why the institutional system was connotated, besides centralisation, by a sharp separation between social services on the one hand, and health services on the other. At the same time action was undertaken by a multiplicity of public and private actors, in a competition which saw private actors advantaged by the prejudice that they were of better quality than public ones, as well as by lax controls even when they were publicly funded. The organisation of services was based on substantially bureaucratic principles: formal compliance and pre-established procedures based on predetermined entitlements. The professionalism of practitioners was constrained by narrow and minutely defined competences and rules.

The professional identity of practitioners was probably affected by the fact that a large proportion of the personnel employed in both social and health services were 'religious'. According to Bassanini *et al.*, (1977), in 1962, hospital staff, excluding doctors, comprised 45,000 religious workers and 40,000 lay workers, (quoted in Manoukian, 1988: p 16). The most solidly entrenched and socially recognised professional groups were the administrative workers that attended to the enormous bureaucratic workload, (the *'pratiche'* or files), that accompanied every welfare case, and the doctors, who wielded an undisputed cultural hegemony which extended well beyond the health services. A still minor role was played by professional groups comprising relatively new actors in the Italian services, like psychologists and social workers. For a detailed critical survey of the frame of reference for both the training of social workers and experimentation with models of intervention see Bortoli, (1997).

Changes during the 1970s

Like many other countries, Italy saw radical changes during the 1970s. New principles and values arose in civil society to be embodied in a series of profoundly innovative laws. Major changes were made to the regulation of family relationships and procreation, with the approval in 1970 of the divorce law (which was upheld despite attempts to abrogate it by referendum in 1974), and of the law on birth control advice in 1971. In 1975 family law was reformed, and in 1978 abortion was legalised. The time was also ripe for a profound overhaul of the institutional structure, a process also made possible by political and administrative decentralisation and the state's delegation to the regional governments of extensive powers—powers that also covered social and health policies.

At the local level, initiatives that for years had been in progress in various areas of health and social service received encouragement and formal recognition. In 1971, communal day nurseries were established, and in 1975 health advisory bureaus for women were set up. In 1978 the courageous campaign against mental

hospitals led to the enactment of a law forbidding further confinements and assigning care for the mentally ill to a welfare system based on de-institutionalisation and action by local community services, (Pirella, 1987; Cazzullo, 1989). There thus arose new types of services targeted on subjects and/or needs that had previously been ignored by the welfare system. A change took place, in fact, in the principles orienting policies and in the criteria on which service provision was planned.

Now predominant was the principle that every citizen is entitled to receive the health care and welfare support necessary for them to take their place in society and lead a decent life. This principle became a commitment by the state and the local authorities to undertake action to enhance the quality of life and of social relations. The logic was no longer that of reparation, therefore, but of prevention. And if this was the objective, services could only be free, and only public facilities could guarantee free access to them and ensure that the supply of services matched the needs of the community, independently of any market logic.

In Zucconi's view, services were no longer a:

> *...molecular and welfarist response to personal needs' but 'infrastructures of social promotion' and the 'means to ensure the political participation of citizens in the life of the local community.*
>
> (Zucconi, 1974: p 47)

Hence, the goal became that of establishing, in Ranci Ortigosa's opinion:

> *...a different individual/community exchange relationship, one alternative to that of exclusion and which can be achieved only to the extent that not only specialists, but society as a whole, in its political dimension therefore, undertake this constant and generalised commitment to socialisation.*
>
> (Ortigosa, 1971: p 376)

The political dimension of the action undertaken by the social-health services both legitimised and imposed mechanisms by which citizens could participate in the planning of services. The decentralisation, therefore, was not solely administrative and functional; it was also a sincere endeavour to construct some sort of 'bottom-up democracy' in this field as well, reducing the distance between the locus of decision making and the arenas in which needs arose and measures were taken to deal with them. The forms and mechanisms of interest representation were still the traditional ones. The political parties and trade unions continued to play a crucial role, conserving their substantial rootedness in society, albeit amid numerous tensions and conflicts.

The radical overhaul of the system of services in Italy culminated in the creation of the National Health Service at the end of 1978. As a consequence, the fragmentation, centralisation, and separateness of the previous system were replaced by a rational and uniform structure able to guarantee unity, homogeneity, completeness, equity and order. The aim of the new policy and the new organisational culture was to supersede the traditional images of care, need and illness. A 'global' vision arose of the needs of citizens— needs which could only be met by equally 'global' responses based on an integration between health and social services, and on co-operation among professional categories that would eliminate long-standing power relations and the social hierarchies which they engendered. The organisational model became that of the multi-professional team, while the figure of the specialist was opposed by that of the 'single operator'. Not by chance the name given to the core organisational level was the 'Unità Sanitaria Locale', (USL), (local social-health). This not only evoked the idea of the aggregation of resources into a single operating unit and the integration of social and health service delivery, but also implicitly emphasised the uniformity of the system throughout the country and the elimination of the shortcomings that had always characterised a large part of previous arrangements. The main formal constraint was still the participation of citizens in the decision-making process, a right which was to be guaranteed at all levels.

It is important to emphasise that the:

> *...creation of this organisation was determined not only by technical considerations but also by socially shared beliefs laden with idealism, which proposed ways to achieve organisational goals bereft of empirical verification, and expressed models for the division of social and professional labour and strategies for the distribution of power.*
>
> (Manoukian, 1988: p 37)

The Crisis Since the 1980s

The system soon broke down, however. This complex set of beliefs and goals could not withstand the test of reality. Although Italy was certainly not the only country whose welfare system entered crisis, it is important to emphasise that this crisis also meant the failure of a cultural, political and professional project which even today has not led to an equally profound and comprehensive revision of individual intentions and projects. One frequently gains the impression that the current situation in Italy is still heavily conditioned by this failure.

The causes of the failure were probably inherent in the system itself. Firstly, the endeavour to change the system began too late, when the conditions for its success had already ceased to exist. There were insufficient resources to ensure full implementation of the programme to modernise, upgrade and standardise the system of services throughout the country. As later sections will show in detail:

> *...general government primary expenditure increased by 15 points of GDP from 1960 to the early 1990s, pushing the primary balance into deficit from 1965 onwards.*
>
> (OECD, 1997: p 70)

The public debt, which averaged 15.9 per cent of GDP in the 1960s, rose to 29.0 per cent in the course of the 1970s, reaching 71.5 per cent in the 1980s, (Golinelli and Mantovani, 1998: p 38). Only in 1997 did the public debt slowly begin to fall; nevertheless it was still 121.6 per cent of GDP (slightly below that of Belgium among the EU countries) (Istat, 1998: p 198). Not everyone seems to be aware of the fact that this financial constraint inherited from the past meant that, in 1997, just under 10 per cent of GDP was allocated to paying off the interest on the accumulated debt—a figure three times higher than the amount spent by the other main European countries, (Commissione per l'analisi delle compatibilità macro-economiche della spesa sociale, 1997). The cost of modernising or even maintaining the welfare system grew impossibly high. But another, equally important, resource was lacking: the social legitimisation of the system. Perhaps the main reason for this was the breakdown in the mechanisms introduced to involve citizens in policy choices and the assessment of needs and results. In some sectors, the bodies set up to perform this exercise in popular democracy were soon drained of their functions and reduced to a marginal and substantially symbolic role. The 'management boards' of the local national health service units were unable to perform their political function of planning services, and instead encroached on the technical-managerial sphere, interfering in professional areas. All too often they changed from participatory and democratic bodies into 'business committees', more or less legal, but nevertheless playing an improper role.

The progressive institutionalisation of the 'new' social and health services eroded consensus concerning the use of democratic styles of management and of co-operation among practitioners with different roles and training. The implicit assumption of the law instituting the National Health Service—that a global and integrated system could be achieved simply by locating practitioners with different skills and training in the same facility—very soon proved to be overly optimistic and ingenuous. The initial innovative thrust rapidly petered out (and in numerous instances was never there in the first place), creating room for 'normal' aspirations for professional autonomy, for the re-emergence of boundaries and barriers within organisations, and renewed competition among professional groups to win positions of authority. This struggle to re-establish hegemonies and privileges has induced both social workers and the social services to scale down their expectations.

The failed reform

It should be pointed out that each of Italy's twenty administrative regions had been given the task of implementing the national law which instituted the National Health Service (in fact, one of these regions, Trentino-Alto Adige, is divided into two autonomous provinces, those of Trento and Bolzano). Although one of the objectives was to make the availability of resources and service delivery as homogeneous as possible among the various parts of the country, there was no ignoring the fact that the initial situation was marked by numerous gaps and substantial organisational

differences. Some of the solutions adopted by the Regions maintained a high degree of differentiation. Mention should be made in particular of the problem of the relationship between health care (which was the direct responsibility of the National Health Service) and social care (administered by the communes). As regards management models, with time the formal separation between social-welfare programmes (run by the local authorities) and health care (provided by the local health units) became residual. There were various forms of integration, ranging from 'associated' management, with full delegation of social-welfare functions by the communes, to 'co-ordinated' management, with separation of powers and linkages through specific instruments covering all or some of the areas of social intervention. However, the story of the integration between the social and health sectors, according to Censis:

> ...highlights the not always happy relationship between the Unità Sanitaria Locale (USL) (the local health and social unit responsible for health services) and the local authorities (responsible for welfare services), the inefficient management of social services by the USL, which were obliged to undertake multiple competences, and the conflict among practitioners and the consequent breakdown of inter-professional co-operation.
>
> (Censis, 1997: p 298)

This inability of practitioners and the social services to achieve full co-operation and integration with the health services should be set in relation to another major weakness in the Italian social-welfare system: the lack of a legal framework to re-organise the social-welfare system and flank the 1978 law instituting the national health service, thereby completing the legal framework in which the health and social services operate. Rei comments that:

> The failure to reorganise the system has preserved a complicated interweaving of actors, levels and competences in the welfare sector.
>
> (Rei, 1994: p 105)

To date a law has yet to be approved which unifies the nineteen schemes developed by various political parties in the course of the last twenty years (such a law is currently passing through the legislation). Below, I shall examine the most interesting aspects of what may be the turning point for the social-welfare sector in Italy.

Characteristics of Social Public Expenditure

An understanding of the constraints under which the social services in Italy operate, and of the heavy legacy with which they must cope on a daily basis, can be aided by figures on the amount and structure of social public expenditure. The level of spending, in terms of incidence on GDP, is lower than that of the other European Union countries: it amounted to 25.3 per cent of GDP in Italy in 1994, as opposed to the 28.6 per cent average of the twelve countries in the EU. In 1994 the figures ranged from 16.0 per cent of GDP in Greece to 33.7 per cent in Denmark (excluding the 34.8 per cent of Finland, which was not yet a member of the EU at the time). Italy occupied 7th place in this classification of incidence on GDP (Eurostat, 1997).

Although in aggregate terms Italy seems to be in line with the other European countries, a significant anomaly emerges if one considers the inner structure of expenditure, which displays two major distortions: one concerning risks, the other concerning protected categories.

As regards risks, the share of resources devoted in 1994 to the protection of 'old age and survivors' was significantly higher: 63.0 per cent as opposed to the European average of 44.3 per cent; only Greece, with 66.6 per cent, spends more than Italy in this area. By contrast, overall spending to deal with the risks and needs of 'unemployment/training', 'family/maternity', 'housing' and 'other assistance' was much lower than elsewhere in Europe (18.4 per cent as opposed to 31.9 per cent). As for health expenditure, which was around 5 per cent of GDP, Italy was in line with the rest of Europe, (Centre for Economic Policy Research, 1999; Commissione per l'analisi delle compatibilità macroeconomiche della spesa sociale, 1997).

The second distortion, relative to protected categories, is apparent if one considers the wide gap between benefits for workers, or ex-workers, employed in the regular labour market, especially in large firms and the public sector, and those for workers in more marginal sectors or for the unemployed. The old-age pension of a worker in the regular labour market may be as much as four times higher than a social pension (in other countries the ratio is around two to one). As regards

unemployment protection, mobility allowances are more than double ordinary allowances in Italy (in other countries, all workers are treated uniformly). Italy also lacks a minimum income scheme for those entirely devoid of means, as well as an adequate network of services to families (Commissione per l'analisi delle compatibilità macroeconomiche della spesa sociale, 1997: relaz03.htm).

Also to be emphasised is the fact that the average level of pensions varies among regions, reproducing the well-known inequalities between the north, centre and south of Italy. According to figures published by INPS (the national social security institute) for 1999, pensions range from an average of 6,952,000 lire per capita (per year) in Liguria to 3,372,000 lire in Campania (figures from the newspaper *La Repubblica*, 17.8.1999: p 12).

Most indicative of the particular nature of the Italian situation is the large share of spending accounted for by pensions, 63.0 per cent of total expenditure. According to Censis:

> ...*there are more pensions than workers in Italy (22 million old age, social, disability, and survivors pensions, compared with 21 million workers).*
> (Censis, 1999: p 1)

Also as the OECD points out:

> ...*pensions have been the most dynamic component of public spending in the post-war period, rising to levels well above those in other EU countries. Pension liabilities were extended to all employees in 1952; to agricultural workers in 1957; to craftsmen in 1959; to workers in commerce in 1966; and to persons aged over 65 with insufficient income through the institution of 'social pensions' at the end of the 1980s. Originally sustained by these extensions of eligibility, the increase in pension spending since the mid-1970s has been driven by higher real benefits, which increased sharply following the shift to an 'earnings formula', the increase in the accrual factor for each year of contribution, and the introduction of indexation, first to prices in 1969 and then to wages in 1986. Pension benefits far exceeded levels provided by a fully funded system. Although average pensions relative to per capita income were broadly in line with other EU countries in 1993, there was a disproportionate number of pensions relative to population. This, in turn, reflected the higher proportion of persons over 60 years of age; the use of pensions as a substitute for passive income support to unemployed and other workers facing risks of dismissal; and favourable access to early retirement through seniority pensions.*
> (OECD, 1997: p 82)

'Seniority pensions' were granted to workers with at least 35 years of contribution, these accounted for around 2 million pensions in 1996, with outlays amounting to 2.5 per cent of GDP. Within this group, 'baby pensions' granted to public workers with at least 20 years of contributions totalled 250,000, with outlays of 0.3 per cent of GDP.

Forecasts of the incidence of pensions on GDP in the future differ little among studies, ranging from the 17 per cent estimated in 2017 by the Commissione Onofri (Commissione per l'analisi delle compatibilità macroeconomiche della spesa sociale, 1997) to the 15.77 per cent in 2035 by Baldacci and Tuzi (1998: p 336), to 16.0 per cent in 2030 by Censis (1994: p 4). More recent projections by the Ministry of the Treasury, based on figures from the summer of 1999, show that a peak in spending on pensions amounting to 23.27 per cent of GDP would have been reached in 2040, if the reforms of 1992, 1995 and 1997 had not been implemented. In reality, under the current legislation the predicted peak in spending will be reached in 2032, but it will only be 15.79 per cent of GDP. Comparison with the forecasts for 2045 shows that the incidence on GDP will be 14.24%, compared to the 23.06 per cent that would have been reached without the reforms (figures from the newspaper *La Repubblica*, 17.8.1999: p 9). This incidence is highly disproportionate, and to a certain extent is an encumbrance on the future development of the welfare system as a whole.

Demographic trends are also to be taken into consideration: according to OECD (1996: p 102) in 2030 the elderly dependency ratio (that is: population aged 65 and over as a per cent of working age population) will amount in Italy to 48.3 per cent versus 39.2 on average in the OECD European countries. It is no coincidence that reform of the entire pensions system is at the centre of heated political debate which has placed the issue at the top of the current government's agenda.

However, this is not solely a matter of public budgetary policy. Social security should be viewed as an institution, in the sense that it constitutes a:

> ...set of social practices which tend to channel, shape and in a certain sense even 'construct' interactions among individuals and the community. These practices are typically disciplined by formal organisations and rules...but they rest on specific cognitive and normative premises.   (Ferrera, 1998: p 9)

Even more than in the welfare systems of the other European countries, and in particular as regards old age pensions, there has arisen in Italy:

> ...an 'entitlement mentality' whereby benefits are regarded as an unconditional right on reaching a certain age (legal old age, which lasts much longer than biological old age) regardless of the amount of contributions paid during a person's working life and/or regardless of their needs.
>   (Ferrera, 1998: p 53)

Ferrara continues and points out that a:

> ...pronounced motivational shift in the collective imagination whereby the pension-vacation, often heavily subsidised by unaware 'third-party payers', has become a due allowance simply because it is envisaged by the law.   (Ferrera, 1998: p 53)

This aspect is closely bound up with two other features entirely peculiar to the Italian welfare system. Already reported some time ago, (Ferrera, 1984), these have led to the coining of the expression 'particularist-clientelistic system', (Ascoli, 1984; Paci, 1984) (this might best be understood as the application of selective criteria). In the other European countries, opportunities for particularist malpractice are not only less frequent but restricted to the services sector, because they depend substantially on the margins of discretion available to those delivering personal services. Italian clientelism (a system of relationships based not on objective merits or rights but on interests and favouritisms) is a specific 'case' because it has been able to penetrate the sector of money transfers (in particular invalidity pensions and unemployment benefits), where other countries apply universalistic criteria with a high degree of 'juridification' (*verrechtlichung*). It should be noted that the political parties have been mainly responsible for particularist malpractice. Ferrera, (1984: p 274), notes that this trend increased in the 1970s, when universalistic principles of free access by all citizens to health and social services were already being asserted.

The second form of deviation in the Italian welfare system is the:

> ...massive concealment of the costs of social policies, as clearly reflected in the anomalous distribution of the fiscal burden and the worrying levels reached by the public debt...In the majority of the European countries, a conspicuous growth of social spending has been accompanied in the last fifteen years by major increases in taxation or social contributions, or

by adequate monetary disincentives against reliance on benefits (charges, tariffs). The visibility of the costs of the welfare state has created a 'fiscal opposition' in the political market which has led to rationalisation or greater rigour. (Ferrera, 1984: p 74)

The Italian political parties in government, tacitly supported by the opposition, have been unwilling to risk their electoral consensus by introducing restrictive measures. They have consequently opted for the massive concealment of costs through indebtedness or by means of accountancy contrivances. Numerous occupational categories which do not benefit directly from the welfare system have been implicitly compensated by substantial tolerance of tax evasion or erosion. As Ferrera argues:

The political parties have thus been able to continue distributing eligibilities without imposing further visible obligations, while the illusion of practically free benefits has spread among the general public. (Ferrera, 1984: p 275)

Under the pressure of the public debt, and as a result of changes in the political situation, the last few years have seen discussion finally begin on the workings of the welfare system. Whatever the merits of the criteria which govern the granting of pensions and other benefits, I would stress that account must be taken of the cognitive mechanisms and the beliefs in 'acquired rights' that have fostered the consensus as well as the innumerable proposals for a change in recent years. Required, that is to say, are not only reasonable 'technical' proposals likely to produce satisfactory economic outcomes, but also a cultural and 'ethical' debate on the principles underpinning the present system, the intention being to instil new ones in society at large.

The 'eligibility mentality' is not only widespread among the 'social clientele' or the 'assisted classes'—these are terms employed by Baier, 1977, (*Soziale Klientelen*) and Lepsius, 1979, (*Versorgungklassen*), and reported by Ferrera (1999). The pension as an economic support for social needs, or to remedy hardship by economic means, soon became one of the main instruments of social welfare. It has been estimated that 90 per cent of public welfare spending in Italy is used for direct payments to individuals and families, and only the remaining 10 per cent finances services, (Artoni and Ortigosa, 1989). This large-scale

reliance on money transfers inevitably has repercussions on the form assumed by social work: there is no doubt that a great deal of personnel, time and professional resources are taken up by legal counselling, help with administrative procedures, the assessment of eligibility, and formal controls. This activity, moreover, takes place amid great uncertainty, as Negri and Saraceno suggest because:

...firstly, the confusion and shifts between social security, welfare and citizenship have made the national benefits system complicated and piecemeal; secondly, they have fostered uncertainty about rights and guarantees enshrined in the Constitution...and mistrust in the legitimacy of collective action. In some cases, they have also created or exacerbated social cleavages. (Negri and Saraceno, 1996: p 34)

Since the last years of the 1980s there has been a substantial oscillation among principles of welfare delivery (based on income and funded by taxes), social security principles (risk-protection and benefits financed from compulsory contributions by workers), and citizenship rights (benefits provided universally regardless of income and financed by taxation) (Negri and Saraceno, 1996: p 33)

The reasons for the crisis

Besides the distortions in the Italian welfare system just discussed, the reasons for its crisis lie at a much deeper and structural level, and they are shared by the other systems of continental Europe. The generosity of economic transfers combined with an inadequate supply of social services, in fact, is distinctive of the continental model of the welfare state, which is markedly familistic in its bias. Esping-Andersen rightly points out that:

...the Christian Democratic principle of 'subsidiarity' has institutionalised familism, in that it has reinforced, by means of transfers, the model whereby it is the task of the man to support the family economically while the woman is relegated to a caring role. (Esping-Andersen, 1995: p 348)

The assumption underlying a social security system like Italy's is that social rights are mainly based on occupational condition, rather than on citizenship or need. Moreover, the rights acquired in this way are implicitly those of the head of household, in effect, the man, which are then extended to the members of his family to create objective bonds of dependency. The system of extended family rights is implicitly predicated on the male head of household in steady employment; that is, on the male breadwinner model (Lewis, 1992). Again according to Esping-Andersen:

> The influence of Catholic doctrine on social matters is still an obstacle against the public supply of services, especially those to do with social welfare and the social reproduction of the family.
>
> (Esping-Andersen, 1995: p 349)

In the history of the welfare state in Italy, the myth of 'family self-sufficiency' closely interweaves with the substantially 'residual' nature of a large part of social policies and programmes as Saraceno argues:

> The fact that services organised on a collective and gratuitous basis were targeted on the poor has fostered a view that the demand for, and the use of, non-market social services is indicative of a family's inability to cope with its own responsibilities and needs. The long-term effect has been that families not poor enough, or desperate enough, or unwilling to be stigmatised for their use of welfare services but nevertheless unable to afford private ones, have been devoid of support.   (Saraceno, 1998a: p 116)

The cultural and social barriers against access to services, but above all the restricted supply of the latter, have severely hampered efforts by women to enter the labour market: indeed, motherhood and career are almost irreconcilable alternatives for Italian women. See, for more details, the results of the survey on the economic and social constraints that condition individual strategies, and the dilemma between postponing and forgoing marriage and motherhood, in Italy contained in De Sandre, Ongaro, Rettaroli and Salvini (1997).

As Esping-Andersen (1994 and 1996) argues, the benchmarks for continental welfare systems are the traditional nuclear family and a 'Fordist' life-cycle. We know that both these presuppositions are rapidly fading. Family relationships have changed profoundly in recent years: the family is a much less stable institution than in the past. It is smaller in size and its internal bonds are weaker, which means that it is much less protective of its members. See, for example, Barbagli and Saraceno (Eds.) (1997) on the changed characteristics of the Italian family. This lesser stability of kinship bonds is a new source of

social risk. It can no longer be taken for granted that individual care needs will be met effectively within the confines of the family.

The phases of the life-cycle are less rigidly patterned and predictable: the critical moments are no longer restricted to its initial (childhood and adolescence) and final (old age) phases. The central phase of productivity, too, is less stable, and the system no longer suffices to protect against the risks of precariousness that with increasing frequency threaten 'insiders' during the central phase of their life-cycle, traditionally, that of stable employment. New needs, new risks, new risk factors reveal the limitations of policies centred on passive income support and a reduced labour supply.

On the one hand, according to Ferrara:

> ...the vicarious role of the family with respect to public policies, able to reduce the disequilibrium of the protection mechanisms and to counterbalance the inequalities of income and opportunities between 'insiders' and 'outsiders', encounters objective limits of social efficiency.   (Ferrera, 1998: p 57)

On the other, the profound restructuring of the modes of production, the fragmentation of the labour market, the emergence of new mechanisms of social exclusion have thrown the traditional devices of social protection into crisis.

Paradoxically, although the Italian welfare system overwhelmingly allocates its resources to economic transfers, it has so far been unable to provide forms of income support such as to ensure a minimum level for all citizens. Only recently have some communes experimented with forms of supplementary benefit, although such measures look set to spread throughout the national system.

To summarise. Only recently in Italy, since the 1970s, have the social services begun to lose their character of services to help the needy and become services for all citizens. This process has nevertheless met, and still meets, a number of obstacles that hinder construction of a universalistic social care system, homogeneously and adequately developed throughout the country. The most critical aspects of the present situation can be specified as follows:

- entitlement to social services is fragmented among a variety of different institutional actors at local and central levels: between different ministries, between state and local administrations, between regions, provinces and municipalities. These actors are not always willing to co-operate and often do not share the same logic and criteria;

- over time, care programmes and practices have become stratified, some of them as answers to emergencies, others as the result of the pressure and influence of particular categories;

- a national legal framework is still lacking, but the state agencies maintain a strong position in the definition of expenditure, particularly as regards money transfers; so that the regions are left with a relatively residual planning role, whilst the municipalities are in charge of the supply of the missing services, but with no power to modify the overall framework;

- there is still a large degree of disparity between the services provided and patterns of access; this adds to and increases the gap between living standards in different areas, particularly between the north and the centre on one hand and the south of Italy on the other;

- eligibility for services still depends on a formal acknowledgement which does not take account of individual differences based on age, gender or living standards. The distorted supply of aid and frauds are mainly induced by these formal labelling excesses, in addition to their clientelistic use by a large number of trade unions and political parties;

- little attention is paid to the new needs and risks related to changes in family and individual life, as well as the increase in poverty risk, both new and old;

- income re-allocation measures are preferred to service supply: more than 90 per cent of expenditure consists of money allowances, while service supply is financed by the remaining 10 per cent, (Saraceno, 1998b).

The Current Reorganisation of the Italian Welfare System

During the 1990s, radical reform of the welfare system has been introduced in Italy, as it has in the majority of European countries. This reform has concerned social policies, institutional arrangements, and organisational models. There has been no radical questioning of the principles of social solidarity and the promotion of the quality of life and social relations. Nevertheless, the shortcomings of the welfare model inherited from the 1970s and 1980s have become evident, while the curbing of expenditure has been set as the priority in every area of public policy.

In Italy, social work seemingly occupies a residual role in social policies, caught between, 'a cumbersome but unfair pensions system and a universal but inefficient health service', (Commissione per l'analisi delle compatibilità macroeconomiche della spesa sociale, 1997). The problem is how to, 'go beyond the fundamental principle of solidarity to fulfil a role of civil and political integration' (ibid.). It is necessary to find, 'a different way to specify the features of measures targeted on the general population, producing a balanced mix of money transfers and services' (ibid.). The welfare system is still too centralised and should be gradually replaced by a network of local systems with the following characteristics:

> ...extension of guaranteed access to public services (education, childcare, care for the non self-sufficient, housing, etc.) according to the combined principles of universal access and means-tested payment; programmes to combat hardship, also by means of selective measures; the prevention of poverty through supplementary benefits and 'rehabilitative' programmes; support for family and community care as alternatives to 'institutionalisation'; promotion of equal opportunities between men and women.   (ibid: p 1)

The result of this long process of overhauling the welfare system should be, 'a large-scale shift of resources from merely monetary redistribution to the supply of personal services' (ibid.) in order to eliminate a situation in which:

> ...it is likely that three-quarters of welfare spending, almost 50 thousand billion lire (25 billion Euro), is distributed according to entirely inadequate, or indeed random, criteria.   (ibid: pp 2–3)

In short, the system must move from 'assistance welfare' (which nevertheless should be preserved and improved) to a 'welfare of opportunities', (Paci, 1997) based on active protection measures covering every phase of the life-cycle. It should enable people and families to cope with needs and crises as and when they arise, also by mobilising individual and family resources, in order to prevent social exclusion and dependence but also 'rent-seeking behaviour' i.e. to transform what should be temporary economic support into a stable permanent rent.

Thus a global project is under way to reform the Italian welfare system, to revise guidelines, to redefine institutional arrangements, and to reorganise structures and facilities. At the same time, however, the urgent need to reduce expenditure has imposed a series of partial measures to 'rationalise' the system. Economic efficiency has become the fundamental criterion when social and health schemes are devised and assessed. The problem therefore arises of determining whether decisions recently taken on the basis of this criterion are compatible with the guiding principles behind the reform of the welfare system described above—whether these decisions effectively anticipate the new models of social and health care that I have discussed. The national health service was first to undergo institutional reform, at the beginning of the 1990s: the new legal provisions were inspired by a, 'model of rationality and administrative order based on the forecasting and monitoring of results', (Manoukian, 1998: p 13).

At the organisational level, the corporate model is taken as the reference standard; although the model envisaged by the legal provisions is based on monocratic and centralised management, and assigns extraordinarily broad functions and powers to the director general (of the former Local Health Unit, now Local Health Company). Thus affirmed is the outdated conception of company organisation, typical of the large industrial firms of the age of capitalist development, but today discounted by the theory and practice of successful and innovative management. The risk is that an organisational culture will be imposed which subordinates all initiatives to economic efficiency, with a seemingly inevitable cultural gap between managers and practitioners. In fact, the managers take curtailed spending to be the crucial criterion: their social and political status, their position *vis-à-vis* the organisations which they are appointed to run on private contracts for relatively short periods of time (typically, five years with only one review), enable them to impose drastic cuts and unpopular measures, the consequences of which those in operational roles (or who work permanently for the organisation) have to deal with. The immediate perception of lower-level workers is that less money and resources are available, and that they are subject to more direct and rigorous control. This breeds, according to Olivetti Manoukian:

> ...*a sense of loss, an uncompensated loss which impoverishes day-to-day work and heightens the more brutal and surgical aspects of the reform.*
> (Manoukian, 1998: p 19)

In effect, the need to curb expenditure is a novelty in the health services, and even more so for the social services. Hitherto, the problem has been addressed mainly in terms of management control, without new directions for organisational action being proposed, and without effective changes being made to the organisational culture. Manoukian continues:

> *The innovative and entrepreneurial challenge to the system as a whole has translated at the operational level into frustrating constraints which are little understood and much resented. The workforce can only resign itself to them, but at the price of demotivation and disinvestment.*
> (ibid: pp 19–20)

A further consequence of the reform of the National Health Service suggested is that:

> ...*services...must have specifically health-care content. Those of a social-welfare nature are to be considered residual and farmed out to the local authorities, which must find the necessary financing, so that they do not burden the economic circuit (of the Local Health Companies).*   (ibid: p 15)

The needs of accounting transparency and a balanced budget have thus further undermined the model of integrated social-health intervention. The professional and cultural basis of the model of global, integrated and multiprofessional action is in danger of succumbing to the imperatives of the division of tasks, the identification of cost centres, the assignment of spending autonomies, and the attribution of running costs. The delicate issue of results assessment may well arise in social work. The corporate logic of promoting efficiency requires that the work of services and practitioners should be made 'visible', and its results 'measurable'. It is not always easy in social work to define assessment criteria, or to fix parameters and reference standards; even less are these aspects distinctive of the organisational culture of workers in this sector. It seems that the social services are engaged in a process of a critical assimilation of the models that have arisen in the health sector, and indeed those of industry. Misunderstandings may arise if an equation is asserted between 'assessable' and 'quantifiable'. That is to say, there is a distinct risk that the diverse forms of social work, its objectives and results, will be reduced to mere 'numerical data'. This may give rise to a new hierarchy between activities that can 'account for' their results in quantitative numerical terms and those that are unable to 'measure' their results. Only the former will receive recognition and rewards, while the latter will be given very little consideration.

Services and practitioners seem to be undergoing a slow but radical change in their culture. To date, their conception of their work and goals has been excessively 'self-referential'. Perhaps unconsciously, practitioners have justified their work by the fact that they deal with forms of 'distress' in a community. The 'residual' nature itself of welfare policies may have fostered the belief that it is only necessary to work with people who 'suffer' or who are 'marginalised' to gain society's support and esteem. The mere fact of working in the social field (and this may partly apply to health as well) gives meaning and direction to one's work. This image (deliberately exaggerated) of social work leaves little space for assessment: as said, the fact alone that certain 'objectives' are set and certain 'problems' are addressed suffices to legitimise the existence of services and to justify the function of those who work for them.

If, as is now happening, the focus is shifted from the definition of goals (planning) to the measurement of results (assessment), this entails a radical change in professional culture and in services, and a profound innovation of professional techniques. It is not that social workers are not already aware of the problem of the effectiveness of their work; the difference is that it is now necessary to set the results

obtained in relation to the resources used. The difficulty resides in making the assessment of results 'objective' and 'replicable', avoiding the pitfalls of self-referentially and subjective judgement on the one hand, and of mere administrative 'accountability' on the other.

But an even more radical and urgent change is required: assessment should no longer be confined to the (single) practitioner/user relation alone; it should be extended to all users, to care activity and the service as a whole, to the entire community in which a service operates. It is analysis that cannot and must not be conducted by the service managers or politicians alone. This approach seems to be somewhat distant from the culture and models at present imparted to social workers during training; and it is the crux of redefining the relationships among the social services and between these and the health, education and other services.

The curbing of expenditure, and the reduced resources consequent upon it, set an indubitable constraint on the action of services and practitioners. It will be interesting to see whether these are perceived as 'fate' which breed resignation or as a 'challenge' which triggers a virtuous circle of organisational innovation and redefinition of the institutional mandate.

A similar stimulus may be provided by the process of 'corporatisation' (the introduction of business principles) that I have described. This may lead to the adoption of obsolete hierarchical models, or else it may induce the culture of social services to accept criteria and instruments attentive to the quality of performance and results. There are those who are understandably alarmed by the huge quantity of business-inspired schemes for training and the reorganisation of services now spreading in the social services sector as well. However, one should not underestimate the positive impact that business principles may have on needs analysis, on planning action, and on assessment of outputs and outcomes, in a sector perhaps still too closely dependent on actors and decision-making processes external to it, and superior to in merely the hierarchical and institutional sense. The risk that the use of these principles will be purely symbolic or rhetorical is evident. Indeed, it is this that transpires from much of the recent national and regional legislation.

The Challenge of the Market and the Third Sector

Like many other countries, Italy has looked for a solution to the sustainability of welfare systems in the introduction of 'market' models and mechanisms which give greater efficiency and effectiveness to social policies. The 'corporatisation' process that I have mentioned is certainly inspired by this redefinition of the fundamental principles of welfare. Equally fundamental has been the distinction introduced between the funders and providers of services. This, too, is more than anything else a terminological specification for symbolic purposes. Nevertheless, it has introduced a conceptual distinction into social and health services which has further legitimised the already important role of actors and agencies in the so-called 'third sector'. In Italy, a private (for-profit) sector has never really developed in the social and health field. The financial and operational links with the public system, run by the state and the local authorities, have always been very close. Also, the role of structures and personnel linked to the Catholic Church has always been supplemented by, and in a certain sense dependent upon, the public system.

The distinction between service funders and providers has assumed especial significance as regards the curbing of public expenditure. The withdrawal of public administration, in fact, has been envisaged mainly in regard to the production and supply of services, rather than to their funding. This is because greater opportunity and legitimacy has been accorded to third-sector actors as the providers of services. The concept of 'market' or 'quasi-market', associated with that of 'welfare mix', introduces 'competition', indeed 'rivalry', among providers. This, of course, is intended to enhance the efficiency and quality of services, while also increasing the weight and influence of users/clients, who are finally able to 'choose' among services and operators according to how well these are able to satisfy their needs. Non-profit actors must inject their capacity for flexibility and their ability to 'humanise' services into this competition, thereby involving public (and private) actors in a virtuous circle which meets the community's demand for care with ever greater efficiency and effectiveness.

It has been frequently argued that the distinctive feature of Italy's third sector is its markedly 'solidaristic' nature. However, also to be stressed is the highly ideological connotation of many of the agencies that have long and creditably operated in this sector, and which, whatever their culture and ideology, have influenced the history of Italian welfare with an explicitly critical and sometimes openly antagonistic stance towards the public sector.

In a highly centralised welfare system, both theoretical debate and political discussion on subsidiarity have been understandably heated. But they have also assumed manifestly ideological tones which, perhaps inappropriately, have fostered a stand-off between not only political and ideological points of view, but also between the practices and culture of public-sector workers, on the one hand, and those of third-sector practitioners and voluntary workers on the other. The contrast between the two sides has been framed more in terms of 'cultural hegemony' than of concrete professional practices and techniques. Perhaps for this reason it has proved particularly difficult to overcome their mutual suspicion, in a situation which instead requires the integration and collaboration of actors and agencies on each side.

Another aspect should be emphasised in relation to increasingly large-scale and institutionally legitimised entry of new actors from the non-profit sector into the Italian welfare system. I have already pointed out the extremely fragmented and unequal distribution of services and resources across the country, and the frequently incoherent nature of social policy at the local level. The activation of third-sector resources has not mitigated these differences or remedied these local-level inequalities. It seems apparent that third-sector initiatives and resources have been concentrated in areas where a well-developed network of public services already exists. Conversely, where public resources and initiatives are fewer and of poorer quality, less effort has been made to set up the associative forms that constitute the social fabric for third-sector initiatives.

But at issue are not solely the differences in the quality of the resources used at the local level. In recent years, the reduced role of the state has created a relatively broad space for local policy initiatives. These local policies have often moved in very different directions, so that frequent use is made of the expression 'unprincipled municipalism' to underline the scant attention paid to coherent linkages among local policy choices. Accordingly, the third sector has probably helped to accelerate this process of local fragmentation and particularism. While it is true that social policies should be determined by local circumstances and therefore targeted on the needs of individual communities, there should nevertheless be a set of general rules, objectives and standards which ensure a minimal level of response to the needs of all citizens, regardless of local peculiarities.

This difficulty in finding common criteria and rules at the local level should be set in relation to the much more general problem of the crisis of interests representation in the Italian political system. During the 1990s, the party system has collapsed, and with it the perverse set of mechanisms that created a particularist and often clientelistic welfare system. Distrust of the political parties and the abandonment of traditional forms of political participation are evident and probably irreversible phenomena. The worrying consequence, which is visible in social policies as well, is the persistent difficulty of finding a locus for political decisions. Put simply: Who is deciding the objectives and priorities of social policies? With what criteria? On the basis of what political mandate? In relation to what values, both political and ethical? There is a danger, it seems, that it will prove impossible to go beyond economic constraints and contingent emergencies. The discussion is monopolised by the technicians, with strictly economic arguments, or by other 'languages' which deliberately avoid political terrain. Not coincidentally, current debate in Italy on welfare reform has been restricted to the pensions system; not just because pensions are (and will be even more so in the future) the largest item in expenditure on welfare, but because the debate is monopolised by technicians and spending forecasts. Against arguments of this kind, political considerations inevitably appear irrelevant and misplaced, whatever their effective capacity to grasp the nature of the problem and to propose 'adequate' solutions. This is because reform of the pensions system has not been included in more general proposals to overhaul the welfare system. One reason—a crucial one—for the failure in Italy to conduct serious and detailed debate on these issues is the distance between the forms and places of political discussion and those of civil society. The inability of citizens to take part in the discussion is also due to the crisis and inadequacy of Italy's system of political participation.

The rebuilding of a system for the representation of interests, at least as regards social policies, could come about on the basis of policy networks; that is, by the set of relatively stable relations, non-hierarchical and interdependent in nature, among collective actors, or public and private organisations which share common interests and/or norms with respect to a policy. These actors undertake exchanges in order to pursue these common interests on the basis of their awareness that co-operation is the best way to achieve their goals, (Börzel, 1998: p 393). These types of networks may be able to produce collective results by means of voluntary bargaining, despite the diverging interests of the actors that make them up. In this context, the achievement of joint results is an intrinsic value for the actors, according to a logic which to a certain extent may supersede that of 'bargaining', which is based on the maximisation of particularist interest through cost/benefit calculations. Within the networks, additional and informal linkages, based on communication and trust, may arise among actors. These linkages may supplement or replace those that depend on formal relations and institutional memberships. Of crucial importance is the level of consensus within the network, consensus which must concern at least 'a fundamental set of values, beliefs about causal relations, and perceptions of problems', (Sabatier, 1993: p 127, cited in Börzel, 1998). A positive activity of problem-solving may start up on this basis. Worth pointing out is Sabatier's opinion that learning with respect to public policies will more probably come about as a consequence of an external shock than following processes of communicative action.

I shall briefly mention two problems which may arise in a situation where policy networks tend to replace more traditional public institutional models. The first problem is the lack of legitimisation often suffered by policy networks because they are not subject to the formal democratic control that more traditional institutional models envisage. It is clear that the crisis of the traditional institutional forms of the public sector has also, and perhaps principally, been a crisis of democratic control. If policy networks are a way to revitalise decision processes and to root them in the community, the risk may be that, because of their dynamic autonomy, they will constitute a system that is entirely autonomous of and an alternate to the institutional one. Linked with this risk, I believe, is that of the fragmentation of the Italian welfare system: progressive decentralisation has come about without a solid reference framework, general and national, being put in place. This has given rise to that extreme diversification of local welfare systems in which one discerns the risks of what Saraceno (1997) has called 'unprincipled municipalism'.

The second problem, that I wish to point out, in relation to policy networks concerns the role and influence of social workers in this negotiation system. I do not wish to resume the long-standing polemic on the political nature of social work; at issue instead is the forms in which social workers can put forward the needs and viewpoints not only of their users but of the community as a whole within the system of interests representation. This requires reflection on the process by which definition is given to public goods—those goods, that is to say, which concern the social quality of life and which are therefore a matter of public and social discussion, decision-making and responsibility. The transition from the private to the public spheres occurs for those issues which become in the words of De Leonardis:

> ...*the terrain of social, public communications, choices, actions and interactions, responsibilities and conflicts.* (De Leonardis, 1996: p 54)

By means of this transfer, which is brought about by social processes and not just institutional and administrative acts, collective debate focuses on goals and values, and an 'uninterrupted definition' of social goods, problems and solutions takes place, (Pennacchi, 1994: p 20).

I do not feel that it is necessary to press for a political involvement of social workers in this process, so that they perform a conscious and explicit role as political actors. Nevertheless, I believe that problems of 'membership' and of 'professional identity' may arise. The crisis of image suffered by many (mainly public) services, and the renewed tensions among professional groups within the services system, may make the role of social workers in the decision processes discussed more difficult and less fruitful.

The Forthcoming Institutional and Legal Framework

For a long time in Italy we have been waiting for a complete re-organisation of the social care system at national level, as was done with the health care system when the National Health System was established in 1978. This institutional re-organisation would be a step of basic importance to overcome the present confused situation of fragmentation and uncertainty within the social welfare system.

On July 2nd 1999 a document prepared by the parliamentary XII permanent commission (social affairs) was released, concerning 'the realisation of the integrated system of social services and intervention'. The draft law combines and summarises the 19 law projects that during the recent years have dealt with the problem of re-organising this sector of the welfare system. We should really be on the eve of the law promulgation; therefore, it may be interesting to shortly analyse its content.

In the commission's report, the wish to move from a traditional conception of the 'care', as a locus of needs that may discretionally be satisfied, to a conception of active social protection, as a locus of citizenship exercise (Relazione della XII Commissione Permanente (Affari Sociali) del 2 luglio 1999, relatore Signorino, n. 332-A, p 7) has been underlined. The declared issue is, 'the establishment of an integrated system of services and interventions', of 'a system including several actors, institutional and belonging to the civil society and to the non profit sector', (ibid: pp 8–9). The system will be characterised by:

> ...*a more advanced balance between services and financial benefits, providing flexible patterns of care, designed according to the persons needs and those of their families.* (ibid: pp 8–9)

In my opinion, during the implementation of this law the greatest problems will concern the relationship between the diverse institutional actors and between the various decision and policy makers. The law in fact aspires to a model of community welfare, based on a strong federalist option. A genuine organisational autonomy is acknowledged to the local systems; the municipalities will have to run them. But it will not be possible to ignore the problems arising from the great inequalities of the current local systems. For example, in Italy the current *pro capite* social expenditure financed by the municipalities amounted to 82,097 lire on average in 1994; but the range was from the maximum of 200,970 lire of the communes of the Autonomous Province of Trento to the minimum of 19,624 lire of the communes of the Region Calabria, (Presidenza del Consiglio dei Ministri, Commissione di indagine sulla povertà e sull'emarginazione, La spesa pubblica per l'assistenza in Italia, Roma, 1997, cit. in Rossi, 1999: p 187). So, it has been necessary to attribute to the state the technical task and the political responsibility of defining 'the minimum, essential levels of intervention', that will have to be defined within the (national) social plan. The constitution of a national 'fund for social policies' should guarantee a stronger stability and a greater transparency of the public expenditure in this field; but the regions themselves will have to share the fund and to assign the budgets to the municipalities.

A certain degree of prudence shows through the definition of the relationship between public and non profit agencies: the law acknowledges the third sector agencies as fundamental actors within the social care system. The governance and regulation roles are assigned to the public actors; it underlines the need of 'shared rules and quality assessment even in the negotiation between public, third sector and solidarity agencies', (ibid: pp 13–14). The government document states that:

> ...the meaning of subsidiarity that the law proposes is engaging, rich, it demands a reciprocal acceptance of responsibility, new tasks for the public agencies as well as for the non profit ones...It is a meaning [of subsidiarity] different than the poorer one that assumes the withdrawal of the public agencies, that at the most should intervene a posteriori, only to cover the expenditure.　(ibid: pp 13–14)

It seems interesting also to consider how the problem of the integration of health and social care has been dealt with. To this end we have to refer to what has already been settled by the health legislation and the health national plan. In particular, the law promulgated in June 1999, concerning the 'rules for the rationalisation of the National Health System', contains the definition of 'social and health services [as] all of the activities apt to satisfy —through a complex care process—individual health needs, that require health intervention and social care action together', (Article 3). The interventions of this kind are divided between health interventions with a social relevance and social interventions with a health relevance. The first are defined as 'the activities oriented to health promotion, the prevention, detection, elimination and containment of degenerative or invalidity outcomes of congenital or contracted pathologies'; the latter are 'all of the activities of the social care system addressed to support a needy person, with a handicap or a marginization problem related to the health condition'.

A subsequent regulation will have to define the interventions at a high degree of health integration. The health and social interventions at a high degree of health integration will mainly concern maternity and child care, elderly, handicap, psychiatric pathologies, drug, alcohol and medicament addiction, HIV infection, terminal condition, inabilities or disabilities due to chronic-degenerative pathologies. Integrated care patterns will have to be set for them, in order to guarantee continuity between care and rehabilitation, even in the long term. In its relationships with the other sectors of the overall welfare system, the social sector will probably have to expiate its delay. Although with some difficulties and contradictions, since its establishment in 1978 the National Health System has progressively tried to adapt to community demands and to find effective solutions at the organisational level; on the other hand, the social care system still appears very uncertain and fragmented. This leads almost inevitably to a smaller weight, to a reduced relevance in the policy making process and in the institutional regulation. This asymmetry emerges at the operational level too, affecting the relationships between professionals and between services; effective co-operation and integration become obviously more difficult to achieve.

One could expect a push towards integration coming from outside the system, through citizens' participation and democratic control. In fact, the new law, which will formally establish an integrated system of social care, doesn't pay specific attention to these aspects; even though regions and municipalities will be allowed to find the appropriate organisational models in an autonomous way, the public health companies appear to be the latent model for the social services as well. At local level there are already some experiences, as in the Autonomous Province of Bolzano, that constitute a Social Service Company, beside a distinct Health Care Company. The law enacted in June 1999 has further accentuated the 'privatisation' of the National Health System, and its managerial re-organisation; to some extent, it has completed the process that has brought it from a (formally) very democratic and participative model to a hierarchical, 'autocratic' one, that assigns a huge authority to the general manager. Some sort of mitigation of this 'absolute power' may result from the introduction of a 'management board', a technical body that should support the general manager in the policy making process at local level. The health care system will deal with the social one on the basis of this strong and congruous model; this factor will probably lead to an assimilation of the two sectors in a unique 'managerial' model. One should also consider that the delays in the social care system rationalisation have caused the health authorities (mainly the Ministry of Health) to deliver quite a large number of rules and 'recommendations' that heavily involve and oblige the social services and professionals.

Concluding Remarks

A reorientation of social policies has been in progress for some time in Italy, and it is a process that has required a radical overhaul of the institutional arrangements of the welfare system. All this is giving rise to a revision of the nature of social work and of organisational and professional models. To sum up, the main challenges faced by social workers derive from:

- the introduction of criteria governing the efficiency of work and the efficacy of performance; criteria which are typical of personal services but relatively alien to the culture and practice of social services (public and private).

- the prospect of a further cutback in the financial resources available for the delivery of services, despite attempts to reduce the amount of spending on monetary transfers (pensions in particular).

- the need to interact, within the welfare mix, with actors from the non-profit sector which, even when they are not an absolute novelty, perform a decidedly more important role and enjoy considerably more social recognition and legitimisation.

- the necessity to revise professional models of social work which have to date been restricted by an interpretation of its role as centred on 'observance of the rules' and circumscribed to domains of 'formal competence', perhaps more concerned with 'constraints' than with 'discretionality'.

- re-definition of the forms and purposes of integrating the social with the health sector (and with other sectors of social policy); institutional solutions aside, room has been created to address, on the functional level, the problems of collaboration between practitioners and services with different cultures and professional competences.

- the opportunity to participate at the local level in the definition of concrete mechanisms for interest representation, in the setting of priorities, and in the allocation of resources; the forms and aims of this participation will determine the political role and influence of social workers in the welfare system.

- the opportunity for social workers to intervene in the reorganisation of the training system, and in a redefinition of the professional profiles and abilities of the various types of practitioner working in this sector; this may be a crucial stage in the professionalisation of many categories which are perhaps still in search of full social and institutional recognition, and precise definition of their technical-professional competences.

Questions for Further Consideration

- In 1978 the creation of a new rational and uniform social security system in Italy was grounded in a vision of the needs of citizens and based on local-social-health units. The reform failed because, among other reasons, of the inability of different practitioners to achieve full and sufficient co-operation. What is the level of co-operation between social workers and other social professionals in your home country? Which are the most important 'co-operation roles' that social workers undertake within different sectors in your home country?

- The shift within social work practice from an emphasis upon the 'definition of goals' to the 'measurement of results' entails a radical change in both the development of a service culture and the nature of professional understanding about social work practice. Is there a similar shift in your home country? If yes, what are the possible measures social workers in your home country might develop to overcome these difficulties?

- The Italian example shows that third sector agencies are crucial actors in a social welfare system. In your home country, how is the third sector involved and encouraged to participate and thus promote the notion of subsidiarity?

Chapter Seven

Social Work in the Netherlands

Geert van der Laan

Introduction

Dutch social work now finds itself in a turbulent environment. The main source of this dynamism is the current reorganisation of the welfare state. People are expected to take more responsibility for their own lives. Public institutions are withdrawing from many types of care provision, assigning a more significant role to market forces.

A second factor that has propelled change is the reorganisation of the health care system, aimed primarily at cutting costs and deinstitutionalising care. This policy prescribes made-to-measure care, to be provided in home settings whenever possible. The social rehabilitation and reintegration of patients has long spearheaded policy in the psychiatric sector, and similar policy lines have now been implemented in other sectors too.

The combined force of these two policy trends has led to the present state of affairs in which people are pressed to assume more responsibility and take more risks. In the terms of the new policy documents, people need to be activated into becoming self-supportive citizens. According to the authorities, the safety net of the 'caring society' has become too much of a 'hammock', i.e. to rest comfortably upon for as long as you like. It needs to be converted into a 'trampoline', i.e. to help individuals bounce back into society.

A certain degree of tension has always existed between social work and social policy, and also between social work and health care. This tension is being keenly felt in the present times of restructuring of social security and reassertion of market doctrines. Social work is expected to deliver care that is closely tailored to the needs of consumers, while at the same time appraising them of their individual responsibilities within a rationalised welfare state.

In the light of such trends, the demand that social work should be more responsive to consumer needs has highly ambiguous implications. One positive implication is that policymakers now think in terms of individuals instead of categories. This does more justice to individual feelings of well-being. The catch, however, is that this process of individualisation stems in large part from the rationalisation of the welfare state. As collective risks are replaced by individual risks, and as the protection of the state is withdrawn, individuals are forced to survive as consumers under market conditions. Dependence on the state is replaced by dependence on the market.

The deinstitutionalisation of care and the emphasis on self-supportiveness mean that Dutch social work now has to relinquish its more therapeutic ambitions and set out once again in search of what is 'social' in social work. Unfortunately, the profession cannot pursue this quest undisturbed. It, too, has to survive in the new social alignment. As it makes choices regarding the content of its work, market forces dictate which of these choices will be valid. This has a far-reaching impact on the professional quality of social work.

Domain

In illustrating the trends facing Dutch social work, I will draw mainly on the most general type of social work. In the Netherlands we call this 'generic social work' (*algemeen maatschappelijk werk*) to indicate that it has a primary care function, comparable to that of the 'general' practitioner in the health care sector. Perhaps it's better to speak of generic social work (this being the usual term for this form of practice). Dutch generic social work has its historical roots in private initiatives. It works at the community level, has a low threshold, and operates at points where social and public health policy intersect. It concerns itself with interpersonal problems, material problems, psychological problems, and how such problems may be interrelated. In the Netherlands there are more than 150 agencies

Table 7.1: Social Workers in the Netherlands

Field of practice	Number of social workers
Generic social work	2500
Occupational social work	1500
Heath care social work	1500
Social work in municipal social services	1000
Non-residential youth social work	1000
School social work	1000
Social work in ambulatory mental health care	800
Probation work	700
Social work services for mentally handicapped people	500
Social work in child protection services	500
Social work in alcohol and drugs counselling	400
Residential youth social work	100
Total	11500

for generic social work, employing some 2500 social workers and reaching about half a million clients every year, or more than 3% of the Dutch population.

The major difference between the Netherlands and other countries in the field of social work probably lies in the vast number of specialisms that Dutch social work has generated. Examples are sociocultural work, community development work, youth work, personnel work, probation work, guardianship, work with caravan dwellers, socio-pedagogical work and social advice work etc. There are between 10,000 and 15,000 social workers in Holland. Statistics covering this entire field of social welfare are hard to come by, which is another reason why I will mostly confine my examination of current trends to the field of generic social work. Concentrating on one type of work will also enable me to analyse developments in more depth. Most such developments are representative for the entire field of social work and health care. Here are in Table 7.1, first of all, some overall figures from an estimate made by Buitink (1993):

Generic social work

As the above summary shows, generic social work is the foremost area of employment. It can be briefly characterised as follows:

> *It is a generic service at the local level, demand-oriented, available and accessible to all, and because of its position at the interface of care and welfare provision, it reaches especially the lower educated, the lower paid and the minorities in our society. Generic social work focuses on the interdependence between material and non-material problems which impede the functioning of individuals in their environment. Its approach is a synthesis between concrete care and service provision on the one hand and process-oriented guidance on the other, in keeping with professional standards of rigour. It endeavours to provide care that conforms as closely as possible to the experiential world of the target group, and to speak clients' own language. The primary objective of generic social work is to get clients to refind their grip on their terms of existence, so they can fully take part in social life.*
>
> (Van der Laan, 1994)

Such premises are not free from controversy. The profile of generic social work has come under increasing pressure from a complex set of developments. The number of clients has practically doubled in 15 years' time, with no corresponding increase in staff strength. Social workers feel that choices have to be made. Some agencies opt for the groups in greatest need. Others try to preserve the broad, generic nature of social work in the community by soliciting supplementary project grants. Some local authorities exert pressure on social work to provide the most concrete, short-term help possible in order to reduce waiting lists. People with severe psychological problems are referred to other agencies if possible, but sometimes for instance the Regional Institutes for Ambulant Mental Health Care promptly refer them back. Clients with material problems are referred if possible to agencies such as social advice centres, but some of these clients also come back to the social workers if their problems are tied to non-material circumstances.

Registration data confirm that the perceived increase in work pressure is based on the objective situation. The growth in the number of applications for aid has not been compensated by staff expansion (Van der Laan and Potting, 1995). Assessments of the nature of the problems being handled by the more highly pressured agencies (as in the town of Apeldoorn) also indicate that many of their cases are time-consuming ones. On the other hand, a decrease was found in the number of home visits (which are time-consuming), and the average number of contacts per client has been reduced. Figures from the town of Groningen show that an increase in work pressure leads to a lengthening of the average duration of provision; contacts are spread out over longer periods. The term 'heavy workload' is obviously an elastic phenomenon, which manifests itself in many different local patterns. Agencies and workers try to regulate the pressure in whatever ways they can. I will highlight two of the many areas in generic social work where this is the case:

- the choice between material and non-material aid

- the choice between caring and activating

But before addressing these two issues I will briefly review the history of social work in the Netherlands.

The Historical Background of Dutch Social Work

Social work has a long history in the Netherlands, and it is closely intertwined with religious traditions of poor relief. Until the period of French rule around 1800, there were strong ties between Calvinism and the Dutch state, and church and government poor relief were scarcely distinguishable. The 19th century, on the other hand, was characterised by a growing antithesis between church-operated poor relief and liberal efforts to expand public relief. It was not until the new Poor Law of 1912 that the public role was defined as secondary to that of private and church poor relief.

The first social work school was established at Amsterdam in 1899, under the inspired leadership of Marie Muller-Lulofs. Yet a recent analysis by Berteke Waaldijk (1996) has shown that the women pioneers of social work made little headway at first against the male-dominated world of church poor relief. After the Second World War, Marie Kamphuis emerged as the leading protagonist of an American-style professionalisation of Dutch social work. This professionalisation process was fuelled by the desire to wrest social work from the hands of the churches. Kamphuis vehemently opposed the religious premise that social workers were to 'suit the action to the Word'. Though religious herself, she felt that such a 'tie-in sale' between aid to the needy (the action) and evangelisation (the Word of God) was impermissible.

The twin pillars, of the State and the Church, in social work initially persisted, however, mainly as a result of the funding policies pursued by the new Ministry of Social Work set up in 1952. Although social work was left in the hands of private and church initiatives, the government provided an ever-growing slice of the funding. The secularising tendencies that swept Dutch society in the 1960s did not leave social work undisturbed. Social workers from the traditional religious and ideological persuasions (Protestant, Roman Catholic, socialist, liberal and humanist) began to converge, resulting in numerous mergers between agencies and between their national-level coordinating bodies. Until the late 1980s, however, some coordinating bodies continued to hold out as exponents of the power of the private initiative in social work (Koenis, 1993).

Waaldijk (1996) has also pointed to the fact that the Netherlands, in contrast to the United States, lacks a strong tradition of historiography that could elucidate the social ideas promulgated by social work pioneers. Social reform and the creation of the welfare state have generally been treated as part of political and economic history. Observers in the 1960s and 1970s did devote a good deal of sociological and philosophical analysis to the disciplinary effects of social work. This was prompted in large part by accusations that social work was overly concerned with adapting people to prevailing social conditions, and too little with the structural reform of society. The 1980s and 1990s, in turn, have been dominated by a New Realism and managerialism, which gives short shrift to social criticism and models itself on the culture of commerce and industry.

For many years now, social work has thus had to run the gauntlet between two 'rows' of critics (Van der Laan, 1996). On one side were those who claimed that the humane façade of social work was a mere smokescreen for its disciplinary and adaptational strategies. On the other side were the champions of a positivist, market-oriented approach to the welfare sector, who argued that social work should deliver a tangible, commercially viable product that will permit its strategic survival in the market. One way or the other, the critics of social work always had a stick to beat the dog with.

The 1990s in the Netherlands began with appeals for social regeneration. This lent new urgency to the issue of how social workers are to justify their interventions into conditions of social deprivation. The key question is how strictly social work should confine itself to people's individual sense of well-being.

The subjective factor: a sense of well-being

In an attempt to document the subjective side of welfare policy, researchers from Utrecht University carried out a study of perceptions of well-being in the Dutch town of Dordrecht (Hortulanus *et al.*, 1992). The municipal authorities had commissioned the study to find out how much support its welfare policies

enjoyed amongst local people. The findings sent a shock wave through Dutch local government.

Broadly speaking, the existing welfare policy in Dordrecht, as in most other places, was based on the assumption that cumulative social problems gave rise to a poor sense of well-being. The traditional indicators for such accumulations of problems were poor education, low incomes, high unemployment and residence in deprived areas. Policy was influenced by suppositions such as:

- social deprivation has adverse effects on social participation

- people who have low incomes, poor educations and no jobs are socially isolated

The researchers discovered to their surprise that only tiny groups of people shared these assumptions about problem accumulation. Objectively poor living conditions did not always foster a subjective sense of deprivation and social exclusion. Many people in deprived areas did not feel disadvantaged at all. The elderly, the chronically ill and the unemployed did not feel any more isolated than other people. The only group to score high on social isolation were the single parents.

The study shows convincingly that people who feel isolated have very different reasons for doing so other than the usual objective indicators of deprivation. Social isolation is more likely to stem from conditions such as poor quality of primary relationships, a lack of self-esteem, or traumatic experiences.

The report depicts these findings in a diagram consisting of a core surrounded by a number of layers. The inner core is subjective well-being, defined as 'fundamental consent to one's terms of existence', more or less in line with the well-known definition by the Amsterdam sociologist Kees Schuyt. The layers surrounding the core are arranged by the strength of their influence on how people feel. These consist roughly of psychological, social psychological, and sociological factors, in that order. In other words, the researchers' conclude that psychological factors have more effect on people's sense of well-being than sociological factors. They especially reject the widely presumed connection between unemployment as a structural factor and people's subjective well-being.

Significantly, the report repeatedly lauds the accomplishments of social work as one of the few fields to concern itself with this individual sense of well-being. As we know, social workers tend to ask their clients questions such as 'How are you feeling?' and 'How do you feel about this yourself?' This 'soft' approach, so often the butt of public jokes, is valued highly by the researchers. In the face of a top-down social policy approach that puts people into categories – which the people themselves cannot identify with, the researchers found – social work approaches social problems from a more subjective point of view. It targets clients' expressed needs, and provides advice and solutions compatible with their experiential worlds and is articulated in the language that they speak. This very focus on individual experience had been the target of policymakers' criticisms in the preceding years. They believed that social workers scored poorly at providing effective solutions to clients' problems as measured by objective indicators. The Dordrecht study firmly countered such arguments.

Obviously we should not attribute too great a significance to this study, with the subjective factor growing into a 'therapeutocracy' in policy or practice.

As we shall see below, Dutch social work has indeed neglected its mission in some ways, modelling itself too much on psychotherapy. Furthermore, social work must be wary of the pitfalls implicit in the unexpected sociological praise for the individualising approach. Individualisation fits perfectly into the project of restructuring the welfare state, and the shift this entails from *institutional* to *residual social policy* (De Gier, 1989) (Figure 7.1). Institutional policy involves solidarity and collectively borne risks. The principle of solidarity is still enshrined in the Dutch legislation on old-age benefits, with the current workforce paying the pensions of their elders; the principle of collectively borne risks is found in schemes such as those for invalidity benefits. Residual policy, in contrast, entails individual responsibility and individual risk. It is up to individuals themselves to see that their risks are covered, either through paid employment or private insurance policies.

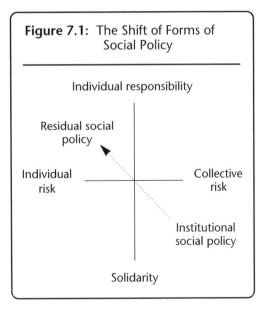

Figure 7.1: The Shift of Forms of Social Policy

Individual responsibility

Residual social policy

Individual risk

Collective risk

Institutional social policy

Solidarity

The restructuring of the Dutch social security system since the 1980s has thus been characterised by trends that run counter to those of the 1950s and 1960s. The route to the welfare state led from individualisation to collectivisation, while the restructuring process takes an opposite course (albeit with some hesitation). This makes individualisation a concept with extremely ambiguous implications.

The Dordrecht study illustrates one other important issue. It highlights a conception of generic social work which had fallen into relative disuse in the Netherlands—that of *social policy in individual cases*.

Social policy in individual cases

Koenis (1993) has analysed the ambiguous role played by social work in the emergence of the welfare state. Both social work and the welfare state have their roots in 19th century poor relief. The ambiguity lies in the fact that the welfare state sought collective solutions to material distress, while social work was left to seek out the individual aspects. Advancing collectivisation created in its wake a sort of residual function for social work. It was to deal with cases for which no collective solution had been found.

Koenis shows that the continuity of social work lies in the tension between particularisation (social work) and collectivisation (social policy). Or, as the Dutch sociologist van Doorn expressed it in the 1960s, the tension between case and institution.

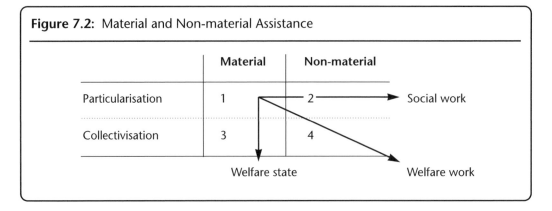

Figure 7.2: Material and Non-material Assistance

This reflects the emphasis social work puts on individual cases—on casework. It also explains its increasing concern with non-material problems. The adoption of the National Assistance Act (ABW) in the 1960s formed the turning point. From that point on, social work began concentrating on the less material aspects of social distress. Koenis also touches on a further tendency: the collectivisation of the right to well-being (Figure 7.2). Based on the contrast between prosperity and well-being, commonly made in the Netherlands of the 1960s and 1970s, the broad field of social welfare ('well-being') work was delegated the task of looking after non-material well-being. As it turned out, however, the accompanying slogan 'well-being for all' was not to survive for long, because it was soon overtaken by the initial symptoms of crisis in the welfare state.

It seems appropriate to explore briefly the concrete implementation of social policy in the Netherlands and the role played by social work in this process (see also Van der Laan, 1997). One outcome of the collectivisation process was that the municipal social services departments were charged with administering the National Assistance Act. An army of civil servants with social work diplomas was hired to implement the scheme. The professional organisation for social workers viewed them more as public officials than as professional social workers, and there was constant debate on whether they were entitled to membership. A similar debate is now underway about the position of graduates from the new professional degree course on social rights services (SJD).

From the moment that social services departments took on the administration of collectivised material assistance, the existing agencies for generic social work (whose origins were in private and church initiatives) began to focus more and more on the non-material needs of individuals and families. This generated a split between material and non-material assistance, even though the social work agencies were largely dealing with the same categories of people as the municipal social services. Benefit claimants applied to the social services department to claim their rights to an income, and then reported to the social work agencies with their psychological and relationship problems. These segregated roles are still very much in evidence, although the new National Assistance Act of 1995 is more alert to the linkage between material and non-material problems. Social workers are increasingly called in to help with rescheduling debts, resolving poor housing conditions and implementing the new policy of reintegrating national assistance claimants into the labour market.

The 'therapisation' of generic social work

We have seen that after the national assistance legislation first took effect in the mid-1960s, generic social workers gradually distanced themselves from a whole range of former tasks that involved material assistance, such as supervising the spending patterns and housing situation of people who were reduced to living on poor relief. They could now stick to the 'safe middle ground', as Draaisma (1979) once stated while observing a shift within generic social work towards 'professionally rewarding areas' such as the personal growth and self-realisation of the middle classes.

Generic social work is concerning itself more and more with activities like relationship therapies…This means it is moving in the direction of mental health care, instead of continuing to focus on 'simple' problems like giving information and advice, helping people to obtain existing provisions, teaching them to fill in forms, mediating in these activities, etc.

(Draaisma, 1979)

In the 1980s, this orientation to the safe middle ground received a new impulse. Especially after the introduction of market principles into social work, even national-level policy began specifically targeting the non-material problems—the 'psychosocial care function' in the public health care funding system. Better survival chances were expected from a social work profile aimed at the medical and therapeutical professions than from one emphasising traditional social work tasks. The welfare image gave way to a health image. At the same time, however, the economic recession of the 1980s was putting material assistance back onto the agenda. A report by the Advisory Council on Government Policy (WRR) designated unemployment and poverty as the two great social issues of the 1980s, especially in the cities. Notably in the period from 1981 to 1985, economic non-activity increased sharply, affecting nearly 50 per cent of the working-age population. These trends in society are mirrored in the registration data for generic social work.

Social work as mirror of society

In the first half of the 1980s, the number of clients that were dependent on social benefit mounted steadily, and so did the numbers of financial problem cases recorded by social workers. The major societal trends of the 1980s and 1990s were similarly reflected in social work caseloads. Unemployment soared in the early 1980s, levelled off around the middle of the decade after the drastic restructuring of industry, and even dipped slightly towards the end of the decade. In 1993 it made a sudden jump, only to decline again by 1996. Figure 7.3 shows these trends as a percentage of unemployed people among the clients of social work agencies and among the Dutch population. Statistical time-series analyses confirm that the trends shown here accurately reflect the trends in society.

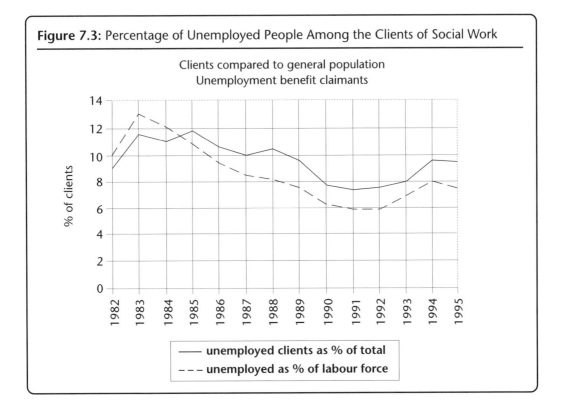

Figure 7.3: Percentage of Unemployed People Among the Clients of Social Work

Clients compared to general population
Unemployment benefit claimants

——— unemployed clients as % of total
– – – unemployed as % of labour force

The upsurge in benefit claims in the early 1980s corresponds to the greater numbers of people applying to generic social work agencies for help with financial problems. We see comparable fluctuations in the percentages of benefit recipients in society, the percentages of benefit recipients amongst social work clientele, and the numbers of applications for help with finances. We may therefore assume that, in some respects at least, social work registration data form a mirror of society.

As we shall see below, the growing need for material help in the 1980s prompted some generic social work agencies to assign parts of their staff to tasks dealing with information, advice, and material assistance. Similar to the therapisation process a few years earlier, the inflow of clients with material problems formed a threat—this time from the opposite side—to social work's traditional concentration on a process-oriented approach to interrelated material and non-material problems.

Two different forces were thus to blame for the bifurcation of generic social work's original comprehensive mission into a 'material' and a 'non-material' stream. The first was market

ideology, which in the 1980s seemed to offer the therapeutic variant the best competitive position. The other was 'the market itself', which caused the explosion in 'demand' for material assistance during the economic malaise of the early 1980s.

A Profile of Social Work Clients

I shall now try to formulate a brief general profile of the clients who make use of generic social work. This profile is based on figures from the uniform nationwide information system set up in the early 1990s to keep track of key social work data. Insight into these typical configurations of problems, should aid us in analysing the relationship between material and non-material social work assistance.

Figure 7.4, below, shows the frequency distribution of clients' problems as of the mid-1990s. One can see, for example, that just under 10 per cent of the clients score positive on psychological problems. (In this database, clients can score on more than one problem.)

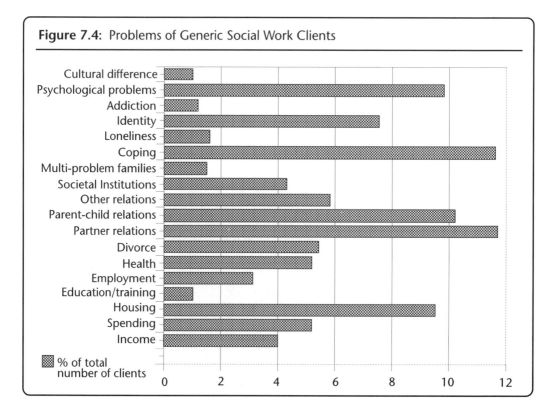

Figure 7.4: Problems of Generic Social Work Clients

Interestingly, many types of non-material problems score high. Although this may seem a first indication that material problems receive little attention in generic social work, such a conclusion needs to be qualified in several ways. More detailed analysis reveals that the material problems mentioned are closely intertwined with non-material ones. It seems that material problems are not always recorded, if they are not specifically addressed in the interventions. Many social workers use non-material problems as a point of access to tackle the long-term solution or prevention of material problems. Relationship therapy may be applied, for example, to teach a couple to communicate better about family expenditures. The most acute financial problems may be referred on to specialised agencies. This nationwide picture differs to an extent from that prevailing in the cities, where far more material problems are in evidence. (Some cities are not represented in the nationwide database.)

The problem categories as depicted above were projected onto a plane by means of a HOMALS analysis in the SPSS statistical program. This produced a plot showing the 'distance' between the various categories and the positions they occupy in relation to one another. HOMALS is a technique which correlates nominal-level data in one or more dimensions. If, for example, a large number of clients have income problems that coincide with housing problems, we can visualise this by saying that these two problem categories are projected nearby each other on a plane. This creates a spatial representation of a problem pattern. If two problem categories (e.g. housing and income) are projected close together, that means that clients presenting to a social work agency with a housing problem will be more likely to have an accompanying income problem than one of the other types of problems in the list.

The HOMALS analysis separates the problem categories into three different groupings. I will try to give names to these below.

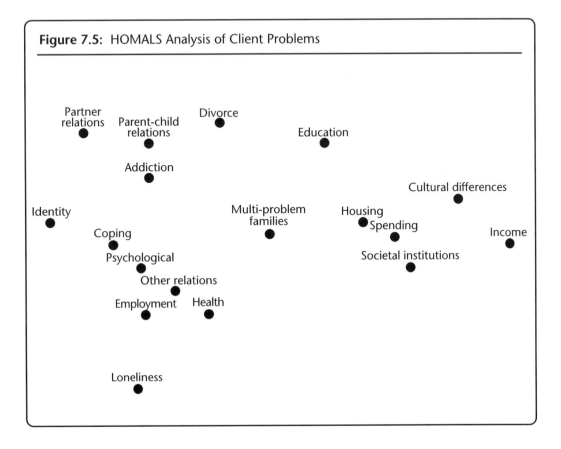

Figure 7.5: HOMALS Analysis of Client Problems

The analysis seems readily interpretable. One rather vague category in the national database, 'multi-problem families' (which actually seems out of place in the list) has been projected at the centre of the diagram. Problems with societal institutions are positioned near the material problems, as are multicultural aspects of problem situations. We know this from other social work databases as well. Problems with employment are associated with psychological problems, health problems and related issues. This, too, can often be seen in the social work records.

If we now perform cluster analysis on the HOMALS distribution, a diagram of three clusters results (Figure 7.6). It provides a clear representation of the problem profiles of social work clients.

The **Interpersonal Problems Cluster** is characterised by:

- a greater proportion of families

- a higher percentage of salaried employees
- more people aged 30 to 50
- counselling as the most frequently applied method

In the **Material Problems Cluster** we see:

- more men
- many disability claimants
- many national assistance claimants
- information, advice, concrete services and mediation as the most common methods
- more contacts initiated by clients themselves
- many clients referred from social services or housing offices
- more liaisons with social services departments and lending institutions

The **Psychological Problems Cluster** contains:

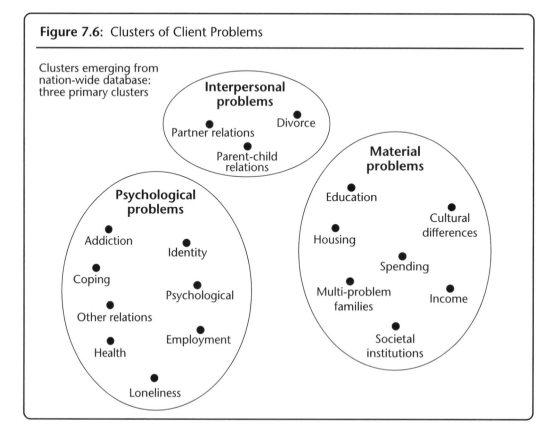

Figure 7.6: Clusters of Client Problems

Clusters emerging from nation-wide database: three primary clusters

Interpersonal problems

Partner relations

Divorce

Parent-child relations

Material problems

Education

Cultural differences

Housing

Spending

Multi-problem families

Income

Societal institutions

Psychological problems

Addiction

Identity

Coping

Psychological

Other relations

Employment

Health

Loneliness

- many older people
- many single householders
- many disability claimants
- group work and guidance as the most common methods
- many referrals from general practitioners, community mental health agencies, police and employment-related organisations

Interrelatedness of interpersonal, material and psychological problems

The above depiction of three primary clusters might give the impression that these can be viewed independently of one another. Closer inspection, though, reveals that this is possible only to a very limited extent. Constructing problem types of optimal purity still says nothing about the number of clients who have *exclusively* material, psychological or interpersonal problems. If we calculate a higher number of clusters, we find that although the first three continue to exist, weaker clusters now also appear which reveal the interrelatedness of the three original ones. Significantly, the weaker clusters contain far and away the greatest numbers of clients. This points to the general conclusion that the majority of social work clients are contending with complex and interrelated sets of problems, and not with simple, straightforward ones.

Many differences between problem aspects come to light within the clusters as well. An analysis of the interconnections between various kinds of *financial* problems recorded by social workers in Groningen (working with a more detailed list of problem categories) reveals that two different types of financial problems exist. There are requests for help with *income acquisition*, and requests for help with the *budgeting of expenditures*. Within the cluster of financial problems, these two types of needs appear to form poles around which the other kinds of financial problems (such as housing costs, indebtedness and bankruptcies) tend to cluster. This impression grows even stronger if we look at the 'carriers' of these problem aspects:

- Income acquisition problems are experienced more by women, single

householders, one-parent families, national assistance claimants, and 'client systems' consisting of one person. Clients in this problem configuration have relatively few debts. I will call it Type A.
- Spending problems are experienced more by men, two-parent families, salaried employees and client systems of two or more persons. This category is more likely to have debt problems. I will call it Type B.

Roughly, then, we are dealing with two different types of clients who have financial problems: those who receive too little and those who spend too much. There is little overlap between the two.

Let us turn now to the linkage between material and non-material problems. For the most commonly occurring financial problems in the Groningen records, it was possible to determine accurately which other problems (of a non-financial nature) accompanied them. Significantly, the problems with income acquisition very often coincided with childrearing problems, and the spending problems not so often. A distinct profile thus emerges for Type A problems. It is determined in large part by the high proportion of one-parent families (by implication most of these are mothers on national assistance benefit). We see further that income acquisition problems are more likely to occur in combination with divorce problems, and are least likely to coincide with relationship problems (within existing relationships). Both types of financial problems in the Groningen database are frequently accompanied by nervous symptoms, conflicts with institutions, social isolation, alcohol consumption, suicidal behaviour or unemployment.

Broadly speaking, we can conclude that the interconnections between different types of financial problems are hardly any stronger than the links between financial problems and other, mainly non-material problems. Poverty in a strict financial sense appears, among social work clients at least, to be strongly bound up with deprivation in other areas of life. This means that help requests for either material or non-material problems can usually be taken to imply simultaneous problems of the other type. Segregating the two aspects is justifiable for only a small segment of the client population.

In spite of this, social work agencies in the Netherlands still routinely separate the two. The growing demand for debt assistance, for example, is still being channelled off to debt specialists, even though research gives ample evidence of the important part social work could play. The very fact that debts are seldom a purely financial problem is an obvious indication for interventions of a more therapeutic nature.

The Re-entry of Material Problems into the Social Work Arena

In a study of problematic debt situations, de Greef (1994) encountered types of clients comparable to those described above—people who spend too much and people who receive too little. He refers to the debts of the former as 'overspending debts', and these occur primarily in higher-than-minimum income brackets. He contrasts them with 'survival debts' and 'compensational debts' (as when one drowns one's sorrows in a shopping spree), which mainly affect families and single people in the lowest income brackets, and which tend to express themselves in accumulated rent arrears and mail-order debts. As a further variant he distinguishes 'adjustment debts', incurred after changes in life circumstances, such as job loss, illness or divorce.

One trend identified by de Greef is that debt problems became increasingly difficult to resolve in the period around the late 1980s and early 1990s, with the debts being both greater and more complex. People's scale of indebtedness mounted so sharply in the course of the 1980s that especially those households with minimum incomes often faced debts far out of proportion to their ability to pay. At the time of de Greef's study, barely a quarter of the repayment arrangements were being successfully fulfilled, and 30 per cent of the households that had agreed debt settlements later lapsed into recidivism. Those households that suffered repeated financial problems generally had higher-than-minimum incomes. In most cases, 'debt recidivism' occurred because households failed to adapt their lifestyles or ceased cooperating with the arrangements made.

There are various types of institutions in the Netherlands that provide debt assistance. The most important of them are the Municipal Credit Banks (GKB), the Municipal Social Services Departments (GSD), generic social work agencies (AMW) and an organisation called Consumer and Household Planning Practice (PCH). The latter is a private, profit-making organisation that charges fees to arrange debt rescheduling. The services provided by these organisations are basically complementary, and various combined arrangements are possible. The organisations can be classified on the basis of their method of debt assistance (behavioural change or setting rules) and on the basis of the range of assistance they provide (material only or also non-material). This can be summarised schematically as follows in Figure 7.7:

Figure 7.7: Methods of Debt Assistance

	Debt assistance method	
Range of assistance	**Setting rules**	**Behavioural change**
Material problems only	GKB	PCH
Material and non-material problems	GSD	AMW

One of de Greef's research conclusions was that generic social work can play a crucial role in debt assistance, for two reasons. First, clients generally express satisfaction with social workers' approaches to debt assistance. They even believe—more so, in fact, than the social workers themselves—that social work made the most effective contribution to the resolution of their debts. Second, social work is capable of analysing the interconnections between material and non-material problems. De Greef reports that households deem the social work method effective because of the way social workers approach their clients:

> *In providing financial guidance, social work essentially has the best qualifications for assessing and influencing human behaviour. This makes its approach the most responsive to the needs of the households with debt problems.* (De Greef, 1994: p 10)

So the evidence is that social work's downgrading of the status of material assistance is unjustifiable. It also forms a strategic disadvantage at a time when the outside world is demanding more and more social work interventions into problems of indebtedness, housing and unemployment.

Material and non-material assistance

It looks as though the classic dilemma of Dutch social work, the choice between health care and welfare work, will remain an issue into the next century. By extension, so will the related choice between a more therapeutic approach directed at non-material problems and a concrete approach dealing with material problems. As we have seen, the push to segregate the generic social work function into a 'material' and a 'non-material' stream was set in motion in the 1980s from two different sources.

Given the increase in applications for material assistance, some generic social work agencies decided to devote extra attention to *concrete aid*. Especially in the cities, Utrecht and The Hague in particular, part of the available social work staff was deployed in the 1980s in service of the information and advice function and the provision of material assistance. The material stream later received additional impetus from the government programme for social regeneration, with its emphasis on less

care and more concrete help and activation. Some 70 per cent of the municipalities joined this policy scheme, whose influence on social work was considerable, especially since the funding and management of social work had been devolved to the local authorities a few years earlier.

The other reason for the trend towards segregation of the material and non-material aspects of social work was what I have called the 'therapisation of social work'. In an attempt to survive the turmoil of the restructuring campaign in the health care and welfare sectors, many social work generalists had begun zeroing in on *non-material problems*—on the 'psychosocial care function' within the system of health care funding—as a domain to be claimed by social work. The professionals in this stream did not encroach on the territory of the social advisers, generic social workers or information and advice bureaux, as the first group did, but on that of the mental health care sector and of the psychologists working in the primary health care sector.

Generic social work is a basic or 'primary' service. Its hallmark is broad accessibility. The appropriateness of this fundamental choice is backed up by registration data and other indicators, and since the late 1980s it has received a strategic boost from the devolution of powers to the municipal level. More than was the case under centralised control, local authorities now call on social workers to deal with problems arising from poverty, crime, nuisance, social isolation, ageing, unemployment, inactivity, debts and other such conditions. However, the problems enjoying the greatest policy interest are precisely those which consume the largest amounts of time and energy—cooperative projects relating to case management, debt management, problem families, chronic psychiatric patients. In other words, the spearheads of policy cost time and money. Social work must make its own choices in policy as a consequence.

Generic Social Work and the Market

Before examining the relations between generic social work and the health care system, I will first illustrate how the restructuring of the welfare state is being combined with the introduction of market principles in the 'contracting out' of social work.

Nowadays the strategy *activating welfare state* aims to reduce apathetic responses by individuals and to increase the participation of its citizens in society. More and more, social workers are enlisted to help achieve these goals. It is assumed that they will activate their clients to take on paid jobs and other socially useful tasks. Activation, however, is also associated with the introduction of a market environment in the social sector. These aspects colour the professional dilemma of social workers as they gently but firmly put the activation policy into practice.

More and more often, social workers are enlisted to help draw up contracts in matters such as naturalisation, activation and rehabilitation for people who have not managed to form any connections with the productive sectors in society.

A good example of the new contract based thinking is a co-operation project in the city of The Hague, the Netherlands, between the Municipal Services for Social Affairs and Employment and the organisation of general social work. In 1992, the management of the social work organisation concluded a controversial agreement with the municipal social services. Under this contract, clients referred to the social work organisation by the municipal social services would be made eligible for regular jobs on the labour market. The social services paid for the services rendered. The social work organisation obliged itself to take on long term unemployed persons with psychosocial problems as clients. Its task was to ensure that the obstacles to taking a steady job were removed, and to activate clients to take up paid work or other 'socially useful activities'. The clients who were referred had obligations of their own: their benefits would be reduced if they did not co-operate. The social work organisation contractually obliged itself to provide help to 400 clients referred by the municipal social services on an annual basis—while guaranteeing a success rate of 60 per cent within a predetermined period. For this 'product', the municipal social services paid three hundred thousand guilders each year. So here we cannot speak of an obligation to make certain efforts, but to produce certain results.

This project is a good example of the transformations between and within the various relations in the present welfare state. Only a decade ago, such a contract would have been inconceivable—at any rate, from the perspective of social work. Far-reaching transformations are at work in a legal-administrative and a social-cultural sense (Van der Laan, 1998).

Several other experiments have been set up in the Netherlands along the same lines of the project in The Hague, in which an altered relationship between government, welfare organisations and members of society can be observed. Although some of these projects have a long history, in the 1990s relations became much more strained by the way in which the projects are positioned on the market.

For example, projects set up for people who have been evicted from their homes, as a result of nuisance or indebtedness, now include their signing a contract with social work *and* for housing. In a nutshell, these contracts offer integrated help and counselling, with the threat of repeated eviction if they do not co-operate. In social work circles, this is referred to as conditional counselling. In fact, it more properly ought to be called conditional housing. After all, in such projects, residents who would be evicted, or who would not be awarded council housing according to the standards of the housing corporations, are given one last chance to obtain housing, on the condition that they sign a contract for counselling.

In debt clearance projects, too, the relationship between client and help provider frequently entails other obligations on the part of the client. Families in very difficult debt situations are given the choice between resolving the situation with counselling or on their own. Only if they opt for counselling does the project negotiate with their creditors to freeze or reschedule their debts while they receive counselling.

These practices are not new either. In the mid-1980s we have already witnessed how social workers were increasingly confronted with local energy companies that would only continue to supply gas and electricity to people who were in default if they concluded a budgetting agreement through the intermediary of the social work organisation. In several sectors, such as working with fringe groups, these practices have been around for a while, but they are being coloured by market-oriented thinking. Welfare organisations have even become dependent on such projects for their very survival. This means that the discussion on the use of professional power in social work no longer primarily takes place within the professional group or adjacent forums, but that the market has taken over this role.

Social Work and the Restructuring of the Health Care System

Generic social work has not only been affected by the transformation of the welfare state and the introduction of market principles, but by the restructuring of the health care system as well. Policy in the health sector seeks to replace an orientation to supply (health care facilities) by a demand-based approach. In combination with a market-based orientation, this effectively transforms clients into consumers. The 'client-linked budget' model is one measure that aims to strengthen the position of clients vis-à-vis the professionals who serve them. In a sense, it transforms clients into employers. The combined effect of all these developments is to strongly constrict the professional role of social workers. In this section I will investigate the implications this has for the choices Dutch social work has to make.

For an adequate understanding of the position now occupied by social work, a brief outline of the structure of the care sector will be helpful. Two guiding principles—differentiation and integration—have long vied for ascendancy in structuring the Dutch care sector.

The differentiation of care tasks into specialisms implies a large geographic scale, since one cannot expect to find a specialist on every corner. The obvious advantage of specialisation is that substantial knowledge and skills are concentrated at a single point. The drawback is that the available services are far away, fragmented and lacking in cohesion. Differentiation results in a loss of integrative potential.

The advantage of an integrated approach is that it allows extensive decentralisation and flexibility. The strength of the generalists is that they can realise integrated service provision on a limited geographical scale. Non-specialist, multidisciplinary teams can cooperate to supply comprehensive, demand-based care. The disadvantages obviously involve their limited ability to apply specialist expertise first-hand.

The Dutch 'echelon' system of care is an attempt to combine both approaches. A first echelon, with comprehensive provision on a small geographical scale (general practitioners and neighbourhood health centres, for instance), is combined with a back-up echelon with specialised functions (as in hospitals) that have much larger catchment areas. In the echelon system as it has traditionally operated in the Netherlands, primary care is immediately accessible to all. It has a before- and after-care task in relation to the more specialised secondary and tertiary care institutions. The 'lines' in the echelon model are regarded as filters to limit the flow to the higher echelons. The usual distinctions are between *peer-based or 'zero-line' care* (family, neighbours, friends, acquaintances, teachers); *primary or 'first-line' care* (generic social work, general medical practitioners, family care, district nursing); *secondary or 'second-line' care* (outpatient mental health or substance abuse care and other ambulatory care); and *tertiary or 'third-line' care* (residential facilities such as mental institutions, homes for older people, young offenders' institutions and drug-free therapeutic communities).

At right angles to these echelons, we can also visualise 'circuits' which vertically transect the echelons. One example is the circuit for care of older people, containing facilities for peer-based care (social networks), primary care (including the coordinated services for older people), secondary care (psychogeriatric sections of ambulatory mental health facilities) and tertiary care (homes for older people, nursing homes). Such vertical connections were originally intended to safeguard continuity in care provision.

Generalist social workers are found in all lines and circuits. Their broadest task is enabling people to take part in social life as fully as possible. This involves reintegration, probation and after-care, and the physical and mental rehabilitation of people who have lost control of their own lives.

In a military model, the soldiers at the front constitute the first echelon. Given that the term 'echelons' (advancing lines) comes from military strategy handbooks, perhaps more of this soldierly vocabulary will be appropriate. General practitioners, home care workers and social workers would be the front-line troops. Characteristic of them is their sharp eye on society: they are to respond to any problem that comes their way, solving it themselves whenever possible. That gives them a broad, general outlook. Whatever they cannot deal with as an 'advance guard' they allow to penetrate to the more specialised 'rear guards' of the second and third echelons.

This echelon model, created in the late 1960s, came under fire during the 1980s from several different directions. The policy of deinstitutionalisation brought on a rapid exodus of clients from residential institutions to primary care. The echelon model itself also came under attack from observers who pointed out that the most vulnerable groups in society repeatedly managed to slip through the net and fall by the wayside (Wolf, 1995).

Registration data in the 1980s reflect this growing pressure on the front echelon. The numbers of clients applying to generic social work doubled in the course of that decade. To make matters worse, the front line not only felt the onslaught from ahead, caused by the increasing demand from society. In effect it was simultaneously 'attacked from behind' by clients being released from institutions. In practically all circuits, deinstitutionalisation touched off a stream of clients towards primary care. Despite the numerous efforts to modernise care, and despite the unfurling of a safety net in primary care which included home care, day care and shelters, the numbers of homeless youth and homeless people with psychiatric problems grew steadily. These are some of the unforeseen side-effects of deinstitutionalisation. Many severe problem cases now receive help that is too 'lightweight'. Such conditions, in combination with wider social processes such as individualisation and unemployment, are driving vulnerable groups more swiftly towards the margins of society.

Musical Chairs

Because the policies just described have produced sizeable 'deinstitutionalised groups'

that need to be socially reintegrated, one might expect social work to have received a tremendous boost in all spheres. However, in many areas generic social workers have been overtaken left and right by professionals from the higher echelons, ranging from nurses to social psychiatrists. Projects like care innovation, case management, sheltered housing, and employment and day care facilities have all set out to 'rediscover' social work, and some types of sociocultural work as well. This has come as a particular surprise to social workers in the primary care sector. In the second half of the 1980s, they had attempted to style themselves as 'psychosocial therapists', in order to compete with secondary care agencies on the health market for funding in the legally approved 'psychosocial care function'. In so doing, generic social work had neglected the more purely social aspects of its task, such as housing problems, unemployment, debt and inactivity. As deinstitutionalisation continues, these are the very gaps that are now being filled by other disciplines. In other words, some circuits have been drawn into a game of musical chairs, in which people's tasks seem to change suddenly without them being fully aware of who is responsible for what and who should be overseeing the process.

The relationship with community development work and sociocultural work

For a variety of reasons, many psychiatric patients are not rescued by the safety net of primary care, but slip through it (Van der Laan, 1994). They end up walking the streets or living in various kinds of shelter facilities. It is here that social work's relationship with welfare work comes into view. In the course of its history, generic social work has loosened its ties with community development work and sociocultural work. Their relationship cooled further during the 1980s, as social work oriented itself to the health care sector. But their contact has revived in recent years under the influence of decentralisation and the social regeneration campaign.

Community development work, or community organization, concentrates basically on issues that go beyond individual interests. It works for safe neighbourhoods, affordable housing, healthy surroundings, a tolerant living climate, affordable child care, public participation procedures, and jobs for unemployed local people. *Sociocultural work* focuses on the education and self-development of the individual, with day activities, recreation and cultural development going hand in hand. Both these types of welfare work maintained a distance from 'individual care' while generic social workers were specialising in psychosocial care for individuals and families. In this way these related professions have drifted apart.

In the early years of welfare work in the post-war period, interventions at micro-, meso- and macro-levels were seen as extensions of one another. In the 1960s, Broekman (1964) distinguished four methods in social work: individual casework, social groupwork, community organisation and social action. Clearly, social work in those days had far fewer differentiations than it has now.

Care or activation

We have seen that Dutch generic social work occupies a strategic position between health care and welfare. But this is more than just a strategic characteristic. It has consequences for the content of the work itself. It means that social work sometimes needs to care for people, and at other times it needs to activate them. Sometimes it has to do both things simultaneously, trying to tap the residual capabilities of its clients. General principles like social reintegration, rehabilitation and probation after-care have

historically been core tasks of social work. The tension between caring and activating makes itself felt in many types of social work. In a study on helping clients with occupational disabilities, Melief (1994) found that social workers provide the best-quality care when they deal with *retrospective* matters. This includes emotional elements (lending an ear, showing understanding and giving encouragement) as well as rational-cognitive elements (creating order and seeking causes). The more *future-* and *action-oriented elements* come off rather poorly. Stimulating the clients to make concrete plans for the future and helping them build a new action repertoire receive comparatively little attention, and even concrete, practical aspects of the problem situation are neglected. 'The further they lie from the consulting room, the less likely they are to be dealt with in the counselling' (Melief, 1994).

According to Melief, generic social work is too strongly oriented to the past and too inwardly directed. Especially for clients who are out of work, whatever the reason, an outward, future-oriented view is called for. Many clients risk sinking into passivity, and an activating approach is essential to keep alive their prospects of renewed social participation.

If we examine the Dutch debate about activational social work, we see it is dominated by a number of antitheses. The most important of them are juxtaposed below in Table 7.2.

The current policy paradigm has shifted the point of gravity in most cases to the options on the right-hand side of the table. Sometimes this manifests itself in innovative practices;

Table 7.2: The Poles of Care and Activation

Care	Activation
Dependence	Self-reliance
Solidarity	Individual responsibility
Social causes	Personal causes (individual failures)
Thinking in problems	Thinking in potentials
Reluctance to intervene (fear of patronising)	Eagerness to intervene ('stepping in')
Retrospective	Prospective
Adjustment-oriented	Action-oriented

sometimes it constitutes no more than lip service to policy. Many people are inclined to translate the terms on the left directly into those on the right. The first pair of concepts is a good example. Forms of caregiving (feeding and clothing someone and helping them calm down and come to their senses) can readily be conceived as a first stage on the road to activation. The activation paradigm promises to be a driving force in social work in the years to come. By applying techniques derived from methodologies such as task-centred casework, social workers try to develop an activating approach to individual counselling.

My analysis so far has shown that in the recent past Dutch social work has somewhat alienated itself from its historical roots. It has become fixated either on therapy or on its clients' material living conditions. It now faces the challenge of reorienting itself to again take up its classic task—that of improving the social participation of vulnerable groups in society.

Methods and Professional Issues

The specific methods applied by social work in the Netherlands derive from many different schools of thought within social work and therapeutic disciplines, ranging from the family system approach to task-centred casework and from gestalt therapy to an ecological approach. Family therapy has had an especially large following. Interestingly, it was mainly the Dutch social workers, through their contacts in the United States, who helped to familiarise Dutch psychologists and psychiatrists with the family approach. The Netherlands has almost no psychoanalytic tradition, nor have behavioural techniques ever found much acceptance.

At present an estimated 10–15,000 social workers are employed in the Netherlands (population 15 million) (see Table 7.1). Only a small proportion of the social workers are organised in the professional organisation NVMW (Nederlandse Vereniging voor Maatschappelijk Werk). In the mid-1980s that organisation drew up a *professional profile* that is now widely acknowledged as delineating the core tasks of social workers. The *professional code* was also revised in the 1980s. In negotiations with the employers' association, the NVMW has recently drawn up a

professional statute governing the relationship between universal professional standards and specific job demands. It specifies the rights and duties of both the employers and the professional employees.

The NVMW also maintains a register of qualified social workers, and it administers the disciplinary regulations and complaints procedures applying to individual social workers. The employers' association has a separate complaints procedure for institutions and agencies. Social workers are covered by the nationwide collective bargaining agreement (CAO) for welfare work.

Client organisations are rare, except where social work is performed in contexts such as the health care sector.

Social Work Education

The Dutch social work infrastructure also includes about 30 initial and advanced training courses, as well as provincial and national-level educational support institutions. Professional education is provided by higher professional schools, which are strictly separate from university education and research. The advantage to this system is that Dutch social workers are generally well-trained for operational practice. Another strong point of Dutch social work is its use of supervisory tutoring as an instrument to improve quality. This is a highly-developed technique in the Netherlands, backed up by an association for supervisory tutoring and a professional journal on the subject.

In 1994 all social work training courses underwent quality assessment carried out by a national review committee. It advised the higher professional schools to improve their quality by putting more effort into applied research, method development and theory development. Hopefully this will narrow the gap between the social work schools and the universities.

Social Work's Mission in a Turbulent Environment

The new situation of professionals under market conditions and the new approach to social security give cause for some profound reflection about the mission and tasks of social work in the Netherlands. Some of the issues that need consideration are as follow:

a) Should social work be willing to deliver 'piece goods', paid for by the unit, and to guarantee their results in advance?

b) Should social work be willing to conceive social problems, such as crime, nuisance, debt, disablement and unemployment, in terms of behavioural change, and to use its professional power to steer clients towards the changes prescribed by the commissioning institutions?

c) Should social work be willing to accept the governing role of the market in such processes?

Unique to the current state of affairs is that these three questions are inextricably linked. As a consequence, the debate is therefore no longer a normative one, carried on by a professional group in relative autonomy. Dutch social workers more or less forfeited that prerogative when they persistently avoided any discussion on the exercising of discipline. The norms are now being prescribed by the market.

For the group of *organised professionals* this means they must now make a concerted effort to preserve their professional standards. After all, professionals have a duty to maintain a position in society *between* the demands of their clients and the financial incentives provided by commissioning institutions.

For *social work education* it means that students should be trained to deal conscientiously with conditional care provision and with the professional use of power.

For *employers* it means a firm acknowledgement of the distinction between professional responsibility and employees' responsibility, and the implications this has both for management and for quality policy.

For *clients* and their organisations it implies a challenge to defend their civil rights, but it also means acknowledging that professionals have a responsibility of their own in assessing client demands.

For *educational support and research organisations* it implies the need to thoroughly investigate what instruments (selection, fees) are suitable for preventing excesses caused by market constraints.

For *public authorities and commissioning bodies* it means conscientiously weighing the intended and unintended consequences of the introduction of market-led instruments of regulation and control. Rather than withdrawing from social security, government ought to take a far more active role when choices have to be made.

Questions for Further Consideration

- The notion of 'activation' is an important idea in social policy in the Netherlands. How might the concept of activation be used and employed in social work in your country?

- In the Netherlands social work is divided into a series of different specialisms and some examples are given in the chapter, such as: community development work; general social work; guardianship; personnel work; probation work; social advice work. socio-cultural work; socio-pedagogical work; work with caravan dwellers; and youth work. What kinds of specialisms within social work are found in your country—how similar or different are these to the Dutch specialisms? What is the justification for these specialisms?

- Recent developments in social work in the Netherlands highlight the tension between understandings and contructions of social work purpose and methods as being to provide material or non-material forms of assistance. How has this tension been resolved in your country, through what mechanisms and with what success?

Chapter Eight

The Development of Social Work in Spain

Montserrat Feu

Introduction

The relationship between social policy, social services and social work in Spain is best understood in the context of the specific political and economic history of the country. In particular, these features have evolved during the country's transition from a dictatorial to a democratic political system.

After the civil war, (1936–39), in which the Republic and the progressive forces in the country were defeated, a period of dictatorship began that did not end until the late 1970s. Social welfare during this period was limited and heavily dependent upon charitable activity. The transition from a dictatorship and the process of democratisation during the 1980s were the starting point for a concerted effort to introduce some form of social protection system and an associated legislative base in the country through the establishment of basic universal rights of its citizens and the provision of professional (as opposed to charitable) forms of interventions within the emergent health and social service systems. The profession of social assistant/social worker has evolved within this changing context from the previous conception of welfare as charity and help, to the current position which is underpinned and sustained by models and techniques associated with professional intervention.

Current European tendencies towards the revision of social welfare systems present a series of challenges and dilemmas for Spain. The welfare system in Spain is still fragile and unconsolidated and any kind of reductions in the level of resources at this stage of its development are likely to considerably increase existing social differences and divisions within Spanish society.

The Spanish Social Service System

The Spanish Constitution

The Spanish Constitution stipulates the transition from a dictatorial, charitable-based and paternalistic state to a democratic state and by law defines and implies that social services are a basic right of all citizens. Article 9.2 of the 1978 Spanish Constitution states:

> It is the public authorities' responsibility to promote the necessary conditions for ensuring a real and effective freedom and equality for all individuals and groups, and to eliminate all barriers to the full participation of all citizens in the political, economic, cultural and social life of the country.

This new approach replaces the previous charitable system with a universal and integrated concept of social services based on social welfare. This process, parallel to the strengthening of democracy in the country, is the result of new political and technical approaches adopted in the country's new legal framework. Although the constitution does not specifically and explicitly refer to a general right to social services, it highlights the need to protect and foster certain population groups such as the family, youth, older people, disabled people and all those needing specific social care and attention. Similarly, the constitution includes the definition of legal principles that have the function of 'regulating social and economic policies' and which involve the public authorities participation— subject to certain specific legal regulations. Specific mention is made of:

- family and child protection (article 39)
- youth support (article 48)
- integration of disabled people (article 49)
- protection of older people (article 50)

Furthermore, the constitution also confers to the self-governed communities (*Comunidades Autónomas*) the right to legislate for social services. Since there is no exclusive competence of the state on the matter, each community is empowered to legislate specifically for those services. As part of the newly founded democratic Spanish State, the Spanish Constitution recognises the different nationalities and regions existing in the country following a principle called 'The Public Administration Decentralisation Principle' which defines a federal state consisting of 17 self-governing regions and their corresponding self-governing statutes. As for the social services themselves, there is no general act defining a framework for the entire country, but 17 different social services acts corresponding to the 17 independent regions. Each region has enacted its own laws and regulations governing social services, although there are a great number of commonalties among the regional laws. In general terms, the 17 self-governed regions have exclusive competence on social services which enable them to determine, implement and operate their own services in co-operation with local authorities, municipalities and provinces.

Social welfare policy in Spain

The political crisis in Spain during the 1930s led to a civil war where the Spanish Republic and the forces of the left were defeated. A dictatorship resulted, in the form of 'franquism' (as Franco's authoritarian regime was known), which lasted until the late 1970s and Spain's subsequent transition to a democracy. Franco's regime was little concerned with social issues, since after the civil war all of the regime's energies were focused on the economic reconstruction of the country. During this period social protection was aimed at working men, as women were discouraged from the entering the workforce and were expected to remain within the domestic sphere acting as wives and mothers.

In 1939, a form of social insurance that provided retirement benefits and long-term sickness income called *Seguro Obligatorio de Vejez e Invalidez* was created which covered industrial workers with low incomes. In 1942, a specific health insurance for this group called *Seguro de Enfermedad* (health insurance) came into effect along with the minimal provision of the *Sanidad Benéfica* (charitable health care) for unemployed people. In 1961, the *Seguro*

Obligatorio de Desempleo (unemployment benefit) was enacted, followed in 1963 by the *Salario Mínimo Interprofesional* (guaranteed minimum wage) and the *Seguro Obligatorio de Enfermedad* (Health Insurance) which covered only 45 per cent of the country's total workforce. In 1966, the Act providing a national insurance system, the *Ley General de la Seguridad Social* was passed. The national insurance system set up a single health care structure which consisted of all the previous independent health care insurance existing in the country, although certain groups such as the self-employed, domestic, agricultural and maritime workers were covered by a different insurance regime.

Between 1957 and 1967 the country went through a period of intensive development with industry expanding in certain areas of the country, in particular in the north of Spain, Catalonia and the East Coast. This process led to a great number of migrant labourers coming from the central and southern rural areas of Spain to the industrialised areas in Spain and other European countries. During these years the dictatorship placed particular emphasis on education which led to the reform of the education system by the Education Act of 1970, the *Ley General de Educación*.

In 1982 a specfic law aimed at the integration of physically and mentally disabled people was enacted (*Ley de Integración*, LISMI). In 1990 an act regulating non-contributory pensions (*Ley de Pensiones no contributivas de la Seguridad Social*) came into effect which covered those citizens who had never contributed sufficiently to be entitled to social benefits.

Since the late 1980s, mainly as a result of the 'welfare state crisis', successive governments have taken steps towards promoting a model of social services which combines elements of both social control and improved performance and efficiency. Measures that have been introduced include the privatisation of services through the encouragement of for-profit and non-profit making private institutions; the promotion of self-help and mutual-help groups and an emphasis upon the family's responsibility for the care of the ill and the elderly. These measures, it is argued, are necessary to foster greater participation and involvement of all citizens in the fulfilment of their own social needs and are necessary to achieve greater efficiency and better performance in the services provided and the achievement of a process of modernisation.

These approaches have been justified within a general argument that emphasises prevention and the need to keep dependent people within their local community and family situation. Nevertheless, such initiatives all too often conceal a political agenda aimed at reducing expenditure on primary social benefits and the reduction of the levels of services and medical care. In practice, this general approach has led to women being left with the responsibility for assuming all home care tasks at the expense of their professional careers.

Social work in Spain

The first Social Work Schools were created during the Second Spanish Republic between 1932–36. Their creation and organisation were strongly influenced by other European schools of social work, in particular those in Belgium and France. In Barcelona a Social Assistance School for Women was founded in 1932. During the early years of Franco's regime, (1939–57), social work was mostly 'charitable and paternalistic' in form; social workers were trained both by religious institutions closely connected with the Catholic Church and the *Sección Femenina*—the feminine branch of the totalitarian party *Falange Española* which embodied Franco's dictatorship. The type of social work carried out, called 'Obra Social' (National Charity) which was enacted under the terms of the 1849 *Ley de Beneficiencia* (Charity Act), was limited in scope and mainly aimed at helping the so-called 'needy'. The construction and practice of this form of social work was essentially due to Franco's regime being highly interventionist and was significantly different from the social welfare models instituted in most other European countries after the Second World War. Between the years 1958–67, all the existing Social Work Schools were formally acknowledged by the state and their degrees were fully recognised. Social action was primarily aimed at the social integration of individuals, groups and communities presenting specific problems. Methodologically, a highly traditional approach, essentially based on casework, group work and community work was used with clients. In spite of the domination of

traditional forms of practice, some sectors within the field of social work expressed a growing concern with the need to ground the discipline and its practice on a scientific basis.

The period 1967–79 was dominated by critical discussion and debate regarding the nature of social work. For example, during the 1970s, the Latin America-based movement concerned with the 're-conceptualisation' of social work gained strong support in Spain. Access to specific publications, especially of Latin American authors previously unavailable, raised many questions about the official role played by the Catholic Church within the field of social work. These new influences gave rise to approaches that were closely linked to the left-wing opposition to the regime.

During this period, there were a number of significant conferences and meetings. In 1967, at a conference held in the Levante, social workers from Catalonia, Valence and Majorca held a critical discussion regarding the goals and objectives of social work in Spain. In 1968, the first National Conference of Social Workers took place, a conference that has continued to be held every four years up until the present. During these first years, progressive professional groups gave speeches concerning the need to promote fundamental social change and asserted the need to play an active social role in support of all Spain's citizens. Methodologically, traditional social work methods were questioned and the development of an alternative 'Basic Method' was proposed.

Of all the discussions involving professional social workers, special mention should be made of the 1977 Pamplona Conference, which took place at an extremely important socio-political moment—when the first free democratic elections were held in Spain. This election, in which all the political parties participated, marked the beginning of the end for Franco's regime. This period was crucial for the development of modern social work practice in Spain, the key issues relating to this period are:

- A general acceptance of the 'Basic Method' which emphasises the importance of the environmental context of social work and an approach that offers insight into the surrounding reality of clients' lives and the need to transform clients' social environments.

- The debates concerning the ideological and political dimensions of social work and the commitment to promoting social change.

- The development of a model of social work aimed at the planning and implementation of social action (in the forms of both assistance and prevention) that is subject to the principle of respect for the self-determination of individuals, groups and communities.

- The attempts to improve the social status of social work and establish it as a discipline, based upon scientific methods.

These approaches to social work developed during the 1970s focused around the need to acknowledge the community as a key player in the political struggle. They gained broad acceptance particularly in the urban areas where the social problems brought about by industrialisation arose and where social groups opposing the dictatorship first emerged.

From 1980 until the present there have been continuing significant developments in social work. For example, in 1983, the professional status of social work was achieved through the adoption of a new system of qualifications. A newly created Diploma in Social Work was introduced and traditional social work schools were absorbed into university faculties—greatly enhancing the status of social work. In relation to the organizational structures of social work, following the introduction of democratic elections in all Spanish municipalities and city councils, departments of social work were established across the country. The main goal behind the establishment of these departments was to end the charitable system and to ensure that the entire population was in receipt of social benefits.

As stated by Sarasa, (1998), social work ideology in Spain has changed over time following the prevailing conditions in the country's socio-political evolution. Nonetheless, some principles have remained constant. At the end of the period of dictatorship two main models of social work co-existed, firstly an 'official' model, based on liberal humanitarian principles and secondly,

an 'unofficial' model which advocated social change and which was closely linked to political activism against the Franco regime. Today, social work is expected to contribute to the implementation and development of the democratic system in Spain, a system based on free elections but still far from possessing all of the attributes of a fully developed democracy. However, for many professionals there remains the inherent contradiction in social work which acts both to reproduce existing relations of class domination and seeks to realise the needs and social claims of the general population through the implementation of social change.

Arising from these developments, large numbers of well-qualified professionals are now employed by the Spanish Social Services Networks. However, there remains a lack of substantial evaluative surveys that have assessed the real impact of the changes that have occurred.

The relationship between social work and social services

The nature of the social services structure has had a great impact on the social work practice carried out in Spain. We would assert that the participation of social workers in the implementation of the public social services system has proved beneficial in lessening social disparities and has led to a service and benefit system which responds to the needs of the general population. However, to date there is a lack of critical evaluation of the contributions made by social workers to this process. Increasingly, there is a trend towards social work practice adopting a 'need/resource' approach, in which the social worker acts primarily as a gatekeeper to resources and benefits. We argue that this approach presents too simplistic a view of what social work actually involves, since this approach only defines the social work task as being to relieve hardship and suffering directly. Such an approach does not, for example, take into consideration preventative and community orientated work.

During the Sixth Conference of Social Workers, held in Oviedo in 1988, Amaya Ituarte pointed to the dangers resulting from the over-identification of social work with social services. She argued that such an over-identification might lead to the loss of the professional identity of social work and she provided the following definition of what should be the discipline of social work's main objective:

> *...to deal with any situation involving human beings needs or difficulties, either on an individual, group or community basis, which might prevent or make it difficult for them to normally develop their abilities and capacities regarding themselves and their social background or develop their social environment in such a way as to achieve social welfare.*
>
> (Ituarte, 1988: p 153)

According to data provided as part of the 1995 survey by the Catalan Social Workers Association, 68 per cent of the professionals interviewed argued that social workers' functions are not sufficiently clearly defined and further 77 per cent considered that social work practice is not appropriately established. Perhaps unsurprisingly, social workers directly dealing with clients were shown to have played little role in the definition of general social policies drawn or developed at senior levels of public administration. Nor has the participation process sufficiently involved target populations through consultation of local associations or social bodies.

The Catalan Social Service System

In order to more fully understand the relationship between the Spanish Constitution, the social services system and the role played by social workers within the country, this section refers to the development of those services in Catalonia, one of the main self-governing communities in Spain.

The 1979 Autonomous Government Statute Book conferred to the local governing authority, the *Generalitat de Catalunya*, exclusive competence to determine the social services and social care systems for the region. The Catalan social services system is thus defined as a co-ordinated set of services and benefits which are the responsibility of different public authorities and managed by public and private institutions. Social services interventions are carried out on the basis of a three-level structure aimed at:

1. The prevention of social problems.

2. The provision of support and care services to combat marginalisation.

3. The promotion of human welfare.

Since all these aims require the participation of citizens, the regional government seeks the active participation of all individuals, groups and public authorities involved in order to achieve an improvement in the quality of life. Primary legislation has been followed by specific regulations with priority given to fulfilling the following needs:

- To support and foster the welfare of the family and other alternative household units.

- To support and foster the welfare of children and youth.

- To support and foster the welfare of older people.

- To support and foster the welfare of physically and mentally disabled people.

- To prevent drug addiction and ensure social rehabilitation of drug addicts.

- To promote actions intended to prevent and eliminate any form of discrimination on the grounds of race, sex or any other pretext.

- To prevent crime and to provide social care to ensure the rehabilitation of offenders.

- To fight poverty and social exclusion.

Whilst the social services are available to all the population, they are targeted at particular individuals and groups who present with personal development or social integration problems and needs, and require specific social care and attention.

The organisational structure of the social services

The legal framework within which the social services operate comprises the following:

- 16. 1985 Act of Social Services.

- 8. 1987 Local Acts.

- 6. 1987 Municipality Regulations Act.

- 4. 1994 Act regulating the Public Authorities Management Decentralisation and Co-ordination of the Catalan Social Services System.

The following essential elements should also be mentioned:

- The foundation in 1982 of the ICASS (Catalan Institute for Social Services and Social Care) which merges all the different social care services previously depending on the Spanish Central Government.
- The law enacted in 1991 on Youth Protection and Wardship, which was subsequently modified by the 1995 Act and the 1996 Public General Act on Wardship.
- The 1987 Decree Regulating Social Services.
- The creation of the Social Welfare Department that is directly accountable to the Generalitat de Catalunya.
- The enactment of the Decree on Reinsertion Allowance (PIRMI) which has subsequently been enacted as a general law; the creation of the Interdepartmental Program between both the Social Welfare Department and the Labour Department of the Generalitat specifically aimed at population groups with low incomes and social integration problems.

The Catalan Social Services are organised according to two different assistance levels: 'Primary Attention Social Services' and 'Specialised Social Services'.

Primary Attention Social Services

'Primary Attention Social Services' are those services concerned with the first level of attention given to the population requiring social care and which mainly provides information, support and guidance. These services are intended to identify social risk situations and to subsequently direct clients to specialised services. Primary attention services are of a multi-purpose nature. They are directed at the entire community, have to deal with all sorts of social situations and conflicts, are intended to both promote and activate the social fabric and co-ordinate local social networks existing in Catalonia. They are based on a personal assistance scheme in which the clients, their families and their social situation are given special attention.

Services are provided by the UBASP (Primary Attention Social Services Units), social care units that are located in each neighbourhood or district. These units are equipped with interdisciplinary working teams consisting of social workers, youth workers and carers who co-operate with other professionals, according to the specific needs of each situation. These services depend directly on the local authorities of those municipalities consisting of at least 20,000 inhabitants or on regional councils of small municipalities. Those situations requiring specialised attention are referred to the various Specialised Social Services units or to those services involving other welfare services.

Specialised Social Services

'Specialised Social Services' provide detection, diagnosis, treatment, support and rehabilitation for individuals and groups with specific needs. These services include day centres, residential centres and support services.

- *Day centres*: these provide leisure activities and community support for individuals and groups as well as offering preventive interventions during daytime hours.
- *Residential care centres*: these are intended to replace the family environment either on a temporary or a permanent basis and are offered to individuals that cannot stay in their homes due to a variety of reasons. They include residential homes, attendance centres, hostels, residential centres, youth hostels and other residential accommodation schemes.
- *Supporting services*: these consist of complementary services to Primary Attention or other Specialised Services intended to facilitate families, provide access to education and employment for individuals and groups in situations of social exclusion or deprivation. They include adapted transportation schemes, custody services and social integration support schemes, etc. All these services are managed by socially or commercially oriented private and public institutions.

These differing levels of primary and specialised social care services are provided by multidisciplinary teams made up of social workers, youth workers, carers, psychologists etc. The team composition varies, depending on the different actions to be carried out and they often include volunteers who act as a social support workforce. The great complexity of most social problems faced by those services requires a multidisciplinary approach within the social services network and requires inter-agency and inter-professional co-ordination. However, the complexity involved in the development and full implementation of the Catalan Social Services System makes it very difficult for this co-operation to be successfully achieved. This is mainly due to political differences in the extent of the legal competence conferred between the public authorities involved both on an autonomous and a local basis, and the different criteria and approaches adopted by the various professionals participating in the project.

The professional organisation of social work

The professional organisation of social work in Spain has undergone a process parallel to the country's social and political changes during the last decades. Catalan social workers have organised themselves in the following manner. In 1958, the so-called *Asociación de Asistentas Sociales* (Female Community Workers Association), an institution linked to the Catholic Church. The association's rules set out the following aims, to:

- Foster a religious, moral, theoretical and practical enhancement of community workers.

- Promote an active co-operation between community workers.

- Preserve, achieve and improve community workers' rights.

These principles show the close connection between social work and the Catholic Church and exemplify that social work is conceived as being primarily a feminine profession. This association is governed by a board of directors whose president is proposed by the association members and who is submitted for approval to the diocese. On the board of directors there is also a diocesan clerical counsellor.

In 1964, the 'Association Act' was passed, which recognises the freedom of assembly, as stated in the *Fuero de los Españoles* (Spanish Common Law), if seeking lawful aims and being subject both to the 'Movement'

Fundamental Principles (the Movement being the one and only legal party ruling the country) and to the religious associations depending on the 'Concordato' (a Catholic Agreement) in force in Spain. This new act provided for the adoption of new association rules for a Community Workers' Association as a non-profit-making public organisation. An important step was therefore taken towards the creation of a strictly professionally oriented association. The primary aims and objectives of the association were to:

- Foster study and research activities on subjects related to social work.

- Promote and foster co-operation between social workers.

- Organise and participate in conferences and workshops focused on key issues concerning social work.

- Make known through specialised publications and other means the task and duties of social workers.

- Create a library specialising in social work.

The association had a board of directors whose members were elected for a three-year term from amongst and by the association members during their annual general meeting. There were also commissions appointed for specific working areas with elected representatives. In 1967, all the different Spanish Social Workers Associations finally merged into the FEDAAS (Spanish Federation of Social Workers). Of the 28 associations created between 1961 and 1968, 25 joined the FEDAAS, which from then on was appointed as the representative body of social workers. Two main issues dominated the work of the federation: the need to create a university degree of social work and the need to create a professional association for social workers.

Although there was a general law (2/1974 Act) governing professional associations, it was not until 1982 that a specific law was passed regulating the creation of 'Social Work Graduates and Social Workers Professional Associations' as corporations with legal personality and full capacity. The associations existing up to that moment became professional associations and membership became a requirement for professional practice and provided social workers with the same status enjoyed by other prestigious professional activities. In 1982, the General Council of Social Work Graduates and Social Workers Associations was created in Madrid and it pursued the initial co-ordination tasks carried out until then by the FEDAAS. In 1990, there were 37 professional associations in Spain and about 20,000 graduate social workers.

In general terms, the functions assigned to the Social Work Graduates and Social Workers Associations were the following:

- To organise the professional activity of its members in order to guarantee the observance of a professional code of ethics as well as the due respect to citizen's rights.

- To provide legal counselling to its members before public authorities and private institutions; to participate on conciliation acts or arbitration proceedings in those professional issues required by its members.

- To provide all the information required to integrate recently graduated members professionally.

- To provide general activities and services both related to social work or demanded by its members, such as counselling or training.

- To foster the co-operation between its members in order to prevent any unfair competence between them. To adopt measures to avoid professional intrusion.

- To regulate minimum working hours for private professional practice.

- To co-operate with and participate in Directing boards or consultative bodies regulating issues concerning the profession. To participate as jury members in competitive examinations for positions in the civil service in the different professional associations.

As the government assigned legislative competence to the self-governing communities, they acquired law-making powers concerning the creation of professional associations. In 1982, the Catalan Parliament passed a law regulating the activity of all the professional associations located in Catalonia and in 1983 further specific rules concerning those associations were enacted.

At the present time, the Catalan Social Workers Association (Collegi Oficial de Diplomats en Treball Social i Assistents Socials de Catalunya) has about 3,800 members. The headquarters are located in Barcelona and the association has four agencies in the other Catalan provinces (administrative divisions), namely in Lleida, Tarragona, Girona and Manresa. The directing board is elected every four years from amongst the candidates proposed by the association members. There are also several working teams dealing with specific professional issues as well as specialised committees appointed by the Directing Board. The association provides a large range of activities and services intended to help its members professional practice including the publication of a magazine specialising in social work entitled *RTS-Revista de Treball Social*, a quarterly publication well-known to most Spanish and Latin-American social workers.

The association has representatives in those bodies of the Catalonian Autonomous Government and in Barcelona's City Council working on social welfare. The association participates in the design of the Barcelona Social Services Integral Plan as well as in the Social Welfare City Council and other social welfare councils and other community associations of Barcelona. Close co-operation is also maintained and joint activities are organised with other related professional bodies such as the Catalan Psychologists Association, the Specialised Educators Association or the Caregivers Association, etc.

The professional code of ethics in social work

Since social work is a professional practice which involves working with human beings, it has a commitment to certain ethical principles that seek to enhance the welfare of individuals, groups and communities and to ensure their full development and rights to freedom. Furthermore, social work is also committed to fight for the adoption of social policies fostering the services and resources required to reach these goals. Accordingly, social work requires a code of ethics which should be adopted by all its members and which should subsequently evolve in reflecting society's norms and values. The need to reach an agreement on this issue and to draw up a code of ethics is undoubtedly crucial to its claim to professional status.

The interest shown by the Catalan Social Workers Association on this issue lead to the adoption in 1989 of a Code of Ethics for Social Workers, the first code of ethics ever published in Spain for social workers This has become a benchmark for the rest of the country's social workers. This code was written by the Ethics Consulting Board of the Social Workers Association, an advisory team consisting of more than 40 specialised professionals from different domains related to social work practice and to legal advice. The main aim of the code of ethics is to provide general criteria for the interpretation of ethical issues in professional practice with regard to both the personal behaviour of social workers and their relationship with their clients, other professionals and institutions. The code is based on the International Bill of Human Rights, the Spanish Constitution principles advocating for a democratic and fairer society, and the 1985 Social Services Act in Catalonia. The code is an attempt to further the aim of securing citizens' access to social services and benefits, and the free and full promotion of personal and community development. The main principles stated are that:

- Every human being is unique, irrespective of origin, belief and social position.

- Every individual, group and community is entitled to participate in and look for the most appropriate means to solve its problems and organise its social life.

- Social workers have a duty to use their knowledge and experience to carry out the professional tasks demanded of them and to use the resources at hand fairly without discriminating against anybody.

The code is divided into five sections:

- The obligations to the clients.

- The obligations to the employer.

- Social workers obligations to professional practice.

- The obligations to colleagues.

- The obligations to society.

The code's wording reflects the evolution and traditions of social work in Spain.

Following the development of this code, the Professional School of Catalonia formed a Council of Ethics, comprising social workers of considerable professional experience, for the purpose of considering the principles outlined by the code and the ethical dilemmas that arise in practice for both professionals and institutions.

Dimensions of Social Work

The education of social workers

Social work education was introduced into the university sector in 1981. In this year, education programmes on social work were incorporated in the recently created *Escuelas Universitarias de Trabajo Social* (Social Work Colleges) which conferred bachelors degrees in social work. The 1983 Decree integrated the existing Social Work Schools within the Central Public University structure. These schools thus became Social Work Colleges. The education programme provided in those colleges is based on a three year BA. Course aims are achieved by means of a division of the curriculum into different aspects of knowledge:

- *Social sciences*: this aspect provides the analytical tools enabling an insight for social work from different social sciences such as sociology, psychology, anthropology, economics, social history, etc.

- *Social work, social services and social policy*: this aspect provides the theoretical and conceptual framework of social work as well as the methodology and specific techniques aimed at social intervention directed to individuals, groups, institutions and communities.

- *Practicum*: this aspect provides for the integration of theory and practice. Fieldwork experience is compulsory and consists of a practical stage conducted by professionals and directly monitored by the college. This professional practice enables the students to learn about the relationship between social workers and clients and to acquire those specific abilities and knowledge required for a serious professional practice.

The main principle underlying this structure is to provide social workers with some key tools aimed at combining a theoretical and a practical education as well as preparing future social workers for multidisciplinary teamwork.

In 1993 and 1994 the LRU (University Reform Act) required a review of university college's programmes thus allowing for a review of the programmes' content. At the present time, a credit accumulation system has enabled the provision of more flexible and appropriate programmes adapted to every university centre and their particular orientations and approaches to the social sciences, enabling students access to a wider choice of studies. Recently, most colleges have reorganised their programmes in order to allow for a greater debate on the profession's main aims and to adapt future social workers' education to social changes, such as the reshaping of the welfare system and the current transformation of the labour market. It is considered necessary for the future that social workers be provided with an education that equips them for developing new projects and participating in new professional environments and domains.

Currently, the main challenges faced by social work education are:

- Professionals have to be able to define and assume a professional profile relevant to a continuously changing social environment, to continuously update and upgrade their skills and to deal with new demands and working conditions beyond the current requirements public authorities put on them.

- On methodological considerations, social workers education has to be aimed at acquiring the latest skills, techniques and research methods relevant to social work.

- Education programmes have to be interdisciplinary in order to allow for the integration of the different disciplines, knowledge bases and analytic frameworks adopted by a range of professions allied to social work.

- Educators have to consider and develop the relationship between social work and other disciplines and the identification and integration of the specific contents for courses that incorporate multidisciplinary approaches and new educational techniques.

- Education programs have to balance compulsory and optional subjects in order to enable the students to create their own academic curriculum relevant to their specific possibilities, abilities and preferences.

- Programs need to participate in Socrates-Erasmus European projects that address European approaches to social work, co-ordinate their content, promote mobility and exchanges between students and teachers and provide a common forum for debate on European, global and in particular Latin American approaches to practice.

- Social Work Colleges have to promote close co-operation with professionals and provide a space for debate as well as a forum for professional associations and other social work related associations.

- Social Work Colleges need to engage in wider debates on the nature and construction of 'social reality' and social dynamics with representative bodies of public administration departments and participate in discussion forums on social policies and welfare benefits.

Finally, the country's progression towards the establishment of a university degree on social work should be noted. The need to achieve a higher education degree became apparent in 1968 on the occasion of the first Social Worker's Spanish Conference and has been repeatedly mentioned in the subsequent conferences. The 1970 General Education Act did not include the acknowledgement of the university degree on social work, a decision that gave rise to protests and a strong political activity such as the students sit-in in the Social Work Schools, the social worker's strike and a strong pressure exerted by schools, associations and the FEDASS itself on the ministries as well as full media coverage of the protests. In 1998, the General Council of the Social Workers Spanish Associations drew up a detailed report on the subject which argued the need to a provide social workers with a higher education degree; however its request for such a degree, submitted to the Spanish University Council, was refused.

Research in social work

In considering both the development, and the current situation of social work in Spain, some important research and literature which has been influential requires particular mention. Hence, between 1969 and 1970, the National Institute of Applied Sociology of Madrid, carried out a nationwide survey entitled *Situación del Servicio Social en España*, reporting the actual state of social services in Spain. This study employed opinion poll techniques and was directed to all the professionals involved in social work at that time. The findings are of less significance now, given the major changes in social work practice and the social and political environment in modern Spain. However, the fact that such a survey was conducted, well illustrates the development of a more scientific approach to social work.

Another early but highly significant piece of research was the 1976 survey of Catalonian social workers by Estruch and Güell, *Sociología de una profesión. Los asistentes sociales* (Sociology of a profession: social wokers). This study attempted to understand and appraise the profession and the public of the true nature of the presumed crisis of social work on the basis of data provided by social workers themselves. This survey provides some insight into those elements that contribute to the enhancement of social work practice, and for the development of appropriate training of future social workers. Amongst the main reasons given by the social workers interviewed that might account for the professional crisis within the sector, the authors highlight the significance of both a general social crisis surrounding the nature of social work practice, as well as the social structures in which social workers are engaged and involved. The conclusions in this report corroborate the initial hypothesis of the authors regarding the existence of crisis concerning the profession of social work. For them, social work in Spain remained subject to a dominant religious ideology. The report argues powerfully for the need to reconstruct professional knowledge and practice from the daily experience of ordinary life rather than remain constrained by an ideology couched within reified religious notions, inflated pretensions and 'myths' concerning the role of social work and its capacity to effect change.

More recently, the work of de Las Heras and Cortajerena (1985) entitled *Introducción al Bienestar Social* (Introduction to Social Welfare) provides a commentary on the difficulties faced by social workers in their professional practice.

In particular this study highlights the lack of a well-defined professional profile for social work, the lack of acknowledgement and recognition of the existence of a qualifying education programme for social workers, a high unemployment rate, professional intrusion and the profession's increasing feminisation, as important factors in the construction of current social work practice. Work by Llovet and Usieto, (1990), *Los Trabajadores sociales. De la crisis de identidad a la profesionalización*, (Social Workers: The Path from Identity Crisis to Professional Status), provides a review of the development of social work in Spain and is based on research focused on social workers from Madrid. One of their main conclusions is that a significant step has been made towards achieving 'greater professional status' for social workers due to both the official recognition of a university degree as well as through an increasing number of qualified professionals joining the labour market. Furthermore, it provides the result of the implementation and strengthening of a welfare system in general which has helped social workers access public and political positions. However, this study does not confirm whether these developments have been directly beneficial to the population, as the research was not intended to appraise the quality of the services provided. The report also notes that the increasing professional status of social work can be directly related to a general trend followed by most professional activities. However, in a somewhat contradictory vein the report identifies the existence of a substantial decrease in social workers' self-esteem and self-satisfaction regarding their own professional practice. The report concludes that social work is faced with the challenge of developing and evolving without falling into an excessive simplicity; and formulating its own theoretical principles and a systematic approach to its practice. Finally, mention should be made of the survey *Els Diplomats en Treball Social i Assistents Socials de Catalunya*, (Social Work Graduates and Community Workers in Catalonia), published by the Catalan Social Workers Association and directed by a PROGRESS (a reasearch and service agency) team in 1997. This study analyses the professional profile, status and prospects of social workers in Catalonia, and although focused on the professional situation in this area, the survey provides information relevant to understanding the process of the development of the profession in the country as a whole. The study provided information on the contribution of the profession to the development of current welfare and social protection system. At the time of writing, 71 per cent of professionals had at one time worked in the public service system. Some 60 per cent of social workers were currently working in 'primary attention services' in the social or health services, the remaining 40 per cent were working in public or private 'specialised services'.

Social work as a unique discipline

Diverse definitions of social work can be found in the professional literature. The General Council of Official Schools of Graduates in Social Work and Social Assistants in Madrid offers the following definition:

> *Social work can be considered as a discipline that relates to a conception of the human being as one which is in permanent interaction with its environment, and having as its specific object human relationships, both between individuals and between individuals and their social environment.*
>
> (Unpublished document)

A definition of social work adopted by the programme of the University School of Social Work-ICESB-University Ramon School of Social Work (Escola Universitaria de Treball Social) is as follows:

> *Social work collaborates and participates in modifications to the social conditions which obstruct the global development of the individual and communities; it facilitates the population in becoming critically aware in order to realise the potential of individuals and communities, and it is also present in the formulation of social policies and in programmes of prevention.*
>
> (Unpublished document)

Rossell, at the 1993 Seminar of the European Regional Group of the International Association of Social Work Schools, argues that there is a growing need to achieve a greater conceptualisation of social work, as a discipline that combines theoretical knowledge with

systematic practice and to transcend the traditional divisions in professional practice. While Palmade, has defined social work as:

> *...a specific set of knowledge principles with specific characteristics deriving from the education, training, mechanisms, methods and subjects involved.*
>
> (Leal and Roig, 1990: p 10)

We consider this definition of social work provides an open approach, which allows for the integration of different theories from the social sciences as well as a variety of intervention methods and methodological tools that can be applied to social work practice. We advocate for an open and flexible approach, involving a wide range of sciences and fields of knowledge, as social work uses different working methods, theoretical and ideological concepts to interpret the social reality.

In Spain, as in other countries, there is a tendency to emphasise the practice rather than the theories of social work as well as a reluctance to develop a systematic theoretical framework for intervention or establish a specific knowledge base for the discipline/profession that can be applied within an interdisciplinary approach to social problems. The debate in Spain on the lack of functions that are specific to the profession has been widely discussed in recent publications and conferences. For example Zamanillo (1992: 59) has argued that:

> *...by restricting social work to mere practice, a simplistic view of the subject has increasingly gained acceptance which, due to its lack of openness, is not producing the knowledge required for a real interdisciplinary approach.*   (Zamanillo, 1992: p 59)

Given the complexity of the contexts and problems encountered by social workers a simplistic approach to defining its function is inappropriate.

Of course some aspects of practice are far more established than others, such as casework, family work, group work, and there have been a number of systematic approaches developed. However, there remains a lack of published evaluations of these projects. In Catalonia, a debate has recently emerged on the need to redefine community work. During the last few years and in most professional sectors this kind of work has been neglected and social workers have increasingly been considered as primarily managers of the social services system resources and benefits, in particular at the first level (Primary Attention Services). Their withdrawal from community work has entailed the involvement of other professionals, namely education social workers and youth workers, who have taken on the work within communities.

The Social Workers Association Study (Col.legi, 1997), has suggested some future tendencies to be addressed by social work in Catalonia:

The scope of social concern: The social protection system will be accessed by a population from a much wider social base, with new demands and problems. This will require:

- The need to cope with increased marginalisation and social exclusion.
- The development of new social policies to promote integration.
- The development and the improvement of skills relevant to new working practices.

An increase in demand for individual support: This increase in demand will coincide with limits to the available resources and calls for greater efficiency. This will require:

- Establishing priorities among client groups.
- Improvements in the instruments of analysis and diagnosis in the process of assessment of need and justifications of their validity and use.
- Mobilisation of individual and community potential in order to respond to increased needs and diminishing resources as the family alone will be unable to support the tensions within the social protection system.
- To consider individual and family intervention within the context of the wider social environment.

Improvements in the quality of the interventions: social work will have to integrate new methodologies and new technologies in its work. On the one hand the social worker will be required to specialise and on the other to forge more interconnections and networks.

Evaluation of effectiveness: This represents a fundamental aspect of the current situation. The increase in the demand and decrease in levels of resources necessitates selection based upon the results obtained from amongst competing service options.

Investigation: The importance of establishing psycho-social indicators in the identification and assessment of social needs and predictions of future demands.

Promotion: The increase in demand for individualised support will necessitate the redefinition of the need for social work intervention at the primary and community levels.

Prevention: Social workers will need to be involved in the early detection of new social problems and conflicts and the development of appropriate preventive programs.

Social work and the crisis of the welfare state

The so-called 'welfare state crisis', resulting from the global economic conditions affecting all European countries and which has led to a redefinition of public policies relating to social protection, has struck at a very young and very weak Spanish welfare state. The first Social Services Act in Spain was issued in 1984, in contrast to most European countries, which have more established welfare systems and may be better able to face the 'welfare state crisis'. In general terms, there is an increasing concern regarding budget cuts, resulting in a weaker role played by governments in ensuring social protection, the switch from tax-funded services to private services and the lack of a guarantee of citizenship rights to basic social benefits.

In Catalonia, the developing welfare system is still insufficient to meet the growing demand and is faced by a number of obstacles arising from both the number of different authorities involved, such as state-level and self-governing local public authorities, city councils, regional public authorities, etc., and also the political orientations of the governing majority during each period of office. These difficulties have led to a lack of general planning and deficiencies in co-ordination between the institutional and professional dimensions of the social services network. Within this context, social workers act as an interface between the public administration and the increasing demands of a growing population. The welfare system is also subject to large population changes. These include a substantial ageing of the Spanish population, great changes in the family structure, new migratory movements, a great shift in the role of women in society, deep transformations in the labour market leading to high unemployment rates, etc. All of these factors are leading to new needs and an increase in demand for social services.

On the one hand, the phenomena of social exclusion and deprivation arising all over Europe, together with a precarious labour market, budgetary cuts and pressure exerted by privatisation and the development of a welfare 'market' has increasingly limited the role of social work to that of relieving or partially meeting service users' needs. On the other hand, the general agenda for social services increasingly emphasises the need to: integrate programmes; work with existing social networks; achieve efficient service provision; to evaluate the results of the interventions undertaken; to come closer to the citizens and also to question free access to the services provided and the contribution required of the citizens to cover costs of services. Hence, there is a widening gap between the social services agenda and debates within the practice of social work, particularly around the role of preventive and community-based approaches that impact on social structures, processes and change. Increasingly, there is a conflict over the definitions of the function of social workers within the public social services system and a questioning of what constitutes social work practice as opposed to those of other professions dealing with social issues such as education advisors, youth workers and psychologists.

In a recent study published by the Catalan Social Workers Association (Col.legi, 1997), the social workers interviewed proposed that the main changes that social protection might undergo in the future were as follows:

- A substantial increase in the number of clients presenting different and divergent needs.

- A growing demand from new groups, in particular unemployed people, requiring new social and economic solutions.

- A substantial decrease in the level of

social benefits provided; a process that will entail the use of new methods of analysis and reliable documentation.

- An increase in the number and importance of private management schemes, leading to a change in employment contracts. As a result, public authorities will reduce, and private institutions will increase, the number of staff that they employ.

- An increase in primary attention and home care services.

If these predictions about the future are correct, they will directly influence social work practice.

Conclusions

The rapid changes that are occurring within the social and professional environments and the practice and educational contexts of social work, both separately and collectively, present a series of challenges that need to be addressed. In particular, we would highlight the following areas of change:

- The institutional context, i.e. the agencies and services from within which or on whose authority professional practice occurs;

- The object of social work attention, and more directly the clientele of social work interventions, as are the particular needs and problems they present;

- The methodology and models that underpin interventions in the context of interdisciplinary working practices with individuals, families, institutions and communities;

- Approaches to and perspectives for the analysis of complex social relationships and systems, which are broadening and crossing traditional disciplinary boundaries;

- The development, reformulation and introduction of new techniques, skills and models for intervention.

In short, almost every aspect and dimension in the field of social work is subject to evaluation, modification and revision, within a climate that also demands 'scientific evidence' to justify and substantiate the method, action and outcomes of professional interventions. Similarly, the theory-practice divide or dilemma at the centre of social work continues to place a strain on the relationships between academics and practitioners as they struggle to reach an agreement over fundamental questions as to what properly constitutes the purpose, form, legitimacy and capacity of social work.

Questions for Further Consideration

- Arising from its particular history, and as a relatively new democratic state, one of the legitimate purposes of social work in Spain is to contribute to the implementation and development of the democratic system. This in turn allows for a continued emphasis upon developing and maintaining preventive and community-based approaches that impact on social structures, processes and change. On what grounds, if any, can social work in your country legitimise preventative and community oriented activity?

- In Spain, the constitution confers the right to the self-governing communities (*Comunidades Autónomas*) to legislate for social services. In practice, this leads to social workers having to operate within a complex network of different authorities (state-level and self-governing local public authorities, city councils, regional public authorities, etc.) as well as being subject to the changing political orientations of the governing majority during each period of office. How does the balance between central direction and regional autonomy impact on social work in your country?

- Evaluation of the effectiveness of social work interventions is of fundamental concern in Spain. However, an increase in demand and a decrease in the level of available resources has necessitated that there is selection from amongst competing service options. By what criteria are different service options selected and evaluated in your country?

Chapter Nine

Social Work Practice in the United Kingdom

Adrian Adams and Steven Shardlow

Introduction

The United Kingdom (UK) consists of the countries of England, Northern Ireland, Scotland and Wales and the smaller Crown dependencies such as the Channel Islands. Each of these countries has different organisational and legal systems, different structures and different laws relating to health and social welfare, although there are many similarities between the core principles that underpin health and welfare services in these countries. It is likely that in the future the differences between each of these countries, in respect of health and welfare, will become more pronounced as the effects of greater devolution of powers to the separate legislatures in each of them, except England, which does not posses a legislature distinct from the legislature for the UK, are felt. This chapter concentrates upon the development of health and welfare in England as the largest country within the UK.

Health and welfare services in England are currently undergoing substantial changes. The nature of these changes constitute a radical re-formulation of the relationship between the state, the individual, the family and communities wherein the balance of responsibility for ensuring social security is shifting away from the state towards the citizen. This shift of responsibility emanates from the belief that the cost of health and social welfare has become prohibitive and as such represents an ideological break with the post-war concept of a welfare state. Collective responsibility for society's vulnerable members has been replaced by a return to liberal values and social policies in a mixed economy approach. Here, the 'mixed economy of welfare' has become common shorthand to describe a mixture of state, private, voluntary and informal provision of care for vulnerable individuals, whereby the role and function of state institutions becomes one of enabling and promoting rather than providing for the needs of the population.

This revised, residual role of the state has given rise to not only a re-structuring of institutions and agencies, which are now required to operate as assessors and purchasers of care working to pre-determined cash limits within marketed oriented principles, but also to a re-consideration, considerable debate and uncertainty as to the function, role and value of professionals working in the fields of social work, care and welfare within both state and independent sector agencies.

In this examination of the role and status of social work practitioners in England, we will trace how definitions as to what constitutes the essential purpose, nature and characteristics of social work practice have been and are currently being reconstructed from its historical origins and traditions through to current practice issues and concerns. In seeking to understand both how social work has and continues to be understood, defined and constructed over time, four dimensions will be considered.

1. The historical development of social services and the place of social work practice within the wider context of welfare policy.

2. The development and occupational status of professional social work in England in the context of its relationship to the state, and the legislative and organisational framework that authorises its practice.

3. The educational basis of the profession and its claim to conferring expert status to social work practitioners.

4. The moral or ethical principles that are claimed to underpin the profession.

An Historical Overview of Social Welfare and Social Work in England

The origins of welfare policy and legislation in England

The origins of the English welfare system can be argued as deriving from, and indeed still refer to, the English Poor Laws of the fourteenth century. The primary functions of the 1388 Poor Law Act were related to the fixing of wages and relief of poverty, to impose restrictions over the mobility of labour, to maintain social order and distinguish between the able-bodied poor and criminal classes. The 1601 Poor Law Act extended this process of classification and subsequent treatment of different classes of persons by providing a system that would ensure:

- correction for the idle and criminal classes

- work for the able-bodied poor

- relief for the impotent poor (the aged, chronic sick, blind and lunatic)

Poor Law relief took the form of either indoor relief in the poor house, overseen by employees of local parish relieving officers, or outdoor relief in the form of pensions, dole or payment in kind.

The 1834 Poor Law Report and Poor Law Amendment Act re-affirmed the principles of 'less eligibility' and the 'workhouse test', that is, the essential characteristics of both relief and deterrence that have endured within the English welfare system. These principles are still embodied as the care and control functions within social work practice.

Industrialisation during the nineteenth century, urban growth and the resulting concerns over housing conditions and public health, provided the impetus for the next major development in welfare policies. The population in England quadrupled between 1800 and 1900. The cholera epidemics of 1831, 1848, 1854 and 1866 led to over 22,000 deaths, although over 50,000 deaths were recorded annually from generalised domestic fevers like typhus, TB, measles, diarrhoea, scarlet fever and smallpox, (Kay, 1832).

The link between unsanitary conditions, poverty and disease and residential zoning in industrial cities, along with the competition and political/social fusion of the aristocracy and middle classes, coupled with the enfranchisement of the urban working class in 1867, led to a massive increase in public health measures, and industrial and education legislation.

However, the nineteenth century reforms also gave rise to technical, economic and ideological concerns that are still evident today, such as who pays for and who benefits from the welfare system, and how can individual rights and liberties be reconciled with collective benefits and civil responsibilities?

The nineteenth century ideological positions emerging from the tensions between the competing principles and interests in the political economy are all still central to current popular and political debates over welfare. These included the regulation of society through government by expertise, problem solving by instrumental reason and public administration, the idea of the reinstitution of the natural order denied to the masses through private individual ownership, utilitarianism and the role of central and local government.

Central to the role and function of social work's position and function within these debates was the emergence during the nineteenth century, (1869), of the Charity Organisation Society, whose purpose was to ensure that the provision of welfare also provided for the moral improvement of the poor through the application of social case work, which called for a rigorous inquiry into the nature of the problem of applicants and their families and the establishment of deserving and undeserving categories of persons.

By the end of the nineteenth century the principles of the 1834 Poor Law Amendment Act had established an English welfare regime that operated a centralised system that combined both relief and punitive treatment of paupers. A system linked to a network of philanthropy and charity aimed at improving the circumstances of the deserving poor which had been considerably eroded. Social surveys on the condition of the poor had led to calls for improvements in housing, medical services, care of children and working conditions, and these in turn had led to the implementation of a wide range of social policies. The emerging middle, commercial and professional classes, and the enfranchisement of the working classes, had created tensions and alliances within and between the dominant Liberal and

Conservative political parties in both central and local government.

These factors, in combination, led to the establishment of a Royal Commission on the Poor Law (1905), which reported in 1909. The Majority Report advised against the removal of the Poor Law, whereas the Minority Report advised on the break up of the Poor Law and its replacement with an administrative structure based on the idea of prevention through the provision of a prescriptive medical service outside of the Poor Law.

The landslide victory of the Liberal Party in 1906, produced a House of Commons that included: 401 Liberal, 157 Conservative, 82 Irish National, 24 Lib-Labs and 29 Labour members. This combination led to a raft of social policy legislation focused primarily upon children, the aged and the temporarily unemployed. The Liberal Government, 1906–22, introduced legislation based upon the principle of social insurance (National Insurance Act, 1911) in respect of sickness benefit and medical treatment and introduced labour exchanges (1909). The possibility of a welfare regime that breached the Poor Law principles of separating out the poor into two distinct categories, that intervened in the relationship between capital and labour and that operated outside of the Poor Law was established. However, in spite of the virtual erosion of the Poor Law, welfare services remained accessed based on selectivity and arbitrary classifications into the first half of the 20th century.

The foundation of the welfare state in the United Kingdom

Continuing concerns over the selectivity of welfare policy, the inter-war boom and recession and the election of the short lived Labour government, (1929–31), led the National Government of 1933–40 to have developed a limited range of socio-economic policies and legislation that could, in principle, be co-ordinated and administered on a universal and comprehensive basis. However, in the popular imagination and scholarly analysis the primary foundations of the welfare state are located in the Second World War.

The impact of factors arising from the Second World War, especially the shared experiences by all sectors of the population such as civilian bombing, rationing, evacuation, the extension and provision of services to all, with free milk for nursing mothers and under fives, state nurseries for working mothers, the emergency medical service and so on, led to the creation of a social climate and established social attitudes and expectations of a better and more just society with welfare provision for all. These aspirations found public expression in the Beveridge Report, (1942), which identified five 'Giants' that plagued society: illness, ignorance, disease, squalor and want. To combat these 'giants' the report proposed the creation of a universal state system of welfare 'from cradle to grave' based on a social insurance scheme. This report established the four principles upon which the system would rest:

- social insurance and assistance
- the provision of family allowances
- the creation of a comprehensive national health service
- the enactment of policies to maintain full employment

The system would be implemented through a social insurance scheme based on a single weekly flat rate contribution to provide for basic sickness, medical, unemployment, widows, orphans, old age, maternity, industrial injury and funeral benefits. Local authorities would be responsible for health and welfare in respect of vaccinations and immunisation, maternity and child care, domestic help, health visiting, home nursing, ambulances and residential accommodation of the destitute.

Following the end of the war and the landslide victory of Labour in 1945, and in spite of resistance from such bodies as the British Medical Association (BMA), legislation was passed to enact Beveridge's plan during the period of Labour government from 1945–51. The range of legislation passed to deal with the five 'giants' included:

- The National Insurance Act, (1946), created the mechanisms to collect social insurance contributions and provided benefits for employed persons, self-employed persons, non-employed persons, maternity benefits, unemployment and sickness benefits, guardian's allowance, retirement pensions, widow's benefits, death grant, industrial injury benefit, disability benefit, and family allowance.

- The National Assistance Act, (1948), providing scales of assistance in respect of: needs and rent and local authority provision of accommodation on the grounds of age and infirmity.
- The National Health Service Act, (1946), giving responsibility to a Minister for Health for the creations of a comprehensive service to include:
  1. Physical and mental health: prevention, diagnosis and treatment of disease.
  2. Hospital and specialist provision— regional boards, hospital management committees, general practice, dental, pharmaceutical and ophthalmic, executive councils.
  3. Local authority health services—health centres, midwifery, health visiting, home nursing, vaccination, ambulances, prevention and after-care, domestic help, and mental health.
- The 1948 Children Act provided a general responsibility for: the care of children deprived of a normal home life, children's committees, boarding out and reception into care.
- The 1944 Education Act provided for: local education authorities, primary, secondary and higher education relating to attendance, special schools, boarding schools, health service, school milk and meals, and transport.
- The 1948 Criminal Justice Act: young offenders, probation service.

In addition to these major pieces of legislation, the foundations were laid for the creation of 'full employment' by the adoption of Keynsian economic policies centred on demand management. These policies attracted cross party support, later to be known as 'Butskellism', and led to a period of unprecedented economic growth coupled with high levels of employment.

A variety of other significant acts of parliament passed by the Conservative governments of 1951–63 consolidated the construction of the welfare state:

- The 1958–64 Adoption Acts, and the 1963 Children and Young Persons Act providing: advice, guidance and assistance to promote to promote the welfare of children—diminish the need for reception into care or come before a juvenile court;
- The 1944 and 1958 Disabled Persons (Employment) Act;
- The 1959 Mental Health Act that defined: mental illness and subnormality, informal and compulsory admissions, discharge of patients and community care under guardianship, tribunals, registration of homes, local authority provision (welfare officers), special hospitals and management of property and affairs;
- The 1963 Nursing Homes Act—regulation of nursing homes;
- The 1957 and 1961 Housing Acts providing for: central government grants to local authorities for house/slum clearance, demolition, construction and loans for purchase, improvements, sale or lease, housing associations;
- The 1958 Local Government Act provided a general grant for relevant expenditure.

Within a period of 15 years following the Second World War, a welfare state system had been established across the UK based upon the principles and assumptions of welfare outlined by Beveridge and economic growth and stability proposed by Keynes. The first twenty-five years of the welfare state from 1945 until approximately 1970 resulted in the creation of services used and valued by the majority of the profession. Social work played a modest part in the provision of services and had little sense of professional identity, consisting as it did of a variety of specialist activities provided by distinct occupational groups such as child care officers, mental welfare officers and hospital almoners. This situation was soon to be rectified. The influence of an American conceptualisation of social work practice pervaded. This conceptualisation operated through individualistic models of social work, grounded in Freudian psychology, with the result that social workers often paid too little attention to the sociological causes and solutions of their clients' problems.

Universalism and genericism: Seebohm and the creation of social services departments

One omission from the framework of the welfare state within England was the lack of provision for a unified and generic form of personal social services. In the mid 1960s, this view received first public recognition in official publications such as:

- *The Child, The Family and The Young Offender (1965)*, which reflected government awareness of growing public concern at the increase in officially recorded juvenile delinquency rates and the related belief in the importance of preventing 'family breakdown', (HMSO, 1965).

- *Social Work and the Community (1966)*, suggested that under ideal conditions social problems could be solved by the individuals, who were involved, themselves, (HMSO, 1966).

However, it was not until the publication of the Seebohm Report, (HMSO, 1968), that the problems for the provision of welfare due to a fragmented organisational structure for social work were fully recognised and documented. The conclusions of the Seebohm Report recommended a unified approach to the provision of personal social services via the creation of a single social services department within each local authority. The purpose of this authority would be to ensure more effective provision of personal social services in relation to meeting consumers need. The Report suggested that there was a relationship between the effective meeting of social need and the particular forms of administrative structure. In addition, the report identified the existing shortcomings in services as inadequacies in the amount, range and quality of provision and poor co-ordination and difficulties in access to services by clients. The report identified the causes of the shortcomings as a lack of resources, inadequate knowledge and divided responsibility. It concluded that there was a case for organisational change:

> The need for a more unified provision of personal social services has been made plain by growing knowledge and experience. There is a realisation that it is essential to look beyond the immediate symptoms of social distress to the underlying problems. These frequently prove to be complicated and the outcome of a variety of influences. In many cases people who need help cannot be treated effectively unless this is recognised. Their difficulties do not arise in a social vacuum; they are, have been, or need to be involved in a network of social relationships, in social situations. The family and the community are seen as the contexts in which problems arise and in which most of them have to be resolved or contained.
>
> (HMSO, 1968: p 44)

The analysis and arguments propounded within the report generated not only proposals for a new organisational structure but also for a new and different role for social work within society. As Seed has identified, the case for a re-organisation of social work was made within the context of an expanding notion of what constituted the concerns of social work interventions and in particular the assumption that responses to social need could be best formulated through particular forms of organisation, (Seed, 1973).

Hence, the Seebohm Report made the case that the most important aspect of the personal social services is social care in the community, therefore implying that 'field' social work is the essential instrument for ensuring its provision. In so doing, the report defined the shape of social care for at least a dozen years. The subsequent establishment of generic local authority social services departments, through the Local Authority Social Services Act, (1970), provided the organisational framework and rationale for social work within the English welfare state model. The notion of the generalist social worker, not necessarily intended in the Seebohm Report, rather than a generalist team, was seized upon and put into practice by the newly created departments. In theory, all social workers were required to have the ability to work with all types of social problem and with all types of people. In practice, many social workers struggled, as they were required to practice in areas where they felt themselves to be lacking in competence through insufficient knowledge, inadequate experience or irrelevant skills.

The Seebohm Report was highly significant in many ways. Not just for the creation of new organisational structures that profoundly affected the delivery of social work or the creation of a new and more broadly based role for social work in relation to society—as if these were not enough. The report also identified explicit principles that were not then current and which have now become so widely accepted that they have become part of the fabric of social work. For example, the first few pages of the report state:

> *We say that this service must be both accessible and acceptable to those in need. We feel this is a very important part of the structure. To be accessible it must be easily located, easily identifiable; and by acceptable we mean it must not be in a forbidding building, but somewhere where people will be encouraged to go, where they can have all the facilities that are required to deal with people in need, where there can be a warm reception, and a place where children can be looked after. It must fit those two main requirements—accessibility and acceptability.*
> (HMSO, 1968: p 9)

The report begins to discuss the need for non-stigmatising services that can be understood and are geographically available to those who need them. Consequently, the report represents the beginnings of making social services responsive to those who use them a core tenet of subsequent good practice. The report and subsequent reorganisation paved the way for many experiments in the provision of social work, for example through 'intake and long term teams' or through 'neighbourhood' or 'locally based forms' of social work practice. Just as ideas contained in the report enabled the formation of a professional body for social work, (the British Association of Social Workers, known as BASW), which, during the 1970s wrestled with notions of its own professional identity as can be seen in the debates about the adoption of a code of ethics for social work, (see Bamford, 1990: pp 18–41). In helping to define social work both in organisational and professional dimensions, the report also laid the foundations for the radical critiques of current forms of social work practice that developed around ethnicity, gender, age, sexual orientation and so on.

Transformation of the English welfare state

The centralisation of the personal social services through local government structures and the mature role of social work emerged relatively late within the English welfare state

system. With the adoption of the 'new right ideologies', following the election of the Conservative government in 1979, the construction of social work became an early victim of the shift from a welfare state to a 'mixed economy of welfare' that now characterises English welfare services. However, the questioning of the role and value of social work-based practice and services had already started prior to the introduction of the new approach.

During this time, the volume of work that fell to departments increased markedly. This was a result of increasing public expectations, partly because the new departments sought to explore unmet needs, and partly because new legislation laid additional duties on local authorities.

> *Some of the new tasks they were expected to perform, like arranging provision of a stair-lift in the home of a handicapped person, hardly seemed to be formal social work, but often required specialised knowledge they did not possess. All in all, it is no wonder that social workers, clients and the public have been puzzled at times about the roles and tasks of social workers and questioned their ability to perform them all adequately when they were described.*
> (National Institute for Social Work, 1982: p 10)

The emergence of a residual or mixed economy model of welfare provided a radical re-conceptualisation of the role and responsibilities of the state in relation to health and social welfare. This approach, in line with general government, (Thatcherite), policies was directed at the production of wealth, that is, low taxation and low inflation, through the privatisation and the introduction of competition and the conversion from state to private production of welfare, and the reduction of subsidies to consumers. It proposed the development of a welfare market as opposed to a welfare state, primarily through a shift in the role of local authority social service departments from one of provider to that of enabler. Implementation of the policy was introduced throughout the 1980s and early 1990s through various legislative and policy statements such as:

- 1981, DHSS Publications: *Care in the Community: A Consultative Document on Moving Resources for Care in England and Community Care in Action.*

- 1983, National Health Service Reforms: Providing for the contracting out of domestic, laundry and catering services.

- 1984, Department of Health and Social Security Publication: *Helping the Community to Care.* Outlining 28 care in the community pilot projects funded to explore ways of moving long stay residents and resources from hospital to the community.

- 1985, House of Commons Social Services Committee Reports. *Community Care with Special Reference to Adult Mentally Ill and Mentally Handicapped People.*

- 1986, Audit Commission Report: *Making a Reality of Community Care.*

- 1988, General welfare policies including Education Reform, Housing and Local Government Finance Acts.

- 1988, The Griffiths Report: *Community Care: Agenda For Action* HMSO;

- 1989, Department of Health White Papers *Working for Patients* and *Caring for People and Community Care in the Next Decade and Beyond.*

- 1990, National Health and Community Care Act: Including the transfer of funding responsibilities of Department of Social Security to local authorities for residential care and nursing homes, (deferred for two years), and publication of *Community Care and the Next Decade* and *Beyond Policy Guidance.*

- 1991, DoH publications *Care Management and Assessment—managers and practitioners guides,* implementing *Community Care: Purchaser Commissioner and Provider Roles.* NHS purchaser-provider reforms and the introduction of local authority complaints procedures and inspection units.

- 1992, First community care plans published.

- 1993, Local authorities given responsibility and funds to assess and support people in residential care and nursing homes. General Practitioner fundholders now able to purchase community health services.

Three ideas have been central in the drive to develop this new model by linking the social to the economic dimensions of welfare services.

1. *The Production of Welfare Approach,* (Davies, 1986), developed by the Personal Social Services Research Unit at the University of Kent, that proposed a framework of general concepts to assemble a repertoire of casual argument and methods for the collection of data. This has been described as, a 'tool bag' for the analysis of equity and efficiency in social and related long term care and the subsequent Social Opportunity Costing Approach, (Netton and Beecham, 1993) assumes:

- There are insufficient resources to match needs or wants.

- The cost of a resource or service is not to be solely determined by its price.

- To measure the cost of a service one must also be able to measure its outcomes or benefits.

This approach identifies two types of outcome measures. First, intermediate outcomes, that is, the workload or throughput, being the number of users supported, the quality of care offered etc. Second, final outcomes, with the changes in user or carer well-being consequent upon the receipt of services, relative to the changes that would have arisen if nothing had been provided. The model operates through a process of costing welfare by identifying and describing the elements of the service, the units of service to which a cost can be attached, the costs of the service elements and calculated unit costs.

2. The concept of managerialism, namely, the proposed need for the management of welfare services and in particular the personal social services and social work practice, through:

- Service planning and resourcing needs by; rational planning—needs led assessment/ eligibility criteria - targeting - separation of purchasing from provision of service.

- Managerial, rather than professional criteria determining priorities.

- New roles and skills being developed e.g. commissioning/service contracts/care management.

- 'Co-ordinated decentralisation': The monitoring and review of sub unit performance using information systems on production and financial data.

- 'Responsible autonomy'. The central control of decisions over criteria and value base, with local autonomy for generating innovation, based on centrally determined criteria and values.

- Objective setting e.g. the NHS Griffiths Review and Audit Commission.

- Managerial accountability for levels of service provided and quality improvement within cost constraints through the emphasis on specification and achievement of measurable objectives, individual responsibility controlled by fixed contracts, performance review—pay and performance.

- Control of professional/clinical budgeting.

- Short term goal setting.

- Performance indicators for resource inputs linked to care outputs Separation of provision from consumption resource allocation linked to demography/need rather than production/capital costs.

- Separation of functions: managing - purchasing - planning and quality control - minimum provision of essential core services.

3. The introduction of consumerism into the welfare arena, whereby clients or service users are re-framed as 'consumers' and service purchasers as 'customers'. The notion of consumerism presumes that managing the welfare state is the same as running a business. This model leads to a re-shaping of services along the lines of:

- Replacing formal arrangements for 'institutional representation' with more informal approaches to 'looking after' the customer.

- Seeking to satisfy the customer with services and goods rather than allowing influence on what is available.

- Offering choices for consumers or purchasers from amongst a range of service providers, determined by the ability to pay.

These three central notions, in the understanding, need for and purpose of social welfare policy in England, have been conceptualised as a process defined as the commodification of care, characterised by:

- The introduction of operational performance targets.

- Specifying and costing input and output measures.

- Separating the purchase and provision of care.

- Monitoring and reporting mechanisms within the workplace.

- The legislative requirement upon local authorities to spend 85 per cent of their community care budget in the 'independent' sector.

- The imposition of a competence based approach to establish national occupational standards for social workers.

Their subsequent impact on the construction of a role for social workers within prevailing policy, highlights the vulnerability of the profession to fluctuating ideologies, and central and local authority agendas. As Henkel argues:

> *...the establishment of social services in 1971 led by the emerging profession of social work was a Pyrrhic victory for social workers. Although the departments were set up on an assumption that they would be defined by professional values, and although social workers continue to hold many of the key roles in them, that assumption has now been effectively reversed: social work practice is largely defined by legal and managerial values.*

> (Henkel, 1995: p 80)

Current debates regarding the nature and value of social work practice in the UK can be understood as having emerged from, and remain located in historical contexts and it's role and purpose as a function of the state, an expert discipline or a moral enterprise.

Current Professional Social Work

As is made clear in this chapter, social work in England is entering a difficult stage in its evolution. There are challenges to the legitimacy of social work from different forces, such as managerialism, de-professionalisation, financial restraint and loss of public confidence. It is by no means clear that social work will emerge unscathed from encounters with these forces. Despite all of these difficulties, there are a range of developments which are shaping the practice arena with some force. Some of these developments are reviewed below.

Children and families

There has always been a tension between the three elements of the system for the care and protection of children and young people, the protection of those who have been abused, the provision of care for those in need and the methods of responding to those who have committed juvenile crime. The Children Act for England and Wales passed in 1989 and implemented in 1991 has created an entirely new legislative framework. The significance of the Act can be found in the frequently quoted words of the Lord Chancellor, Lord Mackay, during the Act's progress through parliament that the Act is 'the most comprehensive and far reaching reform of child care law in living memory', (Hansard). The Act seeks to balance an impossible set of rights and responsibilities, children's needs, valuing children's rights, providing protection for children from harm or damage, supporting and encouraging family responsibilities and kinship ties, (Fox Harding, 1991). This Act has been grounded in the following principles:

- **Paramountcy**
  When children are involved with the state through legal process or social work activities the child's welfare must be 'paramount', throughout his or her childhood. The child's views must also be taken into account—having regard for the age of the child and the ability of the child to exercise independent thought. Similarly, the age gender, race and background of the child must also be taken into account.

- **Parental responsibility**
  The responsibilities of parents for their children have never been clearly prescribed before this piece of legislation. Hence, this is a seminal piece of legislation that seeks to define the legal nature of that relationship and those responsibilities not only in respect of 'troubled children' or children in need but for all children, especially where families fragment due to divorce etc.

- **Partnership**
  The parents of children are expected to be involved in all elements of their children's lives. If the state is required to intervene, for whatever reason, social workers are still obligated to seek to act in this spirit of partnership. This obligation remains even if the parents are suspected of having abused their child (Department of Health, 1995a; Thoburn, Lewis, and Shemmings, 1995).

Actual day-to-day practice is changing slowly in accordance with these principles and in accordance with the sprit of the legislation. A major change has been to encourage a re-focusing of services for children and families. During the 1970s and 1980s, following a series of child deaths (see *A Child in Mind*, 1987; *A Child in Trust*, 1985), child sex abuse scandals (see Campbell, 1988; *Report of the Inquiry into Child Abuse in Cleveland*, 1988; Richardson, 1982) or supposed ritual or satanic abuse, (Lord Clyde, 1992), a very bureaucratic system had been created for the identification and management of child abuse. Consequently, relatively few resources were devoted to helping families after the initial investigation, (Hallet, 1995). This became the primary focus of social work with children, with insufficient resources being devoted to support families. The Act has encouraged and promoted notions of early intervention strategies such as respite care schemes for families under stress, (Bradley and Aldgate, 1994), or increased support from the voluntary sector (Tunstill and Ozlins, 1994). A recent summary of findings from major research projects, (Department of Health, 1995b), is encouraging social services departments to re-focus their activities toward family support yet also to continue to ensure that children are protected.

Major changes are under way in the provision of juvenile justice. The need for a change in the structures and approach to juvenile justice was exemplified in a recent report produced on behalf of the Audit Commission, (Renshaw, 1998). This report confirmed that defects in the youth justice system identified in earlier reports have persisted. These included an unacceptable slowness evident in the court system, which takes too long to process cases from arrest to sentencing, weaknesses in inter-agency work undertaken by different agencies in this field, insufficient resources or time devoted to preventative work and the failure to address offending behaviour. The 1998 Crime and Disorder Act introduced a range of new proposals, such as inter-agency youth justice teams, a new youth justice board, new court orders and sanctions, including new grounds for care orders. These new measures are having an effect not only on the management of juvenile justice but also on a range of issues, including non-school attenders, the failure of parents to properly supervise children and with those children who engage in substance misuse. It is too early to evaluate the effect of this new legislation.

Local authorities have been almost immune from claims for damages or compensation brought against them by children who have or who ought to have been in care and as a consequence have suffered in various ways. In a recent judgement, (1995), the Law Lords, (the judicial function of the House of Lords which constitutes the highest court in the United Kingdom), determined that three girls and two boys who had been abused by their parents between 1987 and 1992, yet had not been removed by the local authority, did not have the right to sue Bedfordshire social services, the local authority where they had been living. The grounds for this decision was that it was not in the public interest. In June, 1998, the case was heard by the European Convention of Human Rights and deemed to be 'admissible' and will subsequently be heard by the European Court of Human Rights. If the case is determined in favour of the children by this court, the ramifications for the relationship of children and local authorities could be considerable.

Major new initiatives have been introduced by the government, for example, through the 'Quality Protects Programme', introduced in the autumn of 1998. This three year programme, with guaranteed additional funds, imposes greater centralisation of standards in child care throughout England. Targets are being set for each local authority and additional funding is only to be provided for those local authorities that meet these prescribed targets. Local politicians will have increased responsibility, and all authorities will have to devise action plans. These action plans will target key initiatives such as to raise the educational attainment of children who are

cared for by the state, reduce the number of placements children have whilst in care and provide additional financial and other assistance to young people in the early years of adult life—if they have been in care and so on. These developments are significant, if as expected they result in a greater control by central government over areas of the welfare state that have previously been determined locally. Other major initiatives are under way such as the development of new 'Frameworks for the Assessment of Children in Need' and proposals for 'Working Together to Safeguard Children': details of these proposals can be found at the Department of Health website, (http://www.doh.uk/).

Probation practice

There has been a long tradition of provision of social work help by the probation service to offenders in England. However, provision of services for offenders is organized differently in Scotland and Northern Ireland; for example, in Scotland there is no separate probation service: social work for offenders is provided through the social work departments within local authorities. The origins of the service are to be found in the work of the Court Missionaries, a nineteenth century philanthropic organisation devoted to rescuing offenders from the courts and prisons. From the very earliest days, the probation service had as a guiding principle the expectation that probation officers would 'advise, assist and befriend offenders' (Walker and Beaumont, 1981). There is not one national service but rather 55 area probation services—all of which vary greatly in size. Each area operates as a quasi-independent body with an appointed probation committee responsible for the conduct of the service within that area. A variety of forms of social work have been offered by the service. Until recently, the primary function of the service has been to provide an alternative to prison for those who have been found guilty of an offence and who express willingness to seek to modify their offending behaviour though social work processes. Other social work services have included help for prisoner's families, through-care (social work during and after periods of imprisonment) and ancillary functions such as the provision of matrimonial counselling and welfare reports on children. During the 1990s, it has become increasingly obvious that government has intended to reshape and recast the basic functions of probation through radically changing the objectives of the probation service. This process is occurring through modification of the ideological frameworks that have constructed the rationale of probation practice and substantial changes in the occupational structure of the organisation. These trends are evident in a range of documents and measures such as the introduction by the Home Office of national standards for probation officers, (Home Office, 1992 and 1995; Home Office, 1995), the Home Office Three Year Plan, (1996), substantial and regular changes in the legislative framework, e.g. Criminal Justice Act 1991 and 1993, and the 1994 Criminal Justice and Public Order Act. The overall aim of these initiatives has been to change the function and ethos of the probation service into an agency for the punishment of offenders within the community, rather than a therapeutic service that provides an alternative to punishment, (Home Office, 1995). A core element in this process has been to de-professionalise the probation service by reducing the independence of practitioners and using ever more bureaucratic forms of organisational control. For example, the national standards for work with offenders (Home Office, 1995), which prescribe how probation officers should work. Prior to 1996 it was a requirement that probation officers were qualified as social workers and possessed the DipSW or its equivalent, but in 1996, this requirement was removed by the then Home Secretary, Michael Howard. Significantly, this approach has not been changed by the incoming Labour Government in 1997. New training arrangements have been established for new probation officers, following employment based training routes. These are designed to encourage mature applicants to enter the probation service with life experience rather than formal academic qualifications.

Care in the community

A series of developments in the mid 1980s and early 1990s have transformed the organisational structures for the provision of

care intended for people living in the community who are not able to fully care for themselves. The government of Mrs Thatcher commissioned a report from Sir Roy Griffiths into the provision of care in the community, and this report, (Griffiths, 1988), was largely adopted by the government and incorporated into their own planning as a White Paper, (Department of Health, 1989). The White Paper famously states, 'the government acknowledges that the great bulk of community care is provided by friends, family and neighbours', (section 1.9).

Based upon the state recognition of the importance of the informal sector, legislation soon followed that introduced major changes to the method of providing care for people living in the community by the National Health Service and Community Care Act, 1990, (NHS and CC Act). Simultaneously, a large amount of government guidance on the implementation of the act and the standards for good practice was published, (see, for example, Department of Health, 1991), in an attempt to regulate the operation of this new legislation. The origins of the ideas and principles underlying this complex package of legislation and guidance derived from two major sources. Firstly, the system of case management in the US which developed as a system and an approach to plan, provide and review the effectiveness of care for people living in the community where the providers of care were highly diverse and fragmented, (Moley, 1989). Secondly, the research of the Personal Social Services Unit at the University of Kent that explored the applicability of the US case management system with an emphasis on cost effectiveness. The reduction of the cost of community care was central to the government's implementation of the reforms, as was a desire to increase the amount of choice provided for those requiring some form of service. Davies, (1986), and more recently Titterton, (1994), have reported success in achieving these two objectives.

The implications for social work practice has been considerable, and some social workers now hold budgets and are directly responsible for the purchase of care for their clients. Although the function of purchasing care has been retained by managers in some organisations, there are a plethora of different organisational forms and structures, (Challis,

Davies, and Traske, 1994). Social workers, or more properly, care managers, act as assessors to help service users identify their needs. Brokers help devise a care package, financial managers purchase packages of care and evaluators monitor and review the viability, utility and effective functioning of the complete package. To ensure that the quality of provision is maintained, local authorities have been required to set up inspection units to ensure that particular services meet minimum levels of provision. These changes in the organisational provision of care have generated opportunities for significant changes in relationships between social workers and service users. For example, there are increased opportunities for the full involvement of service users—a fact recognised and promoted in official guidance, (Stevenson and Parsloe, 1993). Two major developments as part of these trends have provided opportunities to empower service users. Concern has been expressed about the extent to which Black and other ethnic minority groups are excluded from full participation in the development of community care, (Aitkin and Rollings, 1993). If the care in the community developments are to be truly successful they must be fully inclusive.

Self advocacy

Service users have found inspiration to advocate their own needs on their own behalf, with or without the assistance of social workers. The roots of this movement, which can now be identified in several areas of community care, seems to be from people with learning difficulties, (Lawson, 1991). Groups of service users at national or local level are coming together to define, articulate and argue for their perspective on the kind of service they want. For example, Emanuel and Acroyd, 1996, provide an account of the production of a policy document designed to influence strategic developments for adults with physical and sensory impairments involving both able-bodied and disabled people.

Independent living

Before the introduction of the community care legislation some initiatives were taken by local groups to promote independent living, an important national example is the Derbyshire Centre for Integrated Living. This centre has, since the early 1980s, been run and managed by disabled people with the intention of integrating disabled people into economic and social activities. In 1988, influenced by such developments, the government introduced the Independent Living Fund (ILF). This scheme allowed the needs of the individual to be assessed, and in accordance with those needs, people then received a grant to purchase their own services to enable them to live independently. This scheme successfully promoted opportunities for independence but was terminated in March 1993, with over 21,500 benefiting from the scheme, (Sharkey, 1995), when a much reduced scheme was introduced allowing for a top-up on existing provision rather than true independence. The Labour government is now to introduce a Direct Payments Scheme reinstating some of the elements of the ILF. These schemes, when successful, give real power to service users and transform the role of social workers to be true advisors.

The Recognition and Attainment of Professional Status for Social Workers in England

The current uncertainty about the essential nature of social work, its relative value to society and its effectiveness as a means of successfully 'intervening' in the lives of 'welfare recipients' is not new. As an unregulated professional occupation (except in a restricted sense for the probation service which was a regulated part of social work until 1997), social work has historically, and still remains, subject to the dictates and changing agendas of central and local government and employing agencies, and hence beyond the control of any one authoritative body.

The employment and deployment of holders of a professional qualification in social work in England at either qualifying, post qualifying or advanced levels has been and remains, with the exception of approved social workers and mental health officers under mental health legislation, at the discretion of their employers.

In April 1998 it was announced by the Minister of Health, Paul Boateng, that a General Social Care Council would be established, following on from the publication of reports such as Parker, (1990), and the subsequent development of a broad coalition of interested parties to support the creation of a system of registration for social service staff. However, whilst the precise details of how this council will operate are unclear, it will not only regulate social work but ultimately all those who work in the social care field.

But for the present, issues of autonomy in respect of the organisation of social work activity relating to contractual arrangements, relationships with other professional groups, technical competence and activities, occupational ideology and control of the training system inevitably remain open to influence from outside of any single institution or organisation that can claim exclusivity in representing social work.

Recent developments arising from the implementation of the National Health Services and Community Care Acts, and in particular the adoption of the care management approach by local authority social service departments in England, has thrown the question of what distinguishes social workers from other professional and occupational groups into stark relief.

> Social work can no longer count on a pre-eminent role in social care, and this has been reflected in the employment and use of individuals who are not social workers, in roles which were formally undertaken by social workers. Social work clearly has to justify its place amongst other groups performing care managerial roles.
> (Sheppard, 1995: p 13)

Sheppard argues that the source of this failure by social work, to defend itself from the reduction of its control over the traditional areas of its work and its incapacity to resist the currently prevailing powerful ideologies of managerialism and consumerism, can be traced back to social work's historical failure to establish its own professional credentials or expertise. This failure to formulate, or claim a sufficiently robust and unique body of theoretical knowledge and range of effective specialist skills to manage social problems, has itself given rise to the re-framing of social care work as an area more subject to everyday concerns and economic activity, than to one characterised by skilled, professional interventions. The failure of social work to achieve full professional status and thereby the ability to determine the extent of social

worker's competence is also due in no small measure to the public relations disasters, particularly during the 1980s, such as the Cleveland affair, when social workers failed to protect the rights of children and families and were perceived in the mass media to have acted like agents of a police state. Similarly, the Orkney affair, with the removal of children from their families in the belief that those children had been satanically abused and the Beckford case, when social workers were seen to be unable to protect a child in their care. It is no accident that these disasters, all relating to children, helped to construct a public notion of incompetence among social workers in the public mind.

As with any particular professional group, social work's claim to professional status and distinctive characteristics hinges upon the extent to which it is considered to derive its uniqueness from either the professional education that underpins its practice or the occupational status and functions afforded it by employers of social workers. Simic argues that,

> In social services departments there is a dialectic expressed in the battle for ownership of the welfare process between 'management' and 'labour'. In relation to social work, that labour is defined as 'professional labour' in the sense given by Hardy; independent practitioners with a professional code and a career structure independent of the organisational structure.
> (Simic, 1995: p 11)

Two competing traditions can be traced within the historical and ideological debates over the role of social work within the English welfare regime. Firstly, Pinker's view of social work, (re-framed by Sheppard following the adoption of the care management approach in the 1990s), envisages a limited role for the profession, firmly wedded to meeting agency function:

> What then are the essential roles and tasks of social workers, and how can social work activities best be organised? Our present model of so-called client-centred social work is basically sound, but in need of a better and less ambitious mandate. Social work should be explicitly selective rather than universalist in focus, reactive rather than preventative in approach and modest in its objectives. Social work ought to be preventative with respect to the needs which come to its attention; it has neither the capacity, the resources nor the mandate to go looking for needs in the community at large.
> (Pinker, 1982: p 237)

Although this view currently dominates the political and organisational climate of welfare arrangements in England, a second understanding and approach to the social work role, regarding both the immediate needs of individual clients and an understanding of social welfare and the community, embraces a wider vision of social work in respect of its purpose in responding to citizen and community need.

> *It is not the role of social workers, or of social services departments and voluntary agencies, simply to accept things as they are and work silently with individuals and families…Certainly it is for social workers to implement organisational policies, but they need also to be influencing them if consistent patterns of social care planning for the benefit of clients and communities are to be developed.*
>
> (Barclay, 1982: p 110)

Within these two perspectives on what constitutes an appropriate role and function of social workers, as well as more extreme notions of social work constructed for the purpose of achieving social change, but which have found little favour within current organisational contexts, there endures a shared understanding of that which constitutes the nature of the relationship between worker and client, regardless of the particular orientation of the agency or the worker. This understanding is characterised by the twin concepts of client-centred practice and the use of self. The endurance of social workers' attachment to a particular form of relationship with clients provides for the maintenance of a professional dimension that cannot be afforded by either bureaucratic constructions or market forces.

In spite of organisational pressures and bureaucratic measures, applied to achieve standardisation and regulation in welfare practice, the significance of talk, language and the 'relationship' in social work practice remain central to the process of bringing about change in the client's circumstances. Whilst their reports, in the form of official assessments, plans and recommendations may be couched within taken for granted understandings of predetermined, models and definitions of need and presented through formal systems of description and explanation for defining, classifying and responding to clients; the processes by which social workers gather information and establish a sense of

order in the management of their cases is neither well documented, nor readily subject to predefined rules or other regularities or indeed generally understood.

The underlying circumstances of client's difficulties, the discontinuities, variety and complexity of social life require that social workers adopt individual strategies for mediating between the reconstruction of client life narratives and the formulation of agency required reports within the confines of bureaucratic constructs of need, risk, abuse, neglect, entitlement and other 'problems'.

> *When we study whole human beings, we are aiming to interpret others who are themselves engaged in a process of interpreting themselves…It is an effort to approach the understanding of lives in context rather than through a prefigured and narrowing lens. Meaning is not inherent in an act or experience, but is constructed through social discourse.*
>
> (Josselon and Lieblich, 1995: p 20)

Social workers are therefore intimately concerned with their own and their clients capacity for impression management, whether it be for the purpose of establishing a claim, disclosing or exposing an act of 'abuse' or eliciting co-operation or compliance. Each new referral brings with it the creative possibility of a unique encounter where the social worker is not so much concerned with the 'problem' per se, but with people's understanding of and capacity to cope with the 'problem' and 'the infinitely diverse ways in which they create and communicate their experience' (England, 1986: p 17).

The Educational Basis of Social Work

Responsibility for the development, approval and monitoring of professional education and training of social work rests currently with the Central Council for Education and Training in Social Work (CCETSW). The CCETSW, in partnership with the Care Sector Consortium (CSC), and in consultation with government, employers, educational, professional and union representatives, has developed a continuum of education, training and qualifications in social care and social work that integrates the acquisition and assessment of practice competences and academic attainment required of professional social workers at three levels: basic qualification/diploma level, post qualification/bachelors degree level and advanced masters degree level. (For further details regarding the nature of these qualifications see CCETSW, 1990; CCETSW, 1995.)

The current emphasis given by CCETSW to the demonstration of prescribed competences and achievement of specific learning outcomes, as opposed to the process by which learning is acquired, has led to a position in which the acquisition of a recognised social work qualification is in principle achievable via a variety of mechanisms. Conferment of an award, entry to the profession or 'licence to practice' as a social worker is now determined by the demonstration of competence rather than completion of a particular learning process or experience. Furthermore, the competences to be demonstrated are increasingly being determined as much by the organisational, managerial and bureaucratic functions within welfare agencies as by those methods and practices more traditionally associated with social work, (Brewster, 1991; Cannan, 1994).

These tendencies, already evident in the demonstration of competences and the increased control of the professional activity of social work by forces external to the profession seem likely to continue. An announcement by the Minister of State for Health, Paul Boateng, confirmed that CCETSW will cease to operate around the year 2002 and will be replaced by a National Training Organisation (NTO) a body with responsibility for training and education across the field of social care. This new body, along with the General Social Care Council, (see above), will regulate the functions of training and practice across all of the social care field—of which social work is but a small part. The likely impact of this change for social work will be substantial—it is likely to be marginalised by other concerns.

One realm to which social workers have traditionally turned to in establishing a professional identity outside of that defined within the working environment is the educational experience and process for gaining entry to the profession. A reading of many social work texts appears to suggest that practice transcends organisational factors in as much as it is predicated upon the nature of the relationship between worker and client. Attention is focused upon:

> *...the social worker's role and self image as that of reflective practitioner (rather than that of the detached/objective technical 'expert'), where knowledge is 'manifest in and modified by interactions with clients' and emphasises 'the nature of the relations with clients, the way the worker interacts, the process of working and the assumptions which inform that relationship.*
>
> (Yelloly and Henkel, 1995: p 9)

Debates over the knowledge base and credibility of social work and the role of education and training in establishing its credentials are well documented, (e.g. Green, 1978; Sibeon, 1989; Rodger, 1991; Tsang, 1991; Strom and Gingerich 1993; and Cannan, 1994). Current definitions and standards of competence (see, for example, CCETSW, 1995) as applied to professional social work can be seen as having emerged from these and other on-going debates about the essential nature of social work and differing positions and perspectives on what constitutes knowledge and understanding, prescription and judgement, process and outcomes and effectiveness and quality in social work theory and practice. There has been a rash of new publications about how to help students meet these competences, for example O'Hagan, 1996; and Vass, 1996). Since about 1980, when the Association of Directors of Social Services, the principle employers of social workers, first loudly voiced dissatisfactions with the output of social work courses, the debate has been increasingly concerned with the construction of social work standards of competence, with educational programmes increasingly reduced to functional analyses, performance indicators and measures of competence requirements.

Yelloly and Henkel argue for a model of social work education that emphasises reflection and the capacity to think, and that the purpose and value of the educational experience in social work and in particular to small learning groups is to offer 'containment', whereby:

> *...high value is given to creating a space which is somewhat apart from the everyday world, where a reflective mode and a slower pace is promoted, and where it is permissible to allow vulnerability to surface (a view somewhat at odds with the dominant ideas of competence and 'mastery').*
>
> (ibid: p 9)

This argument adopts a definition of the social worker's role and self image as that of reflective practitioner, rather than that of the detached or objective technical 'expert', where knowledge is 'manifest in and modified by interactions with clients' and emphasises 'the nature of the relations with clients, the way the worker interacts, the process of working and the assumptions which inform that relationship'. Similarly, Jones and Joss argue that increased occupational control in the personal social services has created a shift of emphasis from professional characteristics associated with,

> *...the capacity to deal with uncertainty through the exercise of discretion and judgement; to be responsible for continuously improving upon personal performance and to hold a knowledge base of a set of systematic underpinning theories and an explicit practice theory that 'allows the integration of theory with practice and puts an emphasis upon the professional values of practice'; to a concern with competent professional performance viewed as a series of discrete elements of behaviour, each of which can be observed and measured. Competence is inferred and judged from observed behavioural outputs. Little account is taken of the processes by which outputs are generated or the influence or other outputs including the organisational context of professional work.* (Jones and Joss, 1995: p 30)

The Moral Basis and Ethical Principles of Social Work

As with any particular professional group, social work's claim to professional status and its distinguishing characteristics hinge upon the extent to which it derives its uniqueness from not only the formulation of a robust and unique body of theoretical knowledge and range of effective specialist skills but also its adherence to a distinct set of values that underpins its relationship to service clients. As Simic argues,

> *Whatever the profession or vocation, one defining characteristic is the aspiration to a set of values or code of ethics expressed in some realm separate from that ruled by one's employer or one's self-interest.*
> (Simic, 1995: p 11).

Social work in England has traditionally been understood as having a moral dimension, although the nature of that moral dimension is notoriously difficult to define, (Shardlow, 1998). Difficult, both in terms of the overview

taken by practitioners, whether in the form of regulators of the poor and unemployed under the early Poor Laws, the philanthropic work of the 19th century charity organisations, or the radical perspective of social and community workers in the 1960s and '70s, and in respect of an ethical code of conduct regarding the nature of the social workers' immediate relationship with individual clients.

> *Inherent in people work is the fact that it is also moral work. Every action taken on behalf of clients represents not only some form of concrete service, such as administering medication, issuing a welfare grant, or counselling the family, but also a moral judgement and statement about their moral worth. This is because when we work on people who are themselves imbued with values, our own actions cannot be value neutral.* (Hasenfeld, 1995: p 5)

The subtle and difficult work relating to the raising of self awareness and the ways in which social workers, consciously or not, contribute both towards an ideal model of society and of individual human relations, requires an appreciation and understanding of the centrality of moral judgements and the emotional content of personal relationships. Relationships are the medium in which the concerns and practice of social work arise, responses are conducted and outcomes judged, they are the currency of everyday life. Accordingly, social work expertise derives from the understanding and capacity to intervene in everyday social life.

> *The more that social workers can understand and work personally, rather than impersonally with distressed people, the less they will need to resort to legal procedures and bureaucratic guidelines.*
> (Howe and Hinings, 1997: p 28)

Putman and Mumby, adopting a feminist critique, argue that,

> *Emotion, then, is not simply an adjunct to work; rather, it is the process through which members constitute their work environment by negotiating a shared reality...In organisations, emotions are constantly devalued and marginalised while rationality is privileged as an ideal for effective emotional life...When emotions are incorporated into organisations, they are treated as commodities. Feelings are appropriated by the organisation for instrumental ends ...Stripped away from the spontaneity of human interaction, emotional labour can lead to negative consequences for an employee and for his or her work relationships...In particular, the gap between felt and*

expressed emotion marginalises individual experience and the intimacy that typically accompanies personal feelings. (Putman and Mumby, 1995: pp 37–43)

An awareness of service agency agendas, and the way in which service users are required to fit in with the smooth running of the implementation of the health and welfare systems, helps to locate where the difficulties of practice lie. Legislation, central and local government policies, society's values and agency expectations, individual needs and professional judgements, all inform the decisions that social workers are required to reach in respect of their clients. Analysing these sources of the many contradictions and conflicts that social workers are required to contend with can help to address the level of stress that attends their attempts to resolve these disparate demands and help to identify their role within the personal services.

An examination of social work in England, from its origins through to the emergence of current debates over the centrality of anti-racist and anti-discriminatory practice, exposes the moral dimension as a primary determinant of the nature of social work beyond that of the prevailing economic, political and administrative contexts. This moral dimension requires social workers to locate and question agency decisions within a wider framework than current expediency allows for. Furthermore, it allows for a more sophisticated analysis of the nature and cause of social inequality and the legitimisation of social need in the context of power relations within society, rather than within individualised constructs and explanations. In so doing it exposes and presents the distinct rationale of the profession as being to not only embody the institutionalised morality of society, but also to analyse and where necessary challenge it.

The state is not an impartial institution. It actively discriminates, through social policy, legislation and the allocation of resources, between generations, men and women and different ethnic groups. Social work is subject to the dictates and changing agendas of central and local government and employing agencies, and its capacity for autonomous practice in respect of the organisation of social work activity, contractual arrangements, relationships with other professional groups, technical competence and activities,

occupational ideology and control of the training system is continuously challenged by a wide range of institutions and organisations that claim the right to both represent and direct the profession.

Whilst on the one hand, the texts of social work may emphasise the moral and ethical dimension of practice and locate the worker/client relationship at the centre of the action, organisations, on the other hand, are concerned with managing and routinising 'troubles'. For social workers, the personal transactions and intimacies in which the relationship with the client is established is at the same time underscored by the legitimacy and authority of the organisation they work for, they cannot do what they do unless it is legitimated within a service delivery framework. Managing the tension is problematic for social work, (Camilleri, 1996: p 125).

Constructions of good practice in social work continue to recognise the importance, if not the centrality, of the issues of empowerment, anti-discriminatory practice and working with value conflicts in practice. Dominelli argues that the essence of social work is its

...commitment to establishing relationships between workers and users which aim to provide the user with the resources, encouragement (and sometimes coercion) to change his or her existing lifestyle in more socially adaptive and purposive directions. (Dominelli, 1996: p 156).

However, central and local government policies and legislation, as well as agency agendas, all equally inform the decisions that social workers are required to reach in respect of role, function and relationships with their clients. This creates an essential dilemma around the definition of social need, as to whether it is determined by the professional knowledge and value base of the social work profession or by prevailing political and organisational agendas.

Whilst the moral imperative of the profession's value base may provide the social work profession with its justification to serve as more than a mere instrument of the state, its implementation requires that practitioners operate within the regulations and procedures of the employing welfare organisations. This tension, as evidenced within England, is mirrored across the range of welfare systems, where both global factors and local diversity and the inherent ideological tensions between the organisational and practice dimensions compete for influence over the social work enterprise.

Conclusion

In 1996, The National Institute for Social Work issued a briefing note that summarises the key issues currently facing the profession (NISW, 1996), they conclude that:

> *Traditional assumptions about the nature of their work, the skills and expertise required, and relationships with other care agencies and corporate colleagues are being re-examined. Some of the changes are recognised within social services as deriving from professional values. Others are seen as unavoidable demands from external authorities, welcomed by some but often regarded as alien ways of thinking impossible to reconcile with professional activity.*
> (NISW, 1996)

We have sought to demonstrate that social welfare policies, services and practice in England have arisen out of historically located beliefs and understandings about the nature of individual and social needs, rights and responsibilities. These understandings are themselves products of competing ideological positions that seek to integrate moral, political, economic and technological factors in order to achieve the management, if not the resolution, of prevailing social problems.

We have also suggested that the over association of social work practice with a too narrow conception of the operations of the state has led to a limitation on the potential for social work in England to encompass a broader cultural understanding of the nature of social control, diversity and action, and that:

> *...the language of social control fails to capture the ways in which regulatory practices and techniques have come to operate, not through a crushing of wills or a subjugation of desires but through the promotion of subjectivity, through investments in individual lives, and the forging of alignments between the personal projects of citizens and images of the social order.*   (Miller and Rose, 1988: p 172)

Following Miller and Rose, we would agree that a re-conception of government in which to locate social work is needed, and within which is included:

> *...all those programmes which seek to secure desired socio-political objectives through the regulation of the activities and relations of individuals and populations and...in which the conduct of personal life has become a crucial mechanism in the exercise of political power, including the active promotion of social well being and the public good...it is not helpful to relegate knowledges to a realm of ideology, nor to characterise them as disguising or justifying pre-existing interests or relations of power...*
> (ibid: p 174)

Finally, we have argued that, although social workers in England have experienced identity problems from the onset as relieving officers under the Poor Laws, case workers for nineteenth century charitable organisations, professional practitioners with expertise in counselling during the 1950s, '60s and '70s through to their current role as care managers in the new 'enabling' authorities, the impact of the new managerialism, evident both within the workplace and the educational process, has essentially relocated constructions of social work outside of the professional domain. There has been a debate about whether the activities required under the community care legislation constitute social work—not all care managers are social workers—having neither a social work qualification or a background in social work. Further erosion of social workers' right to claim exclusive expertise or role dominance in welfare practices, has arisen from the emphasis given to consumer choice. One study of interdisciplinary assessment of older people identified that:

> *Care management demonstration projects have produced a variety of organisational models with a range of advantages and disadvantages...The data from our study indicates that user preference is determined by the capacity of the individual professional to provide on-going, understanding and pro-active service, rather than membership of a particular discipline.*
> (Hunter, Brace and Buckley, 1993: p 5)

The combined effects of the process of the commodification of welfare, managerial and consumerist ideologies and the interdisciplinary working practices enshrined in the NHS and Community Care Act and epitomised by the care management approach, present a powerful reformulation of the historical challenges to social work.

Questions for Further Consideration

- In the UK, earlier than in many other European countries, discussion started about the relationship between the state, the individual, families and communities. This discussion led to a strong emphasis on citizens being expected to take responsibility for their own social welfare. What are the consequences of this expectation for the role and function of social work institutions in the UK? How does this compare with the situation in your home country?

- 'Commodification of care' is a very central notion of social welfare policy in the UK. What are the notions behind this concept (e.g. 'Production of Welfare Approach', 'Social Opportunity Costing Approach', 'Managerialism' and 'Consumerism')? Which of these ideas play an important role within your home country's construction of social work? Are there some other notions that are even more important?

- The professional debate in the UK illustrates two ways of developing skills as a social worker: i) a competence-based approach which stresses organisational, managerial and bureaucratic functions; ii) a process-oriented approach which emphasises reflection ('reflective practice'). How does this compare or contrast with the situation in your home country?

Chapter Ten

Towards European Perspectives on Social Work

Adrian Adams, Peter Erath, Steven Shardlow and Horst Sing

The various contributions to this book provide evidence in the different European countries represented that the forms of social security systems, the welfare regimes, as well as the construction of theory and practice about and for social work are characterized by both significant differences and commonalties. We argue that through an analysis of common features in these divergent forms across different countries that a critical appreciation of the nature and purpose of social work can be determined. This does not, however, equate with the simplistic presumption that we can necessarily learn from or adapt partial elements of one system of social welfare into another, nor that a unified system of social welfare could easily be developed across Europe—assuming the political will existed. Arising from an understanding of social work and welfare that is grounded in national, regional, and cultural differences we do not envisage, nor indeed advocate, any enforced conformity in social security systems and social work practice. Nevertheless, neither do we propose a renunciation of the possibility of developing any shared orientations within the domain of social work on a European scale. On the contrary, we do argue that certain shared features, particularly with regard to the educational processes leading to professional competence in social work, identity of professional social work and the general commitments and ethical concerns of social workers towards supporting people in difficult situations to live their lives in dignity, require collective and repeated restatement. In particular, we have highlighted that the complex, convergent and divergent forms of social security systems and social work are increasingly subject to the challenges presented by the processes of globalisation. Moreover, that the European 'harmonisation project' cannot be achieved by denying national and cultural differences but only through attempts to understand different points of view within their historical context. For the student of

European social work, the busy manager, or the over-worked practitioner, there are no simple solutions, either in understanding the differences in social work or in being able to transfer ideas and knowledge from one context to another.

We can identify a series of dimensions where comparison is illuminative.

The Effects of Economics: European Monetary Union and Social Security Systems

The differing courses of action taken by individual countries in the field of social security arising from the introduction of European Monetary Union, (EMU), illustrate both how differently the countries in question have reacted, depending on local economic, political and cultural conditions, and the subordinate importance of social security systems and social work to the economic preconditions required for joining the common currency, (Pakaslahti, 1999: p 104). For example, Belgium, France, Germany, and to a certain extent Austria, considered economic criteria very important for EMU and have implemented rigorous financial cuts in their system of social security. However, Portugal, Spain, and Italy, adopted a type of double-strategy, which aimed both at conforming to the criteria for EMU and simultaneously avoiding major changes to their social security systems. Meanwhile, the Netherlands, Denmark, Sweden and Finland restructured their social security systems several years ago in anticipation of EMU, but remain committed, in principle, to their respective models of comprehensive welfare policies. Only in Luxembourg, Ireland, and in the UK, which has not yet joined the currency union, did conformity with the criteria for EMU not necessitate changes in the welfare system, as restructuring measures were implemented earlier for other macro-economic reasons and without any consideration of the need to meet EMU criteria. The contrary is true for the states of the former Eastern Bloc, where in the last few years drastic measures have been introduced in order to cut spending on social security. These changes, and the overall levels of funding for social welfare create a backcloth for the delivery of social welfare and social work in the various European states.

Differences and Similarities in the Organisational Structures of Social Work

The state, the principle planning and organising authority, together with private voluntary and charitable foundations and agencies, self-help groups and volunteers are all providers of social services, and all play an important, if different, role in each of the countries discussed. This becomes evident when comparing, for instance, the important role played by the Christian churches in social work in Germany with the situation in Finland, or when contrasting the importance of private enterprises in the UK to the situation in France. Such organisational differences have important effects on the concrete practice of social work. These differences shape both the philosophical principles that underpin systems of welfare and the experiences of recipients of social help, as, for example, the provision of help from a church which has a very different character to the provision of services from a private company. It will be experienced by the client very differently. Likewise, differences deriving from the essential role and function of the state within the welfare system will affect the nature of social provision. Thus, the position of a social worker in a French youth welfare department is quite different from his German counterparts. Whereas in Germany the state does not perceive itself as an 'intervention-authority' and concedes almost absolute autonomy to the family with regard to educational decisions, the state will intervene at a much earlier point in France.

Increasing administrative deregulation instigated by the European Union may lead to a greater market orientation, and perhaps even to European networks or social corporations in the provision of social work and social welfare. While such developments may change historically developed power-relations on a national level, it is unlikely to result in a common European organizational system of social work in the foreseeable future.

Similar Social Problems, Different Clients

Do social workers across Europe face similar social problems? For example, even though the social situation in satellite towns, characterised by high rates of vandalism, youth crime and drug misuse, is similar across Europe and many social problems, such as increased homelessness and unemployment, occur everywhere in Europe, these problems will nevertheless have to be understood and responded to differently in different countries according to the local cultural context. The situation of maghreb youth in the 'banlieue' of Paris is not identical with the situation of black youth in the suburbs of London. Homelessness and unemployment have a different impact on people in Germany as compared to people in Portugal and Spain, depending on expectations about being employed, the social view of the status of unemployed people, the extent of family support, the availability of state financial support or access to smallholdings and so on. Accordingly, we have to take into consideration that the individual biographies of such people, the behaviours associated with them and their living and social environments are subject to 'national' and 'regional' influences. Any kind of intervention by social work has to be grounded in these concrete living environments, insofar as it does not consist of purely material relief. A cultural awareness and sensitivity is necessary in order to provide appropriate help and a simplistic transfer of generalist methods and concepts to different contexts and cultures should be avoided. With this in mind, social work can recognize that many types of social problems may be universal but interventions must be grounded in local and regional culture and social expectations.

The Common Challenge to European Social Work

Despite all of the significant differences between social security and social work systems, comparisons between the countries in question suggest a number of areas for collective development and endeavour. Such a conclusion arises in the context of the particular challenges posed by:

- The internationalisation of capital and the globalisation of markets.
- The limitation imposed upon practice due to national budget deficits and low rates of productivity within the public sector.
- High structural unemployment due to the uncoupling of the development of economic growth and employment.
- Demographic changes, particularly with regard to ageing and family structures.
- Migration from Central and Eastern Europe and the Southern hemisphere to the European Union and the migration of populations within the Union.

The consequences of such developments are reductions in the level of resources, the re-structuring of services and changes in social work practice, especially in seeking the achievement of increased efficiency and effectiveness, and yet all of these changes occur within the context of increasing social problems and greater social need. Under such conditions, social work is under increasing pressure to establish its legitimacy, its credentials, and realistic, achievable objectives. It is against this background that European comparisons are essential.

Some Proposals

If it is accepted that in the long term some form of social work remains essential to European countries, a number of general issues relating to the establishment of a collective identity and shared status of the profession need to be addressed.

Firstly, the considerable national differences in the arrangements for the education and training of social workers is problematic and counter-productive within the developing European harmonisation process. For example, whereas in Finland a future social worker undergoes a five-year course at a university, a two-year training is sufficient in France. Similarly, in the UK there is a range of possibilities for post-qualifying professional development in the field of social work within a nationally approved framework of post-professional qualifications, even including the possibility of a doctorate. Yet in Germany, there is no such national structure and higher study for doctorate is only possible after an additional four-year course which requires that candidates change in subject to the academic study of pedagogy or sociology, rather than social work. All this after already having received a diploma in social work/social pedagogy! If such differences are to be reconciled, a central issue for resolution will be how knowledge for social work will be selected from the full range and compliment of complex information and discrete disciplines within the university systems, and the criteria to be applied in determining its relevance to practice. In particular, there is the question of how to approach the competing paradigms of the empirically oriented scientific approach to social work with those that emphasise individual and societal subjective processes. The more subjective paradigms, through which the world is experienced and constructed, oblige social workers, within their layered relationships with individuals, organisations and systems, to achieve a form of praxis that satisfies both scholastic and practical considerations.

Secondly, working with people from both a 'shared' or 'different' national, class and cultural identity, in specific problematic situations, requires more from social workers than merely relating to an unknown counterpart from a different social and cultural environment. Whilst it has always been one of the important tasks of social work to respond to the needs of refugees and asylum-seekers, in confronting the 'other' in the professional context, actions cannot rely on either intuition or preconceived notions and stereotypes. The inter- and multi-cultural and national dimensions of social work require the generation of international standards against which interventions can be evaluated. Some of these discussions are framed within the context of anti-oppressive or anti-discriminatory practice. This debate about the nature of anti-oppressive and non-discriminatory practice is still under development within social work, and requires intellectual, emotional and practical rigour in the processes of comprehending its theoretical principles, subjectively experiencing its existence and most importantly, in the development of the confidence to implement strategies for action in practice. Claims for the neutrality of action must be refuted, purely 'anaesthetic' forms of intervention cannot be justified and a capacity for resistance to and autonomy from instrumental procedures that discriminate against or objectify particular individuals, groups or communities must be acquired. Similarly, further debate and critical analysis of constructs of empowerment, self-determination, enablement and participation is required within the profession.

Thirdly, that comparisons between the different systems of social security and social work within the different countries are intrinsically linked to the specifics of the history of the nation state. Particular approaches adopted within any state have been generated, adopted and derive their legitimacy within the historical relationship between the competing tensions generated by bourgeois ideology, monopoly capitalism and the primacy of the individual. Social work acts at the interface between these tensions, and is therefore inevitably grounded in the interplay of different national as well as international forces.

Finally, that historically developed national systems will not simply be replaced by a common European blueprint. Rather, national systems will continue to both converge and diverge within the framework of Europe-wide competition and development, (Pierson and Leibfried, 1998). Even the smallest agencies and individual actors within these systems will be exposed to the conditions of 'multi-level politics' and will increasingly struggle to do justice to offering social assistance according to their own ethical standards and to meeting the expectations of society. The role of social security systems and social work within 'project Europe' relates to the aspiration of achieving a 'social Europe'. These four propositions will be the topics for future examination by the authors of this volume in the linked publication *Key Themes in European Social Work*.

Coda: The Meaning for Practice

Looking across social work in other European states for examples of good practice to apply in one's own national environment is no straightforward matter. Finding good examples in other states may not be so difficult. However, understanding why a particular form of practice is effective in any state requires the kind of historical and contextual understanding that we have sought to develop in this book. Only armed with such understanding is it possible to begin to apply the lessons that might be learned from looking at practice in other states to one's own situation.

References

Introduction

Bonoli, G. (1997). Classifying Welfare States: A Two-dimensional Approach. *Journal of Social Policy*, 26(3): pp 351–372.

Burrows, R., and Loader, B. (Eds.) (1994). *Towards a Post-Fordist Welfare State?* London: Routledge.

Camilleri, P.J. (1996). *(Re) Constructing Social Work*. Aldershot: Avebury.

Cooper, A., and Pitts, J. (1994). Ironic Investigations: The Relationship between Trans-national European Social Work Research and Social Work Education. In Gehrmann, G., Müller, K.D., and Ploem, R. (Eds.). *Social Work and Social Work Studies*. Weinheim: Deutscher Studien Verlag.

Dominelli, L. and Hoogvelt, A. (1996). Globalisation and the technocratization of social work. *Critical Social Policy*, 47(16): pp 45–62.

Donzelot, J. (1980). *The Policing of Families*. London: Hutchinson.

Donzelot, J. (1988). (Trans. Burchell, G.) *The Promotion of the Social. Economy and Society*, Volume 17: Number 3; pp 395–426.

Esping-Anderson, G. (1990). *The Three Worlds of Welfare Capitalism*. Cambridge: Polity Press.

Ferrera, M. (1993). *Modelli di Solidarieta*. Bologna: Il Mulino.

Giddens, A. (1990). *The Consequences of Modernity*. Cambridge: Polity Press.

Giddens, A. (1994). *Beyond left and Right: The Future of Radical Politics*. Cambridge: Polity Press.

Habermas, J. (1976) (Trans. McCarthy, T.). *Legitimation Crisis*. London: Heinemann.

Howe, D. (1994). Modernity, Postmodernity and Social Work. *British Journal of Social Work*, 24(5): pp 515–532.

Howe, D. (1991). Knowledge, Power and the Shape of Social Work Practice. In Davies, M. (Ed.) *The Sociology of Social Work*, pp 202–222. London: Routledge.

Howe, D. (1991). The Family and the Therapist. In Davies, M. (Ed.). *The Sociology of Social Work*, pp 147–162. London: Routledge.

International Federation of Social Workers (1997). *Social Exclusion and Social Work in Europe-Facilitating Inclusion*. Brussels: IFSW Europe.

Kennedy, P. (1996). *Globalization and its Discontents*. The 1996 Analysis Lecture. London: BBC.

Lloyd, L. (1998). The Post- and the Anti-: Analysing Change and Changing Analysis in Social Work.

British Journal of Social Work, 28(5): pp 709–727.

Lorenz, W. (1994). *Social Work in a Changing Europe*. London: Routledge.

Luhmann, N. (1997). *Die Gesellschaft der Gesellschaft 2 Bande*. Frankfurt/M: Suhrkamp Verlag.

Offe, C. (1984). *The Contradictions of the Welfare State*. London: Hutchinson.

Philp, M. (1979). Notes on a Form of Knowledge in Social Work. *Sociological Review*, 27: 1; pp 83–111

Piore, M., and Sabel, Ch. (1984). *The Second Industrial Divide: Possibilities for Prosperity*. New York: Basic Books.

Richmond, M. (1917). *Social Diagnosis*. New York: Russell Sage Foundation.

Ruxton, S. (1996). *Children in Europe*. London: NCH Action for Children.

Schulz, O. (1996). Maastricht und die Grundlagen einer Europäischen Sozialpolitik. Koln, Carl Heymanns Verlag.

Sibeon, R. (1991). *The Construction of a Contemporary Sociology of Social Work*.

Trevillion, S. (1997). The Globalisation of European Social Work. *Social Work in Europe*, 4(1): pp 1–9.

Wilding, P. (1997). Globalization, Regionalisation and Social Policy. *Social Policy and Administration*, 31(4): pp 410–428.

Czech Republic

Chytil, O. and Hubík, S. (1992). *Vysokoškolská příprava sociálních pracovníků*. Acta Universitatis Palackianae Olomucensis, Sociologica – Andragogica. Olomouc: FF UP.

Chytil, O. (1991). Význam terapeutického vztahu v postpenitenciární péči, Postpenitenciární péče na rozcestí. Sborník příspěvků z trest. *Prámava*, č. 3. Praha: Ústav státu a práva ČSAV.

Chytil, O. (1996). Social Work Education: A View from the Czech Republic. *Alumni Journal, Boston University, School of Social Work*, 2: pp 1–3.

Deyl, Z. (1985). *Sociální výoj Československa*. Praha: Academie.

'Důležité údaje' (1999). *Sociální politika*, č. 5: pp 30–31.

Giddens, A. (1993). *New Rules of Sociological Method* (2nd Edn.). Cambridge: Polity Press.

Havrdová, Z. (1997). Rozvoj vzdělávání v sociální práci. *Sociální politika*, č. 10: pp 8–10.

Hekrdla, M. (1998). Globalita jako totalita. *Právo*, č. 115: p 6.

Houser, J. (1968). *Vývoj sociální správy za předmnichovské republiky*. Praha: Academia.

Jochmann, V. (1991) *Výchovad ospělých - andragogika*. Acta Universitatis Palackianae Olomucensis, Sociologica – Andragogica. Olomouc: FF UP.

Kalinová, L. (1993). K podmínkám systémových a strukturálních změn. *Sociální politika*, č. 2: pp 2–5.

Klimentová, E. (1997). Zájem sociálních pracovníků o vzdělávání. *Sociální politika*, č. 7–8: pp 13–15.

Kokta, J. (1999). Informace o aktuální demografické situaci České republiky v mezinárodním srovnání. *Příloha Veřejné správy*, č. 22: pp 1–8

Kosík, K. (1997). *Předpotopní úvahy*. Praha: Torst.

Krakešová, M. (1973). *Výchovná sociální terapie I*. Praha: Ministerstvo práce a sociálních věcí.

Kriminální statistiky (1999). Praha: Ministerstvo vnitra, http://www.mvcr.cz/statistiky

Machonin, P. and Tuček a kol, M. (1996). *Česká společnost v transformaci*. Praha: SLON.

Machonin, P. (1998). Sociální doktrína: ano, a právě teìd!. *Příloha Sociální politiky*, č. 3: p 6.

Machonin, P. (1999). Překonejme bariéru hodnotových přístupů. *Sociální politika*, č. 3: pp 4–6.

Malinová, L. (1994). Harmonizace vzdělávání a restrukturalizace trhu práce. *Sociální politika*, č. 2: pp 1–3.

Matocha, P. (1998). Předvolební politická modlitba: Ve jménu sanačních 160 miliard, amen. *Mladá fronta DNES*, č. 143: p 11.

Možný, I. and Mareš, P. (1995). *Institucionalizace chudoby v Čechách. Přehledová studie*. Praha: Foundation START.

'Národní plán zaměstnanosti' (1999). *Příloha Sociální politiky*, č. 6: pp 1–12.

Návrh věcného záměru zákona o sociální pomoci a jejím financování. č. j. 33303/97. Interní materiál (1997). Praha: MPSV CR.

Novotná, V. and Schimmerlingová, V. (1995). Vývoj profese sociálního pracovníka, forem, sdružování a vzdělávání. *Informace Společnosti sociálních pracovníků* ČR, č. 17: pp 3–6.

Potůček, M. (1994). Trh a správa v teorii a praxi sociální transformace. *Sociologický časopis*, č. 1: pp 43–44.

Potůček, M. (1995). *Sociální politika*. Praha: SLON.

Potůček, M. (1997). *Nejen trh*. Praha: SLON.

Potůček, M. (1999). *Křižovatky české sociální reformy*. Praha: SLON.

Průša, L. (1996). Sociální politika a determinanty jejího vývoje. *Sociální politika*, č. 1: pp 7–8.

Radičová, I. and Potůček, M. (1998). Porovnanie vývoja českej a slovenskej sociálnej politiky po roku 1989. Sborník prací fakulty sociálních studií Brněnské univerzity. *Sociální studia*, 3: pp 97–154.

Roční výkaz o výkonu sociálně právní ochrany dětí a mládeže, službách a dávkách sociální péče pro rodiny s nezaopatřenymi dětmi za rok 1995 v okrese Ostrava (1996). Praha: Ministerstvo práce a sociálních věcí.

Sociální péče a sociální politika (1928). *Deset let Československé republiky, svazek III*. Praha.

'Sociální politika pro příští století' (1997). Příloha měsíčníku. *Sociální politika*, č. 7–8.

Statistika institutu pro kriminologii a sociální prevenci. Nepublikováno (1996).

Tomeš, I. (1996). *Sociální politika. Teorie a mezinárodní zkušenost*. Praha: Sociopress.

Večerník, J (1997). Transformační procesy v socio-ekonomické perspektivě. *Sociologický časopis*, č. 3: pp 259–272.

Večerník, J. (1998). *Občan a tržní ekonomika*. Praha: Lidové noviny.

Vyhláška MPSV ČSR č. 130/1975 Sb., kterou se provádí zákon o šociálním zabezpečení a zákon ČNR o pusobnosti orgánů ČSR v sociálním zabezpečení. (Decree of the Ministry of Labour and Social Affair No. 130/1975 Coll. implementing the Social Security Act.)

Základní ukazatele z oblasti práce a sociálního zabezpecení v Ceské republice (1997). Praha: Ministerstvo práce a sociálních vecí.

Zákon č. 100/1988 Sb., o sociálním zabezpečení. (Social Security Act No. 100/1988 Coll.).

Zákon č. 114/1988 Sb., o působnosti orgánů ČSR v sociálním zabezpečení.

Zákon č. 289/1997 Sb., kterým se mění zákon o duchodovém pojištění, o zaměstnanosti, o životním minimu a o působnosti orgánů ČSR v sociálním zabezpečení.

Zákon č. 20/1966 Sb., o zdraví lidu.

Zákon č. 121/1975 Sb., o sociálním zabezpečení. (Social Security Act No. 121/1975 Coll.)

Žižková, J. (1994). Sociální politika v období transformace. *Sociální politika*, č. 6: pp 10–11.

Žižková, J. (1997). Orientace sociální politiky 90. let - přednosti a úskalí. *Sociální politika*, č. 2: p 2.

'Zpráva o výoji a stavu české společnosti v oblasti práce a sociálních věcí v období 1990–1997' (1999). *Příloha Sociální politiky*, č. 4: pp 1–8.

Finland

Abrahamson, P. (1997). The Scandinavian Social Service State in Comparison. In Sipilä, J. (Ed.). *Social Care Services: The Key to the Scandinavian Welfare Model*, pp 156–177. Aldershot: Avebury.

Compton, B.R. and Galaway, B. (1989). *Social Work Processes* (4th Edn.). Belmont: Wadsworth Publishing Company.

Deacon, B. (1998). The Prospects of Global Social Policy. In Deacon, B., Koivusalo., M. and Stubbs, P. *Aspects of Global Social Policy Analysis*, pp 11–39. Helsinki: National Research and Development Centre for Welfare and Health.

Deacon, B., Hulse, M. and Stubbs, P. (1997). *Global Social Policy. International Organizations and the Future of Welfare*. London: Sage.

Hämäläinen, J. (1998). Die Krise des nordischen Wohlfahrtsmodells und ihre Auswirkungen auf die Sozialarbeit am Beispiels Finnlands. In Göppner, H-J. and Oxenknecht, R. (Eds.). *Soziale Arbeit und Sozialarbeitswissenschaft in einem sich wandelnden Europa Beiträge aus der Sicht verschiedener Länder*, pp 71–79. Freiburg im Breisgau: Lambertus.

Hanssen, J-I. (1997). The Scandinavian Model as Seen from a Local Perspective. In Sipilä, J. (Ed.). *Social Care Services: The Key to the Scandinavian Welfare Model*, pp 109–130. Aldershot: Avebury.

Jaakkola, J. (1994). Sosiaalisen kysymyksen yhteiskunta. In Jaakkola, J., Pulma, P. Satka, M. and Urponen K. *Armeliaisuus, yhteisöapu, sosiaaliturva. Suomalaisen sosiaalisen turvan historia*, pp 71–161. Helsinki: Sosiaaliturvan Keskusliitto.

Lorenz, W. (1994). *Social Work in a Changing Europe*. London: Routledge.

Louhelainen, P. (1985). *Sosiaalityö: kirjalliseen materiaaliin perustuva kuvaus suomalaisesta sosiaalityöstä*. Helsinki: Sosiaaliturvan Keskusliitto.

Mikkola, M. and Helminen, J. (1994). *Lastensuojelu*. Helsinki: Karelactio.

Pulma, P. (1987). Kerjuuluvasta perhekuntoutukseen. In: Pulma, P. and Turpeinen, O. *Suomen lastensuojelun historia*, pp 11–266. Helsinki: Lastensuojelun Keskusliitto.

Ritakallio, V-M. (1997). Toimeentuloasiakkaat ja sosiaalityø. In *Viialainen, R. and Maaniittu M. (toim). Tehdä itsensä tarpeettomaksi?* Sosiaalityø 1990-luvulla, pp 67–83). STAKES Raportteja 213. Jyväskylä.

Rose, S.M. and Black, B.L. (1985). *Advocacy and Empowerment. Mental Health Care in the Community*. Boston: Routledge and Kegan Paul.

Satka, M. (1994). Sosiaalinen työ peräänkatsojamiehestä hoivayrittäjäksi. In Jaakkola, J., Pulma, P., Satka, M. and Urponen, K. *Armeliaisuus, yhteisapu, sosiaaliturva. Suomalaisen sosiaalisen turvan historia*, pp 261–339. Helsinki: Sosiaaliturvan Keskusliitto.

Satka, M. (1995). Making Social Citizenship. Conceptual Practices from the Finnish Poor Law to Professional Social Work. *Publications of Social and Political Sciences and Philosophy*, University of Jyväskylä (monograph).

Sipilä, J. (1999). *How does the Finnish Welfare State Manage to Solve Social Problems?* Paper presented at the conference of the European Association of Schools of Social Work, 'European Social Work: Building Expertise for the 21st Century', Helsinki, June 10–13, 1999.

Sipilä, J., Andersson, M., Hammarqvist, S-E., Nordlander, L. Rauhala, P-L., Thomsen, K. and Nielsen, H.W. (1997). A Multitude of Universal, Public Services— How and Why Did Four Scandinavian Countries Get Their Social Care Service Model?. In Sipilä, J. (Ed.). *Social Care Services: The Key to the Scandinavian Welfare Model*, pp 27–50. Aldershot: Avebury.

Tuori, K. (1995). *Sosiaalioikeus*. Juva: WSOY.

Urponen, K. (1994). Huoltoyhteiskunnasta hyvinvointivaltioon. In Jaakkola, J., Pulma, P., Satka, M. and Urponen, K. *Armeliaisuus, yhteisapu, sosiaaliturva. Suomalaisen sosiaalisen turvan historia*, pp 163–260. Helsinki: Sosiaaliturvan Keskusliitto.

France

Aballea. F. (1996). Crises du Travail Social, Malaise des Travailleurs Sociaux in Recherches et Provisions. CNAF 44: pp 11.

Aron, S. (1980). Histoire Du Service Social. *Revue De L'économie Sociale*, 16.

Autes, M. (1996). Le Travail Social Indéfini. *Recherches Et Prévisions*, 44.

Avenir (1992). Onisep. *Les Métiers Auprès Des Enfants*, 434–435 (Mai-Juin).

Bailleau, F. (1988). Les Entreprises Intermédiaires. *Revue Pour*, 119. Paris.

Besnard, P. (1980). *L'animation Socioculturelle*. Paris: Puf.

Bourquin, J, and Koeppel, B. (1986). Deux Contributions À La Connaissance Des Origines De L'education Surveillée. *Cahiers Du Criv*, 2 (Octobre).

Castel, R. (1995). *Les Métamorphoses De La Question Sciale. Une Chronique Du Salariat*. Paris: Ed. Fayard.

Chauviere, M. (1987). *L'enfance Inadaptée, L'héritage De Vichy* (2ème Édition). Paris: Ed. Ouvrières.

Chauviere, M. (1993). Naissance Et Enjeux D'une Qualification Éducative Spécialisée En France. *Cahiers Du Travail Social*, 20 (Septembre) (Irts Franche-Comté).

Chauviere, M. (1993). Quelle Qualification Pour Quelle Demande Sociale? In Martinet, J.L. *(Sous La Direction), Les Educateurs Aujourd'hui*. Toulouse: Privat.

Commissariat Général Au Plan (1993). *Redéfinir Le Travail Social, Réorganiser L'Action Sociale. Préparation Du Xième Plan*. La Documentation Française.

Demailly, L. (1991). *Le Collège. Crise, Mythes Et Métiers*. Lille: Pul

Dutrenit, J.M. (1989). *Gestion Et Évaluation Des Services Sociaux*. Lille: Éd. Economica.

Dubedout, F. (1983). *Ensemble, Refaire La Ville*. Paris: La Documentation Française.

Estebe, Ph. (1988). L'évidence Locale Des Politiques Sociales. *Revue Pour*, 119. (For more information see *L'ingénierie À L'assaut Du Travail Social*, 119: (Nov/Déc). Ed. Privat.)

Fourcaut, A. (1980). *Femmes À L'usine. Ouvrières Et Surintendantes Dans Les Entreprises Françaises 1930–1960*. Paris: Aubier-Montagne.

Geng (1977). *Les Mauvaises Peusées du Travailleur Social*. Paris: Ed. Sociales.

Girard-Buttoz, F. (1982). *Les Travailleurs Sociaux, Qui Sont-Ils? Que Font-Ils?* Paris: Puf.

Guerin, C. (1980). *Cahiers De L'animation*, (3rd edition). Paris: Hors Série.

Guerrand, R.H, Rupp, M.A. (1978). *Brève Histoire Du Service Social En France 1896–1976*. Toulouse: Privat.

Ion, J. and Tricart, J.P. (1992). *Les Travailleurs Sociaux.* Toulouse: Ed. La Découverte.

Ion, J. (1992). *Le Travail Social À L'épreuve Du Territoire.* Toulouse: Privat.

Ion, J. (1993). Les Travailleurs Sociaux Son-Ils Encore Un Groupe Professionnel? In Martinet, J.L. p 181. *Les Educateurs Aujourd'hui.* Paris: Privat.

Join-Lambert, M.T., *et al.*(1997). *Politiques Sociales.* Paris: Presses De Sciences Po Et Dalloz (671).

Jovelin, E. (1998). Le Travail Social Est-Il Une Profession? La Professionnalisation Du Travail Social Une Mission Difficile. *Revue Française De Service Social,* Volume 189/190: pp 20–30.

Jovelin, E. (1998). Leadership Ethnique dans le Travail Social, Choix du métier et practiques professionnelles. *Déviance et Societe,* Vol. 23: No. 3; pp 231–312.

Jovelin, E. (1998). *Les Travailleurs Sociaux D'origine Étrangère. Vocation Ou Repli Professionnel? Analyse Sociologique D'un Groupe Professionnel.* Doctoral Thesis, Université De Lille 1.

Jovelin, E. (1999). *Devenir Travailleur Social Aujourd'hui. Vocation Ou Repli? L'Exemple Des Educateurs, Animateurs Et Assistants Sociaux D'origine Etrangère.* Paris: Ed. L'harmattan.

Labourie, R. (1978). *Les Institutions Socioculturelles.* Paris: Puf.

Mission Recherche—Experimentation. (1996). *Ministere de l'Emploi et de la Solidarite, in Recherches et Previsions,* CNAF 44.

Mury, G. (1989). La Double Fidélité Du Travailleur Social In Dutrenit, *Sociologie Et Compréhension Du Travail Social.* Paris: Ed. Sciences De L'homme.

Peyre, V. and Tetard, F. (1985). Les Enjeux De La Prévention Spécialisée: 1956–63. In Bailleau, F., *et al. Lectures Sociologiques Du Travail Social.* Paris: Les Éditions Ouvriers/Criv.

Poujol, G. (1978). *Traités Des Sciences Pédagogiques.* Paris: Puf.

Poujol, G. (1978). *Le Métier D'animateur.* Toulouse: Ed. Privat.

Ronsanvallon, J.P. (1982). *La Crise De L'etat-Providence.* Paris: Puf.

Rupp, M.A. (1970). *Le Travail Social Individualisé.* Toulouse: Privat.

Santelmann, P. (1995). L'exclusion sortir des categories. *Revue Francaise des Affaires Sociales,* 2–3 (Avril–Septembre).

Santelmann, P. (1995). A quoi sert le travail social? *Revue Esprit,* 3–4 (Mars-Avril).

Schnapper, D. (1994). Exclusion Et Citoyenneté. *Pouvoirs Locaux,* 23(IV).

Sevron, F, Duchemin, R. (1983). *Introduction Au Travail Social.* Paris: Esf.

Strauss, A. Miroirs, and Masques (1992). *Une Introduction À L'interactionnisme.* Paris: Ed. Métaillié.

Schwartz, B. (1981). *L'insertion Professionnelle Et Sociale Des Jeunes.* Paris: La Documentation Francaise.

Thevenet, A. (1989). *L'aide Sociale Aujourd'hui Après La Décentralisation.* Paris: Ed. Esf, (32).

Vattier, G. (1991). *Introduction À L'éducation Spécialisée.* Toulouse: Privat.

Vattier, G. Un Tournant. In J.L. Martinet, (1993). *Les Éducateurs Aujourd'hui,* p 68. Paris: Privat.

Verdes-Leroux, J. (1981). *Le Travail Social.* Paris: Ed. De Minuit.

Wuhl, S. (1996). *Insertion: Les Politiques En Crise.* Paris: Puf.

Germany

Abrahamson, P. and Hansen, F.K. (1996). *Poverty in the European Union.* Copenhagen: Printed as a manuscript.

Baecker, D. (1994). Soziale Hilfe als Funktionssystem der Gesellschaft. *Zeitschrift für Soziologie,* 23: pp 93–110

Beck, U. (1986). *Risikogesellschaft. Auf dem Weg in eine andere Moderne.* Frankfurt/M: Suhrkamp Verlag.

Beyme, K. v. (1996). Theorie der Politik im Zeitalter der Transformation. In Beyme K. v. and Offe, C. (Eds.). *Politische Theorien in der Ära der Transformation,* pp 9–29. Opladen: Westdeutscher Verlag.

Brieskorn, N. and Müller, J. (1996). *Gerechtigkeit und soziale Ordnung.* Freiburg: Herder Verlag.

Burmeister J. (1991). Unterstützungsformen für Selbsthilfegruppen. In: *Institut für Sozialwissenschaftliche Analyse und Beratung.* Köln: ISAB-Verlag.

Deutscher Verein für öffentliche und private Fürsorge (1993). *Fachlexikon der Sozialen Arbeit. 3. Auflage.* Frankfurt/M: Eigenverlag Deutscher Verein.

Erath, P. (1998) Ökonomisierung der Sozialen Arbeit als Folge von Globalisierungsprozessen? Plädoyer für eine eigenständige und multireferentielle Sozialarbeitswissenschaft. In Göppner, H.J. and Oxenknecht-Witzsch, R. (Eds.). *Soziale Arbeit und Sozialarbeitswissenschaft in einem sich wandelnden Europa,* pp 25–40. Freiburg/Br: Lambertus-Verlag.

Erath, P. and Göppner, H.J. (1996). Einige Thesen zur Begründung und Anlage einer Sozialarbeitswissenschaft. In Weinheim R. P. v. (Ed.). *Sozialarbeitswissenschaft. Neue Chancen für theoriegeleitete Soziale Arbeit,* pp 187–204. München: Juventa-Verlag.

Frankenberg, G. (1997). *Die Verfassung der Republik: Autorität und Solidarität in der Zivilgesellschaft.* Frankfurt/M: Suhrkamp Verlag.

Freire, P. (1972). *Pädagogik der Unterdrückten.* Reinbek: Rowohlt Verlag.

Giddens, A. (1990). *The Consequences of Modernity.* Stanford, CA: Polity Press, Oxford.

Habermas, J. (1985). *Theorie des kommunikativen Handelns* (2nd Edn). Frankfurt/M: Suhrkamp Verlag.

Hamm, W. (1989). Wirtschaftspolitik als Sozialpolitik. *Ordo,* 40: 342–380.

Heinrich, R.B. and Koop, M.J. *et al.* (Eds.) (1996). *Sozialpolitik im Transformationsprozeß Mittel- und Osteuropas.* Tübingen: Mohr Verlag.

Herder-Dornreich, P. and Schuller, A. (Eds.) (1983). *Die Anspruchsspirale*. Stuttgart: Kohlhammer-Verlag.

Huber, J. (1987). *Die neuen Helfer*. München: Piper Verlag.

Ismayr, W. (Ed.) (1997). *Die politischen Systeme Westeuropas im Vergleich*. Opladen: Westdeutscher Verlag.

Kaufmann, F. (1997). *Herausforderungen des Sozialstaates*. Frankfurt/M: Suhrkamp Verlag.

Kirn, M. (1991). *Der deutsche Staat in Europa. Aufgaben und Ziele des vereinigten Deutschland*. Stuttgart: Urachhaus-Verlag.

Klug, W. (1997). *Wohlfahrtsverbände zwischen Markt, Staat und Selbsthilfe*. Freiburg: Lambertus-Verlag.

Kreft D. and Mielenz I. (1988). *Wörterbuch Soziale Arbeit*. 3, Auflage. Weinheim: Beltz-Verlag.

Lampert, H. (1996). *Lehrbuch der Sozialpolitik*. Berlin, 4. Auflage: Springer Verlag.

Lüssi, P. (1992). *Systemische Sozialarbeit. Praktisches Lehrbuch der Sozialberatung*. Bern-Stuttgart-Wien, 2. Auflage: Haupt-Verlag.

Lissabon, (Ed.) (1997). *Die Gruppe von Lissabon: Die Grenzen des Wettbewerbs*. München: Luchterhand-Literaturverlag.

Luhmann, N. (1972). Formen des Helfens im Wandel der gesellschaftlichen Bedingungen. In Otto, H.U. and Schneider, S. (Eds.). *Gesellschaftliche Perspektiven der Sozialarbeit*, pp 21–43. Darmstadt: Luchterhand-Verlag.

Luhmann, N. (1978). *Legitimation durch Verfahren, Darmstadt und Neuwied 3*. Auflage: Luchterhand-Verlag.

Luhmann, N. (1981). *Politische Theorie im Wohlfahrtsstaat*. München: Olzog-Verlag.

Luhmann, N. (1987). Strukturelle Defizite. Bemerkungen zur systemtheoretischen Analyse des Erziehungswesens. In Oelkers J. v. and. Tenorth H.E (Ed.). *Pädagogik, Erziehungswissenschaft und Systemtheorie*, pp 57–75. Weinheim und Basel: Beltz-Verlag.

Luhmann, N. (1997). *Die Gesellschaft der Gesellschaft* (2nd Edn). Frankfurt/M: Suhrkamp Verlag.

Mayntz, R. (1996). Politische Steuerung: Aufstieg, Niedergang und Transformation einer Theorie. In Beyme K v. and Offe, C. *Politische Theorien in der Ära der Transformation*, pp 148–168. Opladen: Westdeutscher Verlag.

Meinhold, M. (1997). *Qualitätssicherung und Qualitätsmanagement in der Sozialen Arbeit*. Freiburg/Br: Lambertus-Verlag.

Merchel, J. (1996). Neue Steuerung in der Jugendhilfe: Handlungsspezifische Differenzierungen im Kontext pluraler Trägerstrukturen. In *Nachrichtendienst des Deutschen Vereins für öffentliche und private Fürsorge*, 7: pp 215–220.

Meyers. Enzyklop disches Lexikon (1978). Stichwort Sozialarbeit. Band 22, Bibliografisches Institut. Mannheim, Wein, Zürich: Lexikon Verlag.

Müller, C.W. (1988). *Wie Helfen zum Beruf wurde* (2nd Edn). Weinheim: Beltz-Verlag.

Nell-Breuning, O. v. (1957). Solidarität und Subsidiarität im Raum von Sozialpolitik und Sozialreform. In Boettcher, E. (Ed.). *Sozialpolitik und Sozialreform*, pp 218–248). Tübingen: Mohr-Verlag.

Neumann, L.F. and Schaper, K. (1998). *Die Sozialordnung der Bundesrepublik Deutschland*. Frankfurt/M., New York, 4. Auflage: Campus-Verlag.

Oppl, H.(1992). Zur Marktposition der Freien Wohlfahrtspflege. *Soziale Arbeit*, 19: 152–154.

Reidegeld, E. (1996). *Staatliche Sozialpolitik in Deutschland*. Opladen: Westdeutscher Verlag.

Ritter, G.A. (1991). *Der Sozialstaat: Entstehung und Entwicklung im internationalen Vergleich*, München, 2. Auflage: R. Oldenbourg Verlag.

Schimank, U. (1996). *Theorien gesellschaftlicher Diferenzierung*. Opladen: Leske u. Budrich Verlag.

Sing, H.(1998). Globalisierungs- und Transformationsprozesse in Europa und die Folgen für die Soziale Arbeit. In Göppner H.J v. and Oxenknecht-Witzsch R. (Eds.). *Soziale Arbeit und Sozialarbeitswissenschaft in einem sich wandelnden Europa*, pp 57–70. Freiburg/Br: Lambertus-Verlag.

Staub-Bernasconi, S. (1990). Das Berufsverständnis der Sozialen Arbweit. In Mühlfeld, C. and Oppl, H. (Eds.). *Sozialarbeit in Europa*, pp 36–49. Frankfurt: Diesterweg-Verlag.

Staub-Bernasconi, S. (1996). Dimensionen Sozialer Arbeit – Annäherung an ihren Gegenstand. In: Staub-Bernasconi, S. (Ed.). *Systemtheorie, soziale Probleme und Soziale Arbeit: lokal, national, international oder: vom Ende der Bescheidenheit*, pp 95–116. Stuttgart, Wien: Haupt-Verlag.

Thomas von Aquino (1985). *Summe der Theologie Band 3: Der Mensch und sein Heil*. Bernhart, J. v (Ed.). Stuttgart: Kröner-Verlag.

Vorlaeuder, H. (1988). *Die NSV. Darstellung und Dokumentation einer National Sozialistischen Organisation*. Boppaid. Harald Bolde Verlag.

Wendt, W.R. (1990). *Ökosozial denken und handeln. Grundlagen und Anwendungen in der Sozialarbeit*. Freiburg/Br: Lambertus-Verlag.

Willke, H. (1987). Strategien der Intervention in autonome Systeme. In Baecker, D. (Ed.). *Theorie als Passion. Niklas Luhmann zum 60.Geburtstag*, pp 333–361. Frankfurt/M: Suhrkamp-Verlag.

Zacher, H. (1992). Stand und Perspektiven der Forschung und Lehre auf dem Gebiet der Sozialarbeit, insbesondere im Rahmen kirchlicher Fachhochschulen. In Deutscher Verein (Ed.). *Sozialpolitik und Wissenschaft. Positionen zur Theorie und Praxis der sozialen Hilfen. Schriften des Deutschen Vereins für Öffentliche und Private Fürsorge. Allgemeine Schrift 269*, pp 361–379. Frankfurt/M: Eigenverlag Deutscher Verein.

Italy

Artoni, R. and Ranci Ortigosa, E. (1989). *La spesa pubblica per l'assistenza in Italia*. Milano: Angeli.

Ascoli, U. (1984). Il sistema italiano di Welfare. In Ascoli, U. (Ed.). *Welfare State all'italiana*, pp 5–51. Bari: Laterza.

Baier, H. (1977). Herrschaft im Sozialstaat. Auf der Suche, nach einem Soziologische Paradigma der Sozialpolitik. In Farber C.V. and Kaufman F. (Eds.). *Soziologie und Sozialpolitik*, pp 128–142. Opladen: Westdeutscher Verlag.

Baldacci, E. and Tuzi, D. (1998). Dinamica demografica ed evoluzione della spesa sociale. In Rossi, N. (Ed.). *Il lavoro e la sovranità sociale 1996–1997. Quarto rapporto CNEL sulla distribuzione e redistribuzione del reddito in Italia*, pp 321–349. Bologna: Il Mulino.

Barbagli, M. and Saraceno, C. (Eds.) (1997). *Lo stato delle famiglie in Italia*. Bologna: Il Mulino.

Bassanini, M.C., Lucioni, C., Pietroboni, P. and Ranci Ortigosa, E. (1977). *Servizi sociali: realtà e riforma*. Bologna: Il Mulino.

Bortoli, B. (1997). *Teoria e storia del servizio sociale*. Roma: NIS.

Börzel, T.A. (1998). Le reti di attori pubblici e privati nella regolazione europea. *Stato e Mercato*, 54: pp 389–432.

Cazzullo, C. *et al.* (1989). La psychiatrie en Italie: Situation actuelle et perspectives d'avenir. *Psychiatrie Francaise*, 20(1): pp 29–44.

Censis (Cento Studi Investimenti Sociali) (1997). *31° Rapporto sulla situazione sociale del Paese 1997*. Milano: Angeli.

Censis (1998). *32° Rapporto sulla situazione sociale del Paese 1998*. Milano: Angeli.

Censis (1999). *La previdenza in Italia: un sistema in apnea*, at http://www.censis.it/ricerche/1999/15041999.html.

Centre for Economic Policy Research (1999). *Le politiche sociali in Europa*. Bologna: Il Mulino.

Commissione per l'analisi delle compatibilità macroeconomiche della spesa sociale (1997). *Relazione finale*, at http://www.palazzochigi.it/onofri/relaz_index.html.

De Leonardis, O. (1996). I welfare mix. Privatismo e sfera pubblica. *Stato e Mercato*, 46: pp 51–75.

De Sandre, P., Ongaro, F., Rettaroli, R. and Salvini, S. (1997). *Matrimoni e figli: tra rinvio e rinuncia*. Bologna: Il Mulino.

Esping Andersen, G. (1994). Pubblico, privato, solidarietà intermedie, in Pennacchi, L. (Ed.). *Le ragioni dell'equità. Principi e politiche per il futuro dello stato sociale*, pp 149–158. Bari:Dedalo.

Esping Andersen, G. (1995). Il welfare state senza il lavoro. L'ascesa del familismo nelle politiche sociali dell'Europa continentale. *Stato e Mercato*, 45: pp 347–380.

Esping Andersen, G. (1996). *Welfare States in Transition. National Adaptations in Global Economies*. London: Sage.

Eurostat (1997). *Social Protection Expenditure and Receipts*, Basic Statistics of the EU. Luxembourg: Eurostat.

Ferrera, M. (1984). *Il Welfare State in Italia*. Bologna: Il Mulino.

Ferrera, M. (1998). *Le trappole del welfare*. Bologna: Il Mulino.

Golinelli, R., Mantovani, D. (1998). Il quadro macroeconomico e la distribuzione del reddito. In Rossi, N. (Ed.). *Il lavoro e la sovranità sociale 1996–1997. Quarto rapporto CNEL sulla distribuzione e redistribuzione del reddito in Italia*, pp 37–90. Bologna: Il Mulino.

Istat (Instituto Nazionale di Statistica) (1998). *Rapporto sull'Italia. Edizione 1998*. Bologna: Il Mulino.

Lepsius, R.M. (1979). Soziale Ungleichheit und Klassenstruktur in der Bundesrepublik Deutschland. In Wehler, H.V. (Ed.). *Klassen in der Europäischen Sozialgeschichte*, pp 21–64. Göttingen: Vanderhoek and Ruprecht.

Lewis, J. (1992). Gender and the Development of Welfare Regimes. *Journal of European Social Policy*, 3: pp 154–173.

Negri, N., Saraceno, C. (1996). *Le politiche contro la povertà in Italia*. Bologna: Il Mulino.

Olivetti Manoukian, F. (1988). *Stato dei servizi. Un'analisi psicosociologica dei servizi sociosanitari*. Bologna: Il Mulino.

Olivetti Manoukian, F. (1998). *Produrre servizi*. Bologna: Il Mulino.

Organisation for Economic Co-operation and Development (1996). *Ageing in OECD Countries. A Critical Political Challenge*. Social Policy Studies no. 20, OECD. Paris.

Organisation for Economic Co-operation and Development (1997). *OECD Economic Surveys 1996–1997, Italy*. Paris: OECD.

Paci, M. (1984). Il sistema italiano di Welfare tra tradizione clientelare e prospettive di riforma. In Ascoli U. (Ed.). *Welfare State all'italiana*, pp 297–326. Bari: Laterza.

Paci, M. (1997). *Welfare State. Chi ha beneficiato dello stato sociale, a chi andrà la nuova solidarietà*. Roma: Ediesse.

Pennacchi, L. (1994). Processi, principi e politiche nella riprogettazione del welfare state. In Pennacchi, L. (Ed.). *Le ragioni dell'equità. Principi e politiche per il futuro dello stato sociale*, pp 5–41. Bari: Dedalo.

Pirella, A. (1987). Institutional psychiatry between transformation and rationalisation: the case of Italy. *International Journal of Mental Health*, 16(1–2): pp 118–141.

Ranci Ortigosa, E. (1971). Una politica per l'assistenza. *Relazioni sociali*, 4: pp 371–392.

Rei, D. (1994). *Servizi sociali e politiche pubbliche*. Roma: NIS.

Rossi, G. (1999). I servizi alla persona in Italia: risorse, obiettivi, norme e cultura. In Donati, P. (Ed.) *Lo stato sociale in Italia*, pp 169–224. Milano: Mondadori.

Sabatier, P.A. (1993). Advocay-Koalitionen, Policy-Wandel und Policy-Lernen: Eine Alternative zur Phasenheuristik. In Héritier A. (Ed.). *Policy-Analyse. Kritik und Neuorientirung*, PVS Sonderheft 24 (166-148). Opladen: Westdeutscher Verlag.

Saraceno, C. (1997). *Riforma di un welfare diseguale. Limiti e prospettive di cambiamenti possibili*. Il Mulino, 1: pp 158–169.

Saraceno, C. (1998a). *Mutamenti della famiglia e politiche sociali in Italia*. Bologna: Il Mulino.

Saraceno, C. (1998b). La riforma dell'assistenza in Italia. In Paganetto, L. (Ed.). *Lo stato sociale in Italia: quadrare il cerchio*, pp 23–42. Bologna: Il Mulino.

Zucconi, A. (Ed.). (1974) *Regioni e servizi sociali*. Milano: Comunità.

Netherlands

Draaisma, A. (1979). *Ordening in de g.g.z.; beleidsvragen op macro niveau*. Beleid en maatschappij.

Gier, E. de (1989a). Terug naar af. Heroriëntatie van maatschappelijk werk. *Intermediair*, 31 March 1989.

Gier, E. de (1989b). Risico's en sociaal beleid. *Filosofie en Praktijk*, 10/1 1989.

Greef, M. de Schuldhulpverlening. *Sociale Interventie* 1994/2.

Hortulanus, R.P., Liem, P.P.N., and. Sprinkhuizen, A.M.M. (1992). *Welzijn in Dordrecht*. Rijksuniversiteit Utrecht.

Kamphuis, M. (1986). *Kijken in de spiegel van het verleden*. Deventer.

Koenis, S. (1993). *De precaire professionele identiteit van sociaal werkers*. NIZW Utrecht.

Laan, G. van der (1990). *Legitimationsfragen in der Sozialarbeit*. Prague, 1997.

Laan, G. van der (1995). Quality of Information and Quality of Communication. In Rafferty, J., *et al.* (Eds.). *Human Services in the Information Age*, pp 339–352. New York: Haworth Press.

Laan, G. van der, (1994). An Etiquette for Social Workers. In Gehrmann, *et al.* (Eds.). *Social Work and Social Work Studies*. Weinheim: Deutscher Studien Verlag.

Laan, G. van der, (1997/4). Sozialarbeit in den Niederlanden. *Sozialmagazin*.

Laan, G. van der, (1998). The Professional Role of Social Work in a Market Environment. In *The European Journal of Social Work*, 1.

Melief, W. (1994). Hulpverlening vanuit het AMW aan arbeidsongeschikten. Utrecht: Verwey Jonker Instituut.

Schell, J.L.M. (1995). *De algemene bijstandswet*. Deventer.

Schuyt, C. (1991). *Op zoek naar het hart van de verzorgingsstaat*. Leiden.

Swaan, A. de (1988). *In Care of the State*. Cambridge: Polity Press.

Waaldijk, B. (1996). *Het Amerika der vrouw. Sekse en geschiedenis van maatschappelijk werk in Nederland en de Verenigde Staten*. Groningen.

Wolf, J. (1995). *Zorgvernieuwing in de GGZ*. NcGv Utrecht.

Spain

Cáritas (1990). *Documentación social*. Madrid: Diocesana 79 (mayo-junio).

Collegi Oficial de Diplomats en Treball Social i Assistents Socials de Catalunya (1989). *Codi d'ètica dels Assistents Socials*. Barcelona.

Col.legi Oficial de DTS i AS de Catalunya (1997). *Els Diplomats en Treball Social i Assistents Socials de Catalunya*. Barcelona: Hacer.

De Las Heras, P. y Cortajerena, E. (1985). *Introduccion al Bienestar Social*. Madrid: Siglo XXI.

Escola Universitària de Treball Social - ICESB (1994). *El sistema català de Sèrveis Socials*. Barcelona.

Estruch, J. and Güell, A.M. (1976). *Sociologia de una profesion los Assistentes Sociales*. Barcelona: Edicions 62.

Fernández, C. (1997). *Els Serveis Socials a Catalunya*. (Syllabus of the course 'Servicios Sociales' of the Social Work College). Barcelona: EUTS-ICESB.

Feu, M. (1995). *Quelle formation pour la mobilité des travailleurs sociaux en Europe?*, Lecture for the IV Journée Nationale d'Étude. METS: Marseille.

Leal, J. y Roig, M. (1990). Interdisciplinarieded: paradigma o ficcion? Butlleti Informatiu de C.I.F.A. N 5 Septiembre 1990 Patronat Flor de Maig. Cerdañola.

Llovet, J.J. and Usieto, R. (1990). *Los trabajadores sociales. De la crisis de la identidad a la profesionalizacion*. Madrid: Editorial Popular.

Rossell, T. (1993). *Reflexiones sobre la Disciplina del Trabajo Social*, Lecture for the Seminar of the European Regional Group, Turin (Italy).

Sarasa, S. (1998). *Cambios ideológicos en el trabajo social de los ochenta*, (unpublished paper). Barcelona: University of Barcelona..

Uarte, A. (1988). *Actas VI Congreso de Asistentes Sociales*. Oviedo.

Zamanillo, T. (1992). *La intervención profesional*, Lecture for the 7th Congreso Estatal de Diplomados en Trabajo Social y Asistentes Sociales: Barcelona.

United Kingdom

A Child in Mind (1987). Report of the Commission of Inquiry into the Circumstances Surrounding the Death of Kimberley Carlisle. London: London Borough of Greenwich.

A Child in Trust (1985). The Report of the Panel of Inquiry into the Circumstances Surrounding the Death of Jasmine Beckford. London: London Borough of Brent.

Aitkin, K. and Rollings, J. (1993). *Community Care in Multi-racial Britain: A Critical Review of the Literature*. London: Social Policy Research Unit/HMSO.

Audit Commission (1986). *Making a Reality of Community Care*. London, HMSO.

Bamford, T. (1990). *The Future of Social Work*. Houndmills, Basingstoke: Macmillan.

Bradley, M., and Aldgate, J. (1994). Short term family based care for children in need. *Adoption and Fostering*, 18(4): pp 24–29.

Brewster, R. (1991). The New Class? Managerialism and Social Work Education and Training. *Issues in Social Work Education*, 11(2): pp 81–93.

Camilleri, P.J. (1996). *(Re) Constructing Social Work*. Aldershot: Avebury.

Campbell, B. (1988). *Unofficial Secrets, Child Sexual Abuse—the Cleveland Case*. London: Virago.

Cannan, C. (1994). Enterprise Culture, Professional Socialisation, and Social Work Education in Britain. *Critical Social Policy Issues*, 42: pp 5–18.

CCETSW (1990). *The Requirements for Post Qualifying Education and Training in the Personal Social Services* (Paper 31). London: Central Council for Education and Training in Social Work.

CCETSW (1995). *Assuring Quality in the Diploma in Social Work -1*. London: Central Council for Education and Training in Social Work.

Challis, D., Davies, B., and Traske, K. (Eds.) (1994). *Community Care: New Agendas and Challenges from the UK and Overseas*. Aldershot: Arena.

Davies, B.P. (1986). *The Production of Welfare Approach: Discussion Paper 400*. Canterbury: PSSRU, University of Kent.

Department of Health and Social Security (1981). *Care in the Community: A Consultative Document on Moving Resources for Care in England and Community Care in Action*. London: HMSO.

Department of Health and Social Security (1984). *Helping the Community to Care: Outlining 28 Care in the Community Pilot Projects Funded to Explore Ways of Moving Long-stay Residents and Resources from Hospital to the Community*. London: HMSO.

Department of Health (1989). *Caring for People: Care in the Community in the Next Decade and Beyond*. London: HMSO.

Department of Health (1991). *Care Management and Assessment: Practitioners Guide*. London: HMSO.

Department of Health (1995a). *The Challenge of Partnership in Child Protection*. London: HMSO.

Department of Health (1995b). *Child Protection: Messages from Research*. London: HMSO.

Dominelli, L. (1996). Deprofessionalising Social work: Anti-Oppressive practice, Competencies and Postmodernism. *British Journal of Social Work*, 26(2): pp 153–175.

Emanuel, J., and Acroyd, D. (1996). Breaking Down Barriers. In Barnes, C. and Mercer, G (Eds.). *Exploring the Divide: Illness and Disability*, pp 173–193. Leeds: The Disability Press.

England, H. (1986). *Social Work as Art*. London: Allen and Unwin.

Fox Harding, L. (1991). *Perspectives in Child Care Policy*. London: Longman.

Green, J. (1978). The role of cultural anthropology in the education of social services personnel. *Journal of Sociology and Social Welfare*, 5(2): pp 214–229.

Griffiths, S.R. (1988). *Community Care: Agenda for Action. A report to the Secretary of State for Social Services*. London: HMSO.

Hallet, C. (1995). *Interagency Co-ordination in Child Protection*. London: HMSO.

Hasenfeld, Y. (Ed.) (1992). *Human Services as Complex Organisations*. London: Sage.

HMSO (1965). *The Child, The Family and The Young Offender*, Cmnd 2742.

HMSO (1966). *Social Work and the Community*, Cmnd 3065.

HMSO (1968). *The Report of the Committee on Local authority and Allied Personal Social Services* (The Seebohm Report), Cmnd 3703.

HMSO (1988). *Report of the Inquiry into Child Abuse in Cleveland*. London: HMSO, Cmnd 412.

Home Office (1992 and 95). *National Standards for the Supervision of Offenders in the Community*. London: Home Office.

Home Office (1995). *Strengthening Punishment in the Community: A Consultative Document*. London: Home Office.

Home Office (1996). *Three Year Plan for the Probation Service*. London: Home Office.

House of Commons Social Services Committee Reports (1985). *Community Care with Special Reference to Adult Mentally Ill and Mentally Handicapped People*. London: HMSO.

Howe, D. and Hinings, D. (1997). Recovering the Relationship. *Community Care*, 31 July–6 August: pp 28–30.

Hunter, S., Brace, S., and Buckley, G. (1993). The Inter-disciplinary Assessment of Older People at Entry into Long-term Institutional Care: Lessons from the New Community Care Arrangements. *Research, Policy and Planning*, 11(1/2): pp 1–7.

Kay, J. (1832). *The Moral and Physical Condition of the Working Classes*. Manchester: Manchester Statistical Society.

Jones, S. and Joss, R. (1995). Models of professionalism. In Yelloly, M. and Henkel, M. (Eds.). *Learning and Teaching in Social Work: Towards Reflective Practice*, pp 15–33. London: Jessica Kingsley.

Josselon, R. and Lieblich, A. (1995). *Interpreting Experience—The Narrative Study of Lives*, Vol. 3. London: Sage.

Lawson, M. (1991). A Recipient's View. In Ramon S. (Ed.). *Beyond Community Care: Normalisation and Integration Work*, pp 62–83. London: Macmillan.

Lord Clyde (1992). *The Report of the Inquiry into the Removal of Children from Orkney February 1991*. London: HMSO.

Miller, P. and Rose, N. (1988). The Tavistock Programme: The Government of Subjectivity and Social Life. *Sociology*, 2(2): pp 171–192.

Moxley, D.P. (1989). *The Practice of Case Management*. Newbury Park, CA: Sage.

National Institute for Social Work (1982). *Social Workers: Their Role and Tasks* (The Barclay Report). London: Bedford Square Press.

National Institute for Social Work (1996). *Managing Social Work* (Briefing No. 14). London: NISW.

Netton A., and Beecham J. (Eds.) (1993). *Costing Community Care*. Canterbury, PSSRU University of Kent.

O'Hagan, K. (Ed.) (1996). *Competence in Social Work Practice*. London: Jessica Kingsley.

Parker, R. (1990). *Safeguarding Standards*. London: National Institute for Social Work.

Pinker R. (1982). An Alternative View. In National Institute for Social Work (1982). *Social Workers: Their Role and Tasks* (The Barclay Report). London: Bedford Square Press.

Putman, L. and Mumby, D. (1993). Organisations, Emotion and the Myth of Rationality. In Fineman, S. (Ed.). *Emotion in Organisations*. London: Sage.

Renshaw, J. (1998). *Misspent Youth '98*. London: Audit Commission Report of the Inquiry into Child Abuse in Cleveland (1988). London: HMSO, Cmnd 412.

Richardson, L.B. (1982). Survey of Final Fieldwork Placements. *Probation Journal*, 29(2): pp 54–56.

Rodger, J.H. (1991). Discourse Analysis and Social Relationships in Social Work. *British Journal of Social Work*, 21(1): pp 63–81.

Seed, P. (1973). *The Expansion of Social Work in Britain*. Routledge and Kegan Paul.

Shardlow, S.M. (1998). Values, Ethics and Social Work. In Adams, R., Dominelli, L. and Payne, M. (Eds.). *Social Work: Themes, Issues and Critical Debates*, pp 23–33. Houndmills, Basingstoke: Macmillan.

Sharkey, P. (1995). *Introducing Community Care*. London: Collins Educational.

Sheppard, M. (1995). *Care Management and the New Social Work: A Critical Analysis*. London: Whiting and Birch.

Sibeon R. (1989). Comments on the Structure and Forms of Social Work Knowledge. *Social Work and Social Science Review*, 1(1): pp 29–44.

Simic, P. (1995). What's in a word? From social 'worker' to care 'manager'. *Practice*, 7(3): pp 5–17.

Smith D. (1987). The Limits of Positivism in Social Work Research. *British Journal of Social Work*, 17(4): pp 401–416.

Social Insurance and Allied Services (The Beveridge Report) (1942). London: HMSO, Cmnd 6404.

Stevenson, O., and Parsloe, P. (1993). *Community Care and Empowerment*. York: Rountree Foundation with Community Care.

Strom, K. and Gingerich, W. (1993). Students For The New Market Realities. *Journal of Social Work Education*, 29(1): pp 78–87.

Thoburn, J., Lewis, A. and Shemmings, D. (1995). *Paternalism or Partnership? Family Involvement in the Child Protection Processes*. London: HMSO.

Titterton, M. (Ed.) (1994). *Caring for People in the Community: the New Welfare*. London: Jessica Kingsley.

Tunstill, J., and Ozlins, R. (1994). *Voluntary Child Care Organisations after the 1989 Children Act*. Norwich: Family Support Network.

Tsang, N. M. (1991). From learning styles to learning strategies. *Issues in Social Work Education*, 12(1): pp 39–56.

Vass, A. (Ed.) (1996). *Social Work Competences*. London: Sage.

Walker, H., and Beaumont, B. (1981). *Probation Work: Critical Theory and Socialist Practice*. Houndmills, Basingstoke: Macmillan.

Yelloly, M. and Henkel, M. (Eds.) (1995). *Learning and Teaching in Social Work: Towards Reflective Practice*. London: Jessica Kingsley.

Conclusion

Pierson, P. and Leibfried, S. (1998). Zur Dynamik sozialpolitischer Integration: Der Wohlfahrtsstaat in der europäischen Mehrebenen-Politik. In Leibfried, S. and Pierson, P. (Eds.). *Standort Europa. Sozialpolitik zwischen Nationalstaat und europäischer Integration*. Frankfurt am Main: Suhrkamp-Verlag.

Pakaslahti, J. (1999). *La dimension sociale de l'Union Européenne*. Brussels: Presses Interuniver Européennes.

Index